AF592640

Lotus Press Publications

# The World of Nomads

**Dr. Shyam Singh Shashi**

Lotus PRESS
4263/3, Ansari Road,
Darya Ganj, New Delhi-110002

**Lotus Press**
4263/3, Ansari Road, Darya Ganj, New Delhi-2
Ph.: 30903912, 23290047
E-mail: lotus_press@sify.com

The World of Nomads
© 2006 Dr. S.S. Shashi
ISBN 81-8382-051-4

All rights are reserved with the author. No part of this publication may be reproduced, stored in a retrieval system or transmitted, in any form or by any means, photocopying, recording or otherwise, without prior written permission of the author.

*Published by:* Lotus Press, New Delhi.
*Lasertypeset by:* Jain Media Graphics, Delhi.
*Printed at:* Ashim Paint Line, Delhi.

***Dedicated to***

***the memory of Mrs. Indira Gandhi,***
***the former Prime Minister of India,***
***who released my books from time to time***
***and inspired me to write on Roma Gypsies***
***and Nomads of India.***


## Acknowledgement

- *I, most respectfully, remember my Guruwar Prof. R.L. Saksena, the renowned Sociologist and Former Vice-Chancellor Kashi Vidyapith under whose guidance, I conducted research on the Gaddis of the Himalayas and got my doctorate in Sociology and later D.Litt. in Anthropology for my research on Roma, the Gypsies of the World.*
- *I pay my gratitude to the memory of Mahapandit Rahul Sankrityayan and Swami Satya Dev Privrajak whose literature inspired me to travel in the tribal belts of India and abroad.*
- *I am thankful to the great writer Mrs. Mahasveta Devi, Gyanpith and Padma Vibhushan Awardee who appreciated my tribal studies and writings. She has herself devoted her major writings to the cause of tribals.*
- *And, finally, I salute the scholarship of the renowned writers—Dr. Karan Singh, Dr. L.M. Singhvi and Dr. Lokesh Chandra for their love, affection, and encouragement.*

*— S.S. Shashi*

# Preface

*Paling in Prime youth*
*A nomadic ray*
*descends slowly*
*Like a fugitive Gaddi maid*
*from the hill-tops of Dholadhar.*
*The snowy rocky*
*and thorny paths*
*have bruised the feet of the*
*tender ray,*
*and the maid of the mount.*
*Coursing through these terrains since ages*
*The thorns no longer string*
*The nomadic Sun goes hopping*
*like the gypsy shepherd*
*to the end of horizon.*
--- *(From 'White Darkness' by S.S. Shashi).*

My quest in search of new man and the nomadic culture is still alive but the circumstances do not allow me to travel any more. In my world-wide journeys, I met thousands of intellectuals, authors, social scientists, journalists and social activists. Many of them have become my friends.

In my childhood, I read some interesting books like '*How to Win Friends*', '*Pushing to the Front*' and '*Indian Scripture*' including travelogues and nomadic literature which inspired me to travel in the Himalayas and tribal areas to study the people of India. Afterwards, my interest in the nomadic world increased and I visited number of countries to study Roma Gypsies of Indian origin. My journey started from the sociological research of Gaddi, Gujjar, Banjara and other nomads, semi-nomads and continued till today. Recently, I studied the descents of nomadic Hoons and Shakas and NRIs of course. A brief description of my life-long research is given in the first chapter of this book.

Needless to say that I used various research techniques including K.V. Young and my own to study the world of Nomads.

In this book, I have reproduced the relevant material from some of my earlier research works and various sources freely to compare my old and new researches.

I am grateful to the social scientists and writers from whose books and research works, I have tried to make my studies more authentic and interesting.

My thanks are due to Dr. Ian Hancock (USA), Dr. Rina Gropper (USA), Dr. Puxan (UK), Dr. Acton (UK), Roma friends and Romanologists.

I am thankful to all my NRI, PIO and other friends to name a few— Pt. Ram Lal (USA), Dr. V.K. Mehta (USA), Dr. Dauji Gupta, Dr. Sudha Om Dhingra (USA), Dr. V.P. Singh (USA) and Members of Vishwa Hindi Parishad, New York, Dr. Padmesh Gupta (U.K.), Dr. Krishna Kumar (U.K.), Dr. Divya Mathur (U.K.), Dr. S.P. Malhotra, Dr. S.P. Ruhela, Mr. Ranjit Naik, Dr. K.M. Metry, Dr. B.K. Ravi, Dr. R.K. Kaushik, Mr. Dev Bhardwaj, Prof. Yogendra Singh, Prof. I.P. Singh, Mr. J. Veerarahvan, Dr. J.K. Sharma and all the Associates of Research Foundation, Bhartiya Vidya Bhavan and a number of organisations I am associated with. I have long list of friends including Mr. M. Bandopadhyay, Dr. Dharmir Mahajan, Dr. Kapse, I always remember.

I can never forget Dr. Eva Aradi (Hungary) and her husband Mr. Martin Aradi, Mr. Miklos Patrubeny (Hungary), Mrs. Katarzyna Polak (Germany) for their wholehearted support.

I am also thankful to my publishers Mr. A.J. Sehgal for reminding me to complete this work as early as possible. My regards and love to all.

**Dr. S.S. Shashi**

# Contents

*Mrs. Indira Gandhi with her father Pt. Jawahar Lal Nehru in tribal costume.*

*The author presenting his books and Research Foundation's literature to former Prime Minister Mrs. Indira Gandhi.*

*The former President Mr. R. Venkatraman awarding Padmashri to the author.*

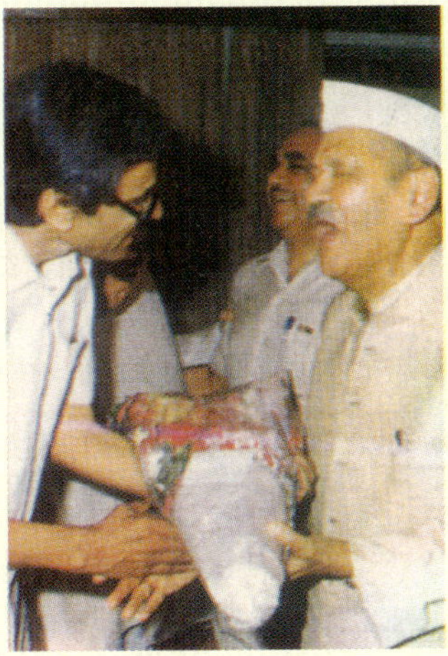

*The author with Dr. Shankar Dayal Sharma, the former President of India.*

*Giani Zail Singh, former President of India honouring the author with garland.*

*Former Prime Minister Mr. Rajiv Gandhi honouring the author with shawl.*

*Author presenting his book 'Nehru and the Tribals' to Mrs. Sonia Gandhi.*

*Author presenting books to Vice President of India Mr. Bhairo Singh Shekhawat.*

*Author with former Union Minister Mr. Vasant Sathe, former Chief Justice of India Mr. R N Mishra and a Japanese Professor in Research Foundation's International Conference (Dec. 1995)*

# 1

# The Journey Begins

My interest in nomadic studies dates back to the years of my young age when I was engaged in sociological research on Himalayan nomads and got my doctorate in sociology from Agra University in 1968 as the first research scholar on the subject. I was fortunate to conduct my research work under the guidance of renowned sociologist Dr. R.N. Saksena. This research work entitled '*A Sociological study of Gaddi tribe in Himachal Pradesh*' was published by Sterling Publishes of Delhi in 1977. I however, came into contact with the Gaddi, Bhotiya and Gujjar nomads even before my graduation during my visits to the tribal belts of Jaunsar Babar of Dehradun district now in Uttranchal and Himachal Pradesh, as a free lance journalist. I also worked as a social worker for sometime in a Gandhian organization- Ahok Ashram Kalsi, situated in the lap of the Himalayas, devoted to the welfare of hill people and edited its monthly journal '*Himalya*' in 1955-56. The organization was set up by a great freedom fighter, learned scholar and social leader of the Himalayas Pt. Dharm Dev Shastri under the patronage of Mahatma Gandhi, Vinoba Bhave and Rameshweri Nehru.

Since I lost my father during my intermediate school, I had to learn and earn, being the eldest son in the agriculturist and freedom fighters' family. This proved to be a blessing in disguise also as I had to work hard and got the first position from 8th to M.A. in my classes. Thereafter, while doing my private and government jobs, I continued my advanced research on pastoral, other nomadic tribes and communities. In course of time, I wrote on the shepherds of India, known as Maratha Dhangar Kshtriya, Kuruba, Dhangar, Nikhar, Pal, Baghel, Gadariya, Gond, Kurumba, Gwala, Yadava, and various semi-nomadic communities of India. I also conducted higher research on Banjara Lambadi, Gadulia Lohar and other nomadic clans. My journey continued from time to time during the period of my regular senior jobs in the government of India as well.

I had a golden opportunity to be invited as an Indian anthropologist by the world Roma Congress to participate in the conference, held in Gottigon city of the then west Germany in 1981. I met many Roma Gypsies and anthropologists and established a good rapport with them. After the conference was over, I began my research tours to Roma Gypsy belts in Europe and America and visited 14 countries in the first round viz the then west Germany, France, Italy, Norway, Sweden, Finland, Denmark, Belgium, Brussels, Holland, Switzerland, England, USA and Canada. During the journey, I had my scholarly interaction with a number of sociologists, anthropologists, poets, writers, journalists, and social activists, in various countries. I also delivered lectures on Indian nomads, Indian culture and vedic religion in European and Amercian universities and research institutes. My earlier research on Roma and later on Shakas and Hoons including a mythological subject on sun-worship in the world are continuing. Besides, I have been writing on literary, cultural, and religious subjects including my poetry since my teen age.

There is an Indian saying— 'if you abandon your home and hearth and join a *carvan*, it will go on far years together and you will meet many co-passengers and like-minded people in your journey.' I am still working on Indian and tribal communities. Earlier, after the Himachal Pradesh got statehood in 1971, I wrote a book *Himachal—nature's peaceful paradise*, based on my research and travelled in the impassable valleys and hills of the Himalayas where many a time, I had a narrow escape from death. In those days, there were no roads and passage through Himalayan terrain was difficult. Dr. Y.S. Parmar, the first chief minister of Himachal Pradesh and a well- known anthropologist, wrote in his foreword to my book on Himachal Pradesh as under—

"It is a great pleasure to see Dr. S.S. Shashi's book *Himachal—Nature's Peaceful Paradise*.

Off and on, useful information about Himachal Pradesh has been appearing in bits and pieces in the past, but Dr.. Shashi's book is the first major attempt to present Himachal as a whole. I hope this will stimulate further study of Himachal, its problems, its past, present and future.

The hills and valleys of Himachal have still to unfold much way of knowledge about their inhabitants, their life, labour and struggle against heavy odds that they have been facing since time immemorial. It is a great story of challenges faced and responses offered.

So far, history has been shadowed by events but it is in the background of events that there lies hidden the saga of the struggle of people and this has still to be recorded in Himachal Pradesh. From eternal snows, Himachalis have derived their peaceful nature, from the ups and downs of the terrain, they have got their hard working nature and perseverance, from ancient *Rishis* and sages they have inherited their calm and from the famous 'Jan Padas' they have imbibed their democratic spirit. It is the great heritage that has to be researched, preserved and presented in proper shape.

I am sure, Dr. Shashi's book would blaze a trail and inspire future writers to drink deep at the *fountain* of history and tradition of Himachal Pradesh to write its fascinating story."

Besides my three hundred books in English and Hindi on variety of subjects including poetry, children literature and encyclopaedic works, I could contribute thousands of articles/write ups also in various newspapers, journals and magazines. One of my leading articles, entitled *Nomads of the Himalayas* appeared on the first and second pages of the magazine section of *Times of India*, dated Sept. 20, 1970 in which I wrote about the Gaddi nomads of the Himalayas—

"The Gaddis of the Himalayas are an unspoilt people, primitive, unlettered yet rich in folklore, they are happy walking their mountains and living from day to day."

In 1982, while studying the man-management and man power planning courses for my another post-graduate degree in Manchester University of England, my interest in nomads of the European countries increased. I visited a number of Gypsy mobile schools in some towns of U.K. and during the vacation, I could find time to visit various countries of Eastern Europe viz Yugoslavia (undivided), Bulgaria, Romania, Greece etc., where I met traditional Roma Gypsy clans and collected lot of research material with participant observation.

I am sorry to say that I was not lucky to be a full time traveller like Columbus, Vasco-de- Gama, Fahiyan and India's famous travelling scholars Bhikku Chaman Lal and Mahapandit Rahul Sankrityayan. However, I managed to collect considerable research material during my world tours that I offered to my readers through my writings. After my voluntary retirement from the post of Director/DG, Publications Division, Govt. of India, I was invited by various literary and academic organizations of Japan, Bangladesh, Thailand, Mexico, Russia, Ukraine and other countries. In my Hindi book on sun-temples of the world, I tried to summarize my long journey from Mexico to Japan and from Thailand to the then USSR and other countries. I arrived at a conclusion that Paganism was one of the oldest primitive religions which is akin to nature-worship of vedic and other mythologies. Nature worship was prevalent all over the world including Arean society. The 'Gayatri Mantra' of the Vedas is also known as 'Surya Mantra' that is worship to Sun God.

In the year 1995, due to my constant research and writings in day and night, I fell seriously ill and underwent spinal cord surgery. I was bed-ridden for two years in various hospitals and nursing homes. On my recovery, I resumed my world tours but in a different way. In 2003, I was invited by World Hindi Council of America, a reputed organization of Non Resident Indians of USA as Chief Guest to address literary functions in various cities of America. During my two-months' stay there, I toured from New York to San Francisco and from Kary, North Carolina to Austin, Texas covering North-South and East-West of USA. I also stayed for sometime at H.D. Swami Prakashanand's Barsana Dham situated in Austin, Texas for studying Indian culture abroad.

My aim to visit the foreign countries was not merely to study the world civilization and culture but to interact with the people of Indian origin abroad and others as well as to spread the message of Indian philosophy of '*Vasudhaiv Kutumbakam*' i.e. the world is one family. I have been trying to create an atmosphere of peace, non-violence, love and brotherhood through my pen and action which are reflected in my books and articles on variety of subjects. As a result, I could establish an international organization, namely, Research Foundation (Anusandhan Sansthan) which was registered by Delhi Government in 1971. The Foundation has organized many national and international conferences in Delhi and elsewhere. Dr. R.N. Saksena, a renowned Sociologist and former Vice Chancellor, Kashi Vidyapeeth was its Founder Chairman. After his demise, Prof. Yogendra Singh, Dean of social sciences Jawhar Lal Nehru University, Padma Bhushan Awardee Mr. T.N. Chaturvedi Governor of Karnataka , Prof. I.P. Singh, Head, Anthropology Department Delhi University and other well-known personalities who are no more in this world, viz eminent Journalist Mr. Akshaya Kumar Jain, former MPs—Mr. Aziz Iman, Kunwar Mohan Swroop, Mr.Chandu Lal Chandrakar helped me in running the organization as Presidium Members/ Presidents of the Foundation.

A number of social, cultural, religious and political leaders also contributed in our mission of world peace, brotherhood and value education as advisors, patrons and associates, former president of India, Dr. Shankar Dayal Sharma took a lot of interest in Foundation's activities, particularly in compilation of Hindi Encyclopaedia of Social Sciences. Mrs. Indira Gandhi, former Prime Minister of India released two books edited by me and she also inaugurated World Roma Banjara (Gypsy) Conferences held in Chandigarh under the chairmanship of Padamshri awardee Mr. W. R. Rishi. In course of time, the Centre for Roma Art and Culture, International, Institute of Nomadic Studies and Culture, Shiksha Bhavan, Educational Centre and other wings of sister organizations were established in Foundation's building named as—'Vaidik Mandir' (charitable) in Rohini, Delhi. A detailed report about our nomadic studies, culture and other fields can be seen in the appendices.

Incidentally, I would like to add some salient features of caste system in India. There are many wrong notions and hypotheses pertaining to caste studies. The caste formation in India cannot be studied properly unless the social scientists attain a complete knowledge of the *gotras*, *alhs* and *sept names* prevalent among the Indian castes and tribes. Many *gotras* are the same in higher and lower communities. One can find *'Vashit'* and *'Bhardwaj' gotras* among Brahmins and Vishwakarmas—carpenter and blacksmith communities also. Similarly, 'Chauhan' is a *gotra* among Kshtriya communities intermingled with OBCs and Dalits also.

It is a well-known fact that in the past, there were Surya Vansh (Sun dyansty) and Chandra Vansh (Moon dyansty) among Kshtriya communities as well as *Kul gotras* and *Rishi gotras.* In course of time, many new clans emerged in Indian society due to emigration, invasion, nomadic transformation, tribal Hinduization and punishment to outcaste on trifling matters by the caste Panchayats to a person who had no way out than to join a lower community. However, he didn't forget the name of his *gotra* and observe the same in matrimonial relationships. Banjaras, Vishvakarmas, sheep and cattle rearing and agricultural communities are the best example who have many Kshtriya and Brahmin *gotras* including 'Shaka' and 'Hoona' —the international *alhs*.

To accommodate martial nomads, gorilla fighters and people belonging to other lower Kshtriya *gotras* and tribal Rajputs, a new 'Agnivansh' (fire dynasty) was formed by the Brahmin priests. They declared Shivaji as 'Chatrapathi Maharaja' only after they were given a handsome gold and money as *Dakshina* by him. Scindia, Gaikwad, Holkar and many other martial clans pertaining to Jat, Kurmi—Backward, Tribals and Dalit Communities were also recognized after the similar rites. There is a cycle of social change. Varna system which was based on work and jobs in the past but later on, due to various reasons, the birth of an individual became the basis of this system which further created a number of castes. There were many interpolations in *Manusmriti* and Vedantic scriptures. Thus the Hindu society was divided into thousands of castes and sub-castes. Some de-notified communities who fought against British regime, were declared as criminal castes by them. My book entitled '*A Socio-History of Ex-Criminal Communities OBCs*' is referred for further studies on this subject.

In this book, I have tried to summarize my life—long research and depict the philosophy of '*Charaiveti*' i.e. go on or nomadism through the ages. In India, we have Buddhist monks, Jain Munis, Hindu Sanyasis and Vanaprasthis who travel as a part of their religious traditions whereas the nomadic communities travel for their livelihood and grazing their cattle in forests and fields. I have included in this volume my research studies on Gaddi, Gujjar,

Bhotiya and Khampa of Himalayas, Banjara, Lambadi and Gadulia Lohars belonging to various states of India and Roma Gypsies, Sintis of Europe and America alongwith the primitive nomadic clans like Shakas and Hoonas in India and Hungary.

In 2004, I was invited in the capacity of a Nomadic-Cultural Anthropologist and Sociologist by the World Federation of Hungarians to participate in the conference held in Budapest, Hungary. While writing a research paper to present in the conference on primitive nomadic people—the Hoons and Shakas, I was amazed to find many historical evidences and strong links between their ancestors of Hungary and India. As *gotra,* one can find them among Gujjars, Jats , Kshatriyas, Shepherds and other nomadic and semi-nomadic communities and tribes of India. This was a new chapter to my earlier research on nomadic world which has been included in this volume. After having a close interaction and intensive discussions with the participant scholars, experts and social activities of various countries, I travelled from Budapest to Berlin via Czech Republic and Slovakia by train. In Germany, I stayed with a Roma family also and observed new changes in their social structure and culture. I am sure that my journey will never end even when I am no more in this world. The *carvan* of travellers will go on carrying the message of Indian culture Vasudhaiv Kutumbakam and *Manav Dharma* to create an atmosphere of world peace and globalization.

---

While the final proof copy of this book was being sent to the press, some scholars and social activists of South Indian nomadic communities viz., Budgajangam, Domibidasaru, Dombaru, Raj Gond, Dhangar shepherds of South and North met the author on 15th Jan 2006 in Delhi. I found many similar ties as mentioned above. Incidentally, I discussed the problems of nomads with Gyanpith and Padma Vibhushan awardee Mrs. Mahasveta and Mrs. Ramanika Gupta and Dr. K.M. Metry, Mr. Balagurumurthy etc. — Activist a social.

# 2

# Sociology of Nomads

Nomadism in the Himalayas, according to Sir Edward blunt and S.D. Pant as in the mountain communities of the Balkans, Alps, Carpathians, Pyrenees, Andes and Tian Shan, shows some common characteristic features. Life long among the nomads, has revolved through regular and successive changes of place. It alternates between permanent and temporary habitations, according to the cycle of the seasons. It is intimately connected with property, with proximity of permanent habitations, and with the existence of pastures lands which are dependent upon geographic conditions and the seasons. Every where these periodic migrations result from the necessity of finding new pastures and ensuring a food supply.

The long -established customs, traditions, and superstitious from the chief means of social control among the nomads. All migrations imply a lack of stability and specialized skill and the frequent break-up of family life. But unlike the alpine nomads, the Himalayans have to traverse considerable distances and have large areas of land at their disposal. In the Alps the family seldom accompanies the nomad, but in the Himalayas the families also migrate. Goats and sheep are not normally milked, and cattle are more or less non-existent. The alpine nomads are agriculturists and herdsmen, but the Bhotiyas are shepherds and merchants combined. The Gujjars rear cattle, whereas the Gaddis are shepherds and farmers too.

### The Forest and Pastures

Below the highest inhabited regions, and towards the south, are patches of forest, consisting of horse chestnuts, red rhododendrons, oaks and pines, while white rhododendrons, kingpins, yews, and juniper grow at greater altitudes above them. Birch and goat -thorn are found on the edge of the snow-line. These forest patches are quite unreclaimed, except that a few of them are exploited for fuel. To a man, coming from the extremely barren Tibetan passes, these forests afford a pleasing contrast. Their gorgeous vegetation interspersed with dense undergrowth and flowering shrubs, greatly delights his eyes, wearied of sterile monotony. In March and April, at the higher levels, the brilliant red rhododendrons form a beautiful contrast with the snowy peaks behind. As we travel downwards, the vegetation changes. The following list gives the limits of this plant succession :

| | |
|---|---|
| 13,000 feet | Vegetation entirely ceases. |
| 12,000 feet | Birch and blue pine. |
| 11,000 feet | Himalayan silver fir spruce, larch, yew, ground cypress, variegated bush rhododendron with flowers of all colours (pink, blue, purple, and white), grassy slopes common. |
| 10,000 feet | Sycamore, rhododendron and chestnut limit. Grassy slopes begin. |
| 9,000 feet | *Tilanj* (*Quercus dilatata*) and *Kharsu* (*quercus semicarpifolia)* chiefly found. |
| 8,000 feet | Oak limit. Hardier oak found with Himalayan silver fir. |
| 7,000 feet | Pine limit; oak and rhododendron and himalayan cypress in abundance. |
| 6,000 feet | Deodar limit; oak and rhododendron (red) begin to give way to pine. |
| 5,000 feet | Pine in abundance. |
| 4,000 feet | *Sal (Shorea robusta)* limit. *Haldu (Adina cordifolia) tun (Cedrela Toona), Sain (Terminalia tomentosa)* and *Dhauri. (Lagerstroemia parviflora).* |

Above 10,000 feet, and immediately adjoining the highest habitations, are fine grassy slopes. These pastures— *bugyal* or *payer as* they are termed locally— stay buried under the snow during the winter months. The snow begins to melt by the end of March, and the tops of the hills, which are moderately flat and open between

10,000 and 12,000 feet, become covered with verdure, and afford splendid grazing for sheep. The pastures grow poorer towards the line of perpetual snow. The grass growing there is known among the Joharis as *finchi*, and is considered to be the favourite food of sheep and goats. It is said to be so extremely nourishing and invigorating that only a few days' grazing is thought sufficient to refresh and fatten the jaded and famished animals. In point of quantity it is regarded as inexhaustible. The consumption during the day is more than compensated by the growth at night. Such ideal conditions for pasturage at such heights are possible on account of the high humidity due to altitude and the gentle slope and impermeability of the rocks. All these factors favour the growth of succulent vegetation.

These pastures, the best known among which are those of Dhankuri and Rokangsain, with those near Milam in Almora and Badrinath in Garhwal and Dhar in Chamba are utilized only when the inhabitants adopt the habit of nomadism. The animals have to be shifted from pasture to pasture in search of new grazing grounds as soon as the nearer ones are exhausted. In order to meet the needs of the flocks that support him, man adapts himself to the environment and becomes a nomad.

**The Nomad : Derivation**

The term **'Nomad'** is derived from the Greek word, 'nemo' which means to pasture. It refers to people who herds of cattle, but with no land of their own and consequently no permanent home. They roam about with their herds of cattle, in search of grazing grounds for them.

The word 'nomad' does not, exclusively, refer to all those persons, who constantly wander hither and do not lead a settled life. They neither posses any land of their own, nor have any home. They migrate with all their belongings either on foot or on burden animals like *yaks*, asses or mules, ponies, or horses, bullocks or buffaloes or camels or in carts either at their will or on their being forced by circumstances, in order to find out better living conditions for themselves. They roam as acrobats or rope-dancers, magicians, oracles, fortune-tellers, palmist, musicians and dancers, quack-physicians or surgeons, veterinarian, peddlers or petty merchants, carriers or artisans. Their way of life has a similarity to that of the Gypsies, Roma, known all the world over, as great wandering communities.

An American anthropologist, Jacob Baegart has described the Californian primitives way of living and ascribes to it the same such as Yerkulas and Chenchu of South India and Gujjars and Bakarwals of Jammu and Kashmir, Punjab and Himachal Pradesh of North, to take to this life. To quote Jacob Baegart:

> "The Californians themselves spend their whole life, day and night, in the open air, the sky above them forming their roof and the hard *sil* the couch on which they sleep. During the winter, only when the wind blows sharp, they construct around them (but only opposite the direction of the wind) a half-moon of bush-wood, a few spans high, as a protection against the inclemency of the weather. It cannot be otherwise with them; for if they had houses, they would be compelled to carry their dwellings along with them like snails or turtles; the necessity of collecting food urges them to wander constantly about. I am certainly not much mistaken in saying that many or them change their night quarters more than hundred times in a year; they hardly sleep three times successively in the same place and the same part of the country. Wherever the nights falls, they will be down to sleep."

So, in the case of the 'California primitive', as he moved along the unexplored country, accompanied by his women and children, he should have been meeting friends as well as foes, with whom he had to enter into welcome and unwelcome relationship, as the case might be. Though the primitive man undoubtedly wanted a woman, he never bargained for a wife and least of all one, who would impose on his unfettered freedom, curbs and controls, liabilities and obligations. It must have been atleast a mating arrangement, dictated more by biological considerations than those relating to property, inheritance, family unity or affinity. Just as he did not think of a permanent home, he did not think of a permanent partner in life.

When he wanted to enlarge his group-unit for purposes of offence and defence, he admitted his parents or brothers, his sisters, their husbands and their off-springs.

The conception of a social unit, larger and wider than the family unit, did not as yet influence him. He had no idea of a group or class affinity, much less a tribal feeling. The elements of a social-structure had not yet taken shape and collective thought and collective actions were still unknown to him. Villages and townships which were the fruits of much later development, had not sprung and all concepts of common social life were totally absent and unheard of.

## Adoption of Nomadism

It is in this state of human development and behaviour that the primitive man adopted nomadism as a practical, quite suitable and comfortable of life. This pattern was adopted by the early people because they liked it. It is so, even now, despite its incongruity in the midst of modern civilisation, its discomforts, its pinpricks and hurdles. It must not be difficult to recall to our mind, even at this colossal distance of time, the picture of a muscular, hardy, unshaven, naked, hairy man striding silently across the shady jungles, either all alone or leading a small group of equally naked women and children, trekking along, criss-crossing foot-paths, in their endless and perhaps aimless journey of life. Their belongings must have been quite few, consisting of a sharp edged digging sticks, a dead deer or a stag for the night meal, one or two dogs as pets, few skins for serving as mattresses or wearing apparels, hollowed bamboos or wooden receptacles for eating and drinking; they, trotting at a speed that would devour distances. The men and women could not have been sullen; the journey could not have been wearisome; the time would not have been heavy; though no songs were sung, no drums were sounded and no stories were told to enliven the march. There could not have been mirth wanting either. An unwary struggling deer would be felled; a tree-top honey-comb would be pierced; a handful of pebbles from the slings of the urchins would bring down clusters of mangoes, black-berries and ripened tamarind; the way-side wild myriad-coloured flowers would be plucked and tucked in the tufts; the stupid cuckoo would be mimicked and teased; the butterflies and beetles chased the ant-nests ground into pungent pastes; peacock's dances enjoyed; hares, wild-pigs, jungle-fowls and edible snared and netted.

I share the theory propounded by V. Raghavaiah

Once the day's journey came to an end, heralded by falling dusk, twinkling stars, and the fading path, the little republic settles down in the open or occupies the abandoned huts of previous campers and lights the flint fires for roasting their meat. Food roasted, all the members squat around the fire which, by, the way, helps to keep off the wild beasts, and finish their meal recalling the day's adventures, past experiences, and cracking racy jokes. The drum made of hollow tree trunks and extended leather, is then pulled out, heated on the embers and then the dancers would leap into the air, prance and frolic, writhing their shapely bodies to the beat of the drum, till all their known tunes fully exhausted and their limbs get tired.

When the night's merriment had come to a close and the waning moon had crept behind the clouds, it is time for getting wrapped up in the slumber, the enduring calm of all troubled minds. Nothing disturbs them till the sharp rays of the morning sun pierce their peace, not of an ominous wolf, not the buzzing bites of wild wasps, or other malignant vermin, not even the reverberating roar of a prowling tiger.

Some of the members may sometimes be employed for keeping by turns, night long vigils for protecting the group from the ravages of wild animals or attacks of preying foes. The pet dog might occasionally lodge a loud protest against the approach of an untamed rival from the adjacent jungle. A harmless star might start a gallop at the familiar ramblings of a distant wild beasts, but the nomad continues to enjoy his well-earned rest, which even nature dare not choose to disturb.

It may be argued that the 'Theory of Resedue' might hold good in the case of some of these nomads, specially of Sansis, Banjaras and Doms; that may be the survivors of those primitive tribes of hoary past and might have decided to cling on to the life, their fathers had led, preferring this free and unfettered life, full of romance, to the one, popularly known as civilised; punctuated at every step by pulls and restraints. But on closer scrutiny we find that some of those people took to nomadism due to various other reasons and not of their own volition.

### The Gypsies (Roma)

According to the top-most Gypsologists of Europe and America the Gypsies are found all over western countries of Europe and America, in millions. They were highly civilised and had a culture which may be termed as superb. They are believed to have migrated from their original home, (India) about 2,000 years back. Their emigration or exodus began at the time of the invasion of Alexander, the great (about 300 B.C.) and continued till the invasion of Mahmood Ghazanavi. These people had to leave their hearth and home and take to this life purely as a patriotic move, because their honour was at stake, which they wanted to keep unblemished and their entity intact, pure and unsullied. Instead of submitting to the atrocities of a tyrant intruder, they migrated from their 'fatherland' to unknown destinations, weathering the vicissitudes of nature and embracing with glee the hardships of worst type.

Mrs. R Bhatnagar quotes some other nomadic people of the Gaduila or Gadia Lohars of Rajasthan. The stray ramblers, are found almost in all important towns of India, with their entire house-hold packed in a bullock cart. They are seen constantly on move from one town to other, alongwith their kith and kins, young as well as old, even babies in the arms of their mothers and their centenarian aged parents, all accommodated in the same bullock cart.

Historians bear witness to the fact that originally they were all rajputs belonging to the valiant warrior clan of Mewar. But, after the tragic fall of Chittor Garh, in an encounter with Akbar, they bid adieu to their beloved motherland with a heavy heart and took to the life of aimless wanders, earning their livelihood by the sweat of their brow, fabricating agricultural implements and iron tools of everyday use. They took to iron—smithy, simply, because being a warrior race, they would have swords, spear-heards, *katras* and khukries—all made of iron dear to them, and also because by handling iron day and night, in season, they know the sources where to iron-ore and how to smelt and shape it.

The circumstances that compelled them to lease their hearths and homes and the great vow, their ancestors took, while leaving Mewar—their place of birth— that they would never lead a settled life until their beloved motherland was set free from the tyrant's yoke still haunts their memories. True to the vow their ancestors took about 400 years back, these valiant people have stood the text of time and by their firm determination and loyal and sincere devotion to duty, they are still roaming about as a free and unconquered people.

## The Pastoral Nomads

The history of pastoral nomads is different from those whom we have mentioned above. Their nomadism is directly connected with the needs of their herds, which contribute as the chief source of their livelihood. Their nomadism is not at random; it is centred or focused around temporary centres and is directly dependent on availability of food.

The social life of these pastoral nomads is democratic and their social organisations are controlled by council of elders. They have a homogenous and social order and women enjoy a status at par with men, with a strict division of labour between sexes. Normally men tend, while women milch. They are characterised by frugality and content with just one meal a day, eaten, in the evening.

Bakarwals, Gujjars, Todas, Gollas, Gaddis, Rebaries, Idyans, and Kurumbas, are classed as nomads or semi-nomads. Some of them have permanent homes to which they periodically return after the grazing hours or the period of migration.

Bhartiya Ghumantu Jan (*Khana Badosh)* Sevak Sangh has done tremendous job in studies and welfare of the Nomadic people of India. To quote J.P. Bharal :

> "Nomads have stable, social and economic organisations, which have been influenced by the exigences of nomadic existence. There are definite territories which they traverse at different periods of the year. They have a definite cycle in their movements. They are conspicuous for their frugality and endurance and as a result of their nomadic life, they have a love for freedom and dislike for controls and limitation, imposed upon them by modern society. They dislike settled occupation, which deprive them of their freedom. Generally, they move from state to state and village to village and look toward the rich society to patronise their art of music and

dancing, magic, fortune-telling, acrobatic feats, etc. Many a times they prescribe talisman which are often spurious. Some are traders, who purchase grains, salt and other articles from areas where these are cheap and sell them, where a marginal profit is possible."

Besides these nomadic groups, there are groups of people who have their own homes or land and periodically return to subsist on their earnings. Their nomadism very often involves moving with the family and belongings to location, where arable lands are available and from where they return later, when harvesting has been completed. Such groups of people are classified as semi-nomadic groups.

## Classification

Bharal classifies the nomadic and semi-nomadic groups, on the basis of their occupation in four categories— pastoral nomads; trading nomads; nomads rendering specialised services, and miscellaneous groups.

The economy of the pastoral nomad is mainly dependent on the herds they posses and their nomadism is directly connected with the needs of their herds. Animal and animal products (wool, hide and skin) and sale or exchange of their animals are the main constituents of their economy. In India, such nomads are confined mainly to the Himalayan regions.

Among the pastoral nomads, Changpas an Bakarwals of Himalayan region are typical. To supplement their income from herds, they carry on other activities like hunting, fishing, collecting medicinal herbs and roots for sale in urban areas.

As mentioned earlier, trading nomads generally purchase grains, salt and other articles from the areas, where these are easily available at a cheaper rates. They sell them in the areas, where these commodities are scarce and where a marginal profit is possible. Some of the trading nomadic groups have established themselves in business, like selling of vegetables, milk, medicinal herbs, drugs, etc., and as brokers of cattle, goats and sheep, etc. The notable example among trading nomads in India are Banjars who are found in most of the states.

Nomadic groups render socialised services too. They have specialised themselves in professions like basket-making, rope-making, mat-making, smithy, house-construction, selling of medicines and drugs, etc. Beldars, form a typical group, who move from village to village and engage themselves in construction work. They move alongwith their families. They are hard-working, quiet and co-operative.

A few of the nomadic groups are black-smiths and prepare agricultural implements and other requirements for the settled communities. Lohars, quoted before, are a typical example under this category. Attempts for their rehabilitation were made but little success has been achieved so far.

Nomadic groups like Sikligar, wander from one place to another and sharpen weapons like razors, knives, sickles, etc. prepare household furniture. Some nomadic groups wander as drug sellers and quack surgeons, like Singi-walas. They pretend to cure all sorts of diseases, connected with impurity of blood.

There are some other nomadic groups like Nats, Kalbeliya and Jogis. The former show acrobatics and physical feats and also beg food grains. The Kalbeliya are snake charmers, who move from village to village, showing snakes and asking for food-grains in return. There are various types of sooth-sayers, palmists and astrologers among the Nomadic and Semi-nomadic groups. They are called Budubudiki, Budgajangam Gondhali Joshi in Karnatak (Mysore) State. They have Brahmin gotras and go about houses predicting the fortunes of people, and collecting money, grains, clothings, etc. The Gadulia Lohars are descendents of Maharana Pratap the great Kshatriya king of India.

Thus the nomod goes on.......

# 3

# Himalayas: The Land of Gods

*In a hundred ages of the gods,*
*I could not tell Thee of the glories of Himalayas.*

— *Skanda Purana*

"Though superficially well-known today, the Himalayas still are little explored, and yet they offer a highly rewarding field of research. For, like all great mountain ranges they have, in the course of time, offered a refuge to races, cultures, religions and arts which elsewhere are forgotten, wiped out or merged beyond recognition into other social units or later form of civilization. Many interesting problems which confront the ethnologists, historians and archaeologists, may await their solution in those valleys."

*Hermann Goetz : THE EARLY WOODEN TEMPLES OF CHAMBA*

From time immemorial, the Himalayas have had a profound fascination for Indians and foreigners alike. Their attractions have been irresistible for the saint and the poet alike, for the pleasure-seeker and the *bon viveur*. The sages of Rig Veda referred to them as Himavat, while Valmiki, the poet who set the *Ramayana* to verse, immortalised them as Shailendra. Hindu mythology has it that Mount Kailash is the traditional home of Shiva—the destroyer among the Hindu Trinity of Gods —and of Parvati, his consort, the daughter of 'king of all mountains'.

It is the grandeur, the beauty and the splendour of the Himalayas that captivate a visitor and grip him. The glitter of the morning sun on a snowy peak, the iridescence of a glacier's edge when it breaks under its own weight , the majesty of a rugged monolith, the infinite peace of a meadow strewn with daisies, forget-me-nots, buttercups and wild primulas, the silence of a starry night in the depth of the Himalayas, the exquisitely sensuous joy of bathing in the cool waters of mountain stream are things to be seen and experienced. You cannot describe them nor can you read about them in books. When travellers bring back stories of the moon looking like a plate of burnished silver, "so close you could stretch out your arm and seize her in your hand ", or of blue and purple rocks painted against a yellow sky, of a rainbow circling the midday sun in a cloudless sky, of clouds fading away with an incredulous smile. "Traveller's tales" , you say under your breath and dismiss them.

## The Lore of the Himalayas

Besides the wild natural beauty, the variety and the majesty, which the eyes behold, the Himalayas have something which no other mountains possess. One is overcome by a strange sense of peace and a feeling of spiritual joy when one enters the Himalayas. Some people believe it to be a kind of magic worked by sages and *rishis* who have gone and lived in the mountain solitude since time immemorial and invoked the blessings of gods.

The call of the mountains is alluring, but the call of the Himalayas is irresistible. As ever since the sons of Pandu, who after the battle of *Mahabharata* renounced their kingdom and alongwith their dog took recourse to the Himalayas, this magnetic force has been attracting and captivating sages and saints, pilgrims and travellers, artists and scientists, mountaineers and anglers, or just lotus-eaters who love to lie basking in the sun in the middle of a meadow covered with daisies and violets at a height of 2,743 m. (9,000 ft.) above sea level. The Himalayas have something for every temperament and taste.

Few places in the world have exercised greater fascination over the minds of men than the Vales of Kashmir, and the western Himalayas. A land of vast forests and meadows, placid lakes and bubbling springs orchards and paddy fields, ringed by stupendous snow-crowed mountains, it has aptly been described as "an emerald set in pearls". In fact, Kashmir has been the dreamland of tourists through the ages. The grand Mughals regarded it as "the earthly paradise". Akbar gave it the noble *chenar* tree to enhance its beauty. Jahangir likened it to a beautiful woman and , as he would a woman, he adored it. His last words, as the emperor lay on his death-bed, were "Kashmir and nothing else".

The first visit to Kashmir is always a memorable experience. The beauty of the valley makes a sudden and strong impact on the visitor and overwhelms him by a felling of wonder and unmixed delight. The nature of the landscape changes the moment one crosses the Pir Panjal, the high mountain range, which lies along the southern fringe of the valley. On one side lie the yellow-brown hills of Jammu, almost arid in their aspect, but as you emerge from the tunnel at the Banihal pass, you see the other side — a vast stretch of rich green fields with rivulets and tiny hills meandering through them. In the distance, a narrow grey ribbon, flanked by a double row of poplars, runs out to disappear into the denser confusion of a patch work panorama. This is the motor road to Srinagar. The poplars were planted by the Mughal emperors, and as they aged and wither, new ones are planted to take their place. Around all this stand the glorious amphitheatre of the northern Himalayas with their snow covered peas. It has justly been said that the Kashmir valley is a jewel set in the heart of rocks. In his famous poem, *Lalla Rookh,* Thomas Moore exclaimed through the lips of his hero, Aliris, the King of Bucharia:

> "Who has not heard of the Vale of Cashmere
> with its roses the brightest that earth ever gave.
> Its temples and grottos and fountains as clear
> As the love-lighted eyes that hang o'er their wave!"

**Physical Features**

Geographically, the great mountain range can be divided into three longitudinal zones:

(1) The great Himalayas, which is the innermost line of the high ranges, has some of the highest peaks in the world and rises to a height of about 25,000 feet at places. A few amongst them, such as Kanchanjunga, Dhalulagiri, Nanaga Parbat, remain a standing challenge to mountaineers.

(2) The lower or the middle Himalayas about fifty miles in width is no more than 12000 to 15000 feet high at its highest point. Some of the best known hill stations of northern India are situated on the slopes of the middle Himalayas.

(3) The outer range or the Siwaliks constitute the foothills of the Himalayas with an average height of 3,000 to 4,000 feet.

Dotting the valleys and the slopes of this great mountain range are numerous temples and shrines; amongst them, Kailas, Manasarowar, Badrinath, Kedarnath are important places of pilgrimage where devotes go in their thousands every year.

The Himalayas are unique for another reason too. The restless human spirit is always in quest of fulfilling extra human relationships. People go there for seeking communion with their personal God, after withdrawing themselves from the attachment of a life of social participation,. Others went there in self-rejection and escape. Hundreds of hermitages thus sprang up along the banks of the holy Ganga, which offered shelter to the thousands of seekers after truth; this tradition survived into the middle ages. For instance, Sankaracharya, the great religious philosopher of the eighth century, did not think his mission complete until he had established a temple of Badrinath and the Monastery of Joytirmath in the heart of the Himalayas, and for this purpose, he had to travel several hundred miles from the extreme south.

## The Hill Stations

Except for Kashmir and Almora, we owe most of our hill-stations to the British who found the heat of the plains unbearable and developed salubrious summer retreats where they could work peacefully away from the enervating heat. The middle Himalayan region with its pleasant climate, sparkling streams, gushing revulets, green meadows and Alpine forests offered ample scope for such hill stations. Along the lower slopes of the great mountain range, there thus grew up a number of new towns and cantonments.

The hill-stations like Simla, Nainital, etc., on the lower spurs of the Middle Himalayas— from Almora in the east to Dalhousie in the west— are islands of modern civilization in a region which has a culture and way of life all of its own.

## The Hardy People

As a result of the conflict between man and nature, there has developed in these regions a mode of life which is rugged, yet colourful. The fertile terraces on the Himalayan slopes are a testimony to the adaptive skill and patient labour of the hill people.

But where man was unable to tame and harness nature, he migrated in search of new lands and means of livelihood. The method of shifting cultivation practised in the past by Bhotiyas of the Kumaon hills, and Gaddis of the Chamba valley, the Gujjars of Kashmir and the other nomadic tribes adversely affected the fertility of the land. With every change of season, they migrate in search of fresh land. It is a sight at once sad and impressive to see groups of men and women walking precariously along narrow hill paths, carrying their entire belongings with them, and followed by flocks of sheep, goats and cattle and ferocious looking watch-dogs.

Obviously, the life in mountain region is hard. Every moment is a struggle with the elements. Yet the great difficulties of the environment have not been able to suppress the initiative and adventurous spirit of man. On the other hand they have evoked a high degree of adaptive skill and uncommon vigour, which is responsible for the self-sufficient agricultural economy of the region. The picturesque terrace fields on the slopes bear testimony to the extraordinary degree of strenuous toil and sourcefulness.

## Perturbed Front

The Himalayas being the perturbed front of India since the Chinese invasion, it has become a national problem to study the nomadic people, particularly the Gujjars, Gaddis and Bhotiyas of this region intensively with integrated approach. The writer had the privilege to work among them as a participant observer. One who ever had been in those difficult areas, can never forget the Brahmaur valley possessing a very narrow gorge flanked by almost perpendicular cliffs on either side of the Budual stream which joins Ravi in a majestic manner.

A number of villages in Himalayas have their separate deity or god, around whom the community life revolves. Shiva and Parvati are popular god and goddesses there. It is a common belief that

Shiva and Parvati can give a son to the sonless. In Kullu valley, there is a tribal god *Jamlu* who is like Kuber, the cashier of the nomad gods and who gives money to the tribals on their demand. In fact, the priest brings as much money from a dark chamber as the God Jamlu wishes the nomads to spend. In Kullu valley, many villages are believed to be governed by the local deities. A colourful procession of village gods can be seen on Dusshera festival in Dhalpur *maidan* of Kullu which is no doubt the peaceful land of gods.

# 4

# Gaddis : Nomads of the Himalayas

## THE GIGANTIC HIMALAYAS

*The gigantic mountain chain of Himalayas,*
*Its torrential life streams, sky scaling snow peaks,*
*Valleys full of rolling grasses and its forest and mineral wealth*
*Have been a great attraction to the pilgrims,*
*Tourists and the traders;*
*Yet the people who live there*
*Continue their endless battle against grinding poverty*
*And the threat of hunger, a perpetual reality.*
*The land is anguished by the severity of nature,*
*The indifferences of rulers and fleeing down*
*Of its educated and enterprising sons.*
*Neither the enchanting beauty of its landscape*
*Nor the spirituality of the faithful,*
*Who go there for pilgrimage and mediation*
*Have been of any help to the people*
*Who are born there and must there die.*
*The Himalayas today call for workers with*
*Talent, energy, zeal and combination,*
*To serve and give their best;*
*Workers who could identify themselves*
*Completely with the life of the people,*
*Who will respond not to snow speaks,*
*But to the starving humanity*
*And endow it with hopes of its future.*

This is how one poet has described the mighty, magnificent and majestic Himalayas, who are threatening yet benevolent, inviting, entertaining who are malignant, yet munificent; who are severe in winter and beautious and bountiful in summer and demonically devastating during the rainy season. Yet who are so attractive, soul elating and irresitibly enching that they draw people from far and near into them.

The Gaddis reside exclusively upon the snowy range which divides Chamba from Kangra. A few have wandered down into the valley which skirts the base the Chain but the great majority lives on the highest above. They are found from an elevation of 4,000 ft. to 7,000 ft. above which altitude there is little or no cultivation. A large number of tribals lives in Chamba and Kangra districts of Himachal Pradesh.

## The People and Habitat

The Gaddis are semi-nomadic, semi-agricultural and a semi-pastoral tribe. They spend six months in migration in search of grass and fodder for their cattle and seasonal employment for themselves and six months in their village for sowing and harvesting their crops.

As a race, they are very simple, fierce, stalwart and virtuous people and as a whole are very interesting tribe. They are frank, peaceful and merry in their manners. Sturdily built, very often bow legged, the tribals are accustomed to enduring great hardships during any sort of weather owing to their migratory life most of them lead. Due to exposure to Sun and rain, they have a slightly dark wheatish complexion. The women folk are pleasing and comely and have the reputation of bearing—modest and chaste. They are bashful and courteous too. Raja Sansar Chand II of Kangra was infatuated by the beauty of a tribal girl and married. She was called a Gaddi Rani. And this event is rightly the theme of a popular folk song—

*The Gaddi was grazing his goats*
*And Gaddan her cows*
*Her earthen pitcher broke on the rocks*

*The cow ate grass*
*Raja Sansar Chand beheld a young face*
*He fell in love*
*And married the lass.*

## SOCIAL STRUCTURE

Gaddis follow patriarchial and patrilineal types of family system. Father, the head of the family, is responsible to look after the interests of each member of the family. But mother is equally responsible and works hard and to some extent, harder than father in field and in the house too.

The *Gaddi* is an occupational name, means shepherd and includes the following castes:–

1. Gaddi Brahaman;
2. Gaddi Rajput;
3. Gaddi Rathi;
4. Gaddi Sipi;
5. Gaddi Rehra.

There is not much distinction of work. Each community is shepherd by profession but in social hierarchy the caste among the tribes are normally placed as above.

The caste composition is based on the age-old tradition which they brought with them while migrating from Punjab, Rajasthan or Bengal in the good old days. There are various theories and folktales about their migration, prevalent among the scholars as well as the tribals.

A popular saying goes:

*"Ujrya Lahore*

*Te Vasya Brahmaur"*

or Lahore was vacated and Brahamaur populated.

**Nomads in Migration**

A real nomadic life of the Gaddis can be observed while they are in migration with their flock. A shepherd carries some light utensils of aluminium and an iron pan. He invariably keeps a *hukka* in one hand. With a *khalru* of cereals and other essential and limited articles, loaded on his back, he follows his flock. He carries his tobacco in a leather pouch. He does not have any spare clothing with him and wears the traditional *chola* in which some newborn kids or lambs sleep.

A Gaddi woman can be seen in migration carrying loads equal to that of a man. She carries the luggage on her shoulders and ties her little child to load, holds some utensils in one hand, helps another child of hers with the other hand and covers the inaccessible and impassable paths in the Himalayan valleys. Thus, she accompanies her husband through thick and thin, sharing his trials and tribulations as a real better-half. (Now there are social changes).

During the journey, a shepherd cooks simple food consisting of maize-flour bread, *masuri dal* or vegetable if available. Sometimes, salt, green chillies and raw onions fill the plate.

The tribal does not keep any tent with him and sleeps under the open sky. During inclement weather, he lies under the shade of a tree, a projecting rock or in a cave. In the absence of these he doubles himself with a bundle and lies among sheep and goats. A blanket is as good as his bedding and the *dora* (200 feet long woollen rope worn by every Gaddi around the back) serves as pillow.

The dogs of the Gaddis are so fierce that they can repel the attack of a bear or even a panther. They watch their master's flocks and protect them. The Gaddis are very fond of their dogs. They would not easily part with them for love or money.

The *malundi* (Shepherd) sells his sheep and goats if the bargain is favourable or if he is in need of money. Being god-fearing and superstitious, he sacrifices a he-goat on certain difficult passes. He never takes bath, seldom cleans his teeth and thus leads absolutely nomadic life. But is surprising to note that despite his carelessness, he is very healthy and quite happy.

He covers between 5 to 7 miles a day. He has to exert himself much in keeping his flocks on the right path. This work is done with the assistance of the dogs or by whistling to which the sheep and goats amazingly respond.

The nomad invariably carries a flute with him. When he plays a folk tune, the hills echo and the hill girls suspends her work under its influence which cannot be expressed in words.

Man is, of course, an organism adapted to Nature. As such, he is ultimately dependent on his geographical environment. Wide fluctuations in geographical conditions set limits. However, in given relative stability of natural conditions, such as man now enjoys, he can become master of his natural environment rather than remaining its slave. But the Gaddi fabric of life seems to be different. They are still slaves of nature and depend on traditional professions.

A Folk song goes:

*Ho truti mere chhikan ri*
*Kachhi vo baria bhale ho.*

*Ho kachhi na truti-truti*
*dile ra paritam ho.*

*Ho bura hunda Bhattia ra rahana*
*Vo baria bhale ho.*

*Ho bura hunds Jhangra ra jina*
*Vo baria bhale ho.*

A newly married couple is in migration, crossing the inaccessible paths of Himalayas. The wife is tired and feels pain in her legs. She complains that she did not enjoy even a single night peacefully after her marriage. She blames her husband that this is all due to their migratory life.

### The Glorious Past

The Gaddis have their glorious history. According to a well known historian, J. Hutchinson, Brahmaur (Chamba) was the oldest principality in India. Maru was the first to settle in this place. He was a man of religious disposition and belonged to the ruling family of Ayodhya. Renouncing his age-old kingdom, he wandered from place to place in quest of peace and ultimately reached Chamba.

Narad Pal waged a war for 12 years with Chamba, whose forces advanced to Madankot near Mandi. This war is still recalled in folklores. The Gaddi army, as the Chamba force is correctly called, besieged the Rana of Manali in the lower fort on the "Gaddi Padhar" for three months. Eventually, the Kulu people got rid of these invaders by treachery. Luring them across the Kothi gorge, after a peace had been patched up by inviting them to a social gathering, they took away the bridge in the darkness.

During all the military expeditions, the armies, of the Kings of Brahmaur must have consisted in bulk of Gaddis and that was why even after the shifting of the capital to Chamba their forces were generally called the Gaddi Army. Even today, there is a good number of brave soldiers belonging to this tribe serving in the Indian Army.

## RELIGION AND MAGIC

"Men generally believe that their conscious being will not end at death, but will continue indefinitely or for ever, long after the frail corporeal envelope which lodged it for a time has mouldered in dust," says J.C. Frzer, a great anthropologist in his book, *The Fear of the Dead in Primitive Religion.*

Religion, indeed, has played a very important role in the life of our country. It is the centre around which the whole of Indian social life rotates. Each one of thousand and one sect has dissented only to come back to the fold within about three generations, contributing its own special technique of normative, theleological goal seeking patterns of behaviour to the broad general stream of Indian design. Hence, Indian religion is essentially traditional way of life.

They fellow Hindu traditions and religion in their own way. Their religion presents some interesting feature and play a vital role in their life. Animal sacrifice is a very common characteristic of their rituals. Most of their gods and deities are considered non-vegetarians and on any religious ceremony an offering of goats and sheep is made.

Lord Shiva is the supreme deity of Gaddis. This is the only god who creates the world and destroy it on doomsday. They worship Him but their worship is catholic to a degree. A folklore on Shiva goes:

*"The Gaddi was grazing his flock*
*The Gaddan offered incense to Shiva*
*To the Gaddi He gave sheep*
*And to the Gaddan—beauty."*

This shows their faith in Shiva who is supposed to give them health, wealth and beauty. He fulfils all the desires of his devotes. It is because of this pervasive faith of the people that this land is called *Shivabhumi*–the land of Shiva. The Chaurasi area in Brahaur has a magnificent temple of Harihar with a number of Shiva-lingas. In Brahmur proper, there is no temple dedicated to Laksmi Narain, Krishna and Rama, although the people observe Janmashthmi and to a certain extent, Ram Navami too. During our survey, a *gurudwara* was located in this area but neither any Arya Samaj mandir nor a mosque or a church could be traced.

*Spirits:* The Gaddis believe in several evil spirits, which are propitiated on certain occasions. They are known as Avtari spirits raised to the level of local deities out of fear and awe. An Avtar is the spirit of a person who died issueless. It causes sickness and warns of impending mishaps in dreams. He creates panic in the heart of the person who later falls sick. To scare away the ghost, Jamanwala is performed. The sick person dons cloths, which are made for the spirit with a silver image of the dead and then worships the Avtar's idol, which is usually set up near any stream. Goats are sacrificed to please these spirits.

Kailu Bir or Kailung is believed to be a demon causing abortion. He is believed to cause harm to a pregnant woman. To propitiate this spirit, a pregnant women puts aside four copper coins with her necklace in the name of Kailu. Two or three months after delivery, the priest alongwith the woman worships the demon which is sanctified by reciting *mantras* and worshipped with an offer of he-goat which is sacrificed on this occasion.

Gunga is another disease-spirit believed to attack cattle particularly cows. The powerful demon is worshipped by setting aside an iron pan in its name. A peace of iron is made and the deity taken into the cattle shed where he is worshipped by the sacred fire. A he-goat is killed and some drops of blood are sprayed on the iron. Soon after cakes are offered and a part is eaten by only members of the household and the left over are buried.

*Banglands.* The tribals believe that if the rituals regarding *Devo-samskar* are not performed properly, the deceased soul would not get peace. Thus, the angry soul may harm his relations. The dead is believed to visit his descendants and relatives' homes in dream. To pacify the soul, people voluntarily construct small houses in the name of the deceased. These houses are called *Banglauds* or *Badangs.* These are built on the outskirts of the village in open places. The travellers also stay in these houses. But above all, the soul of the dead one lies in eternal peace and may bestow benefits on the relatives of the deceased.

*Rituals and Sacrifices:* A priest is attired in the typical Gaddi dress wearing a silken turban, a golden *Kantha* round his neck and some gold rings in the ears but no shoes. He carriers a heavy silver mace and a *thali* with articles of *pooja,* vermilion, rice, flowers, a piece of red cloth, the ball, shankh and milk. The pujari, is generally a Brahaman, but it is a peculiar feature of their religion that a priest (*chela*) belonging to a menial group is considered to be the best of all. In some parts of the country a lower caste man cannot enter a temple, whereas a priest there belongs to a lower community.

The animal meant for a sacrifice is first bathed. *Fulast* (flower and rice) is offered on its head and water is dropped with *drub* (grass) and the devotee holds a copper coin in his hand. If the animal shivers, it is an indication of God having accepted the offering. After this, a third person kills the animal. The priest chants some *mantras* and receives skin, head and one leg of the animal and the rest of the body goes to the slaughterer.

The sacrifices are mostly made while putting new fields under plough; removing the incapacity of a field for growing wheat; laying the foundation stone of a house and laying the central beam of a roof; celebrating births and marriages; on the 12th and the 14th day of a death before a journey and for propitiating evil spirits.

Here is an interesting event which I can never forget. Two days before I reached the Budhal river, young man fell into a river and died instantaneously. On hearing the news of the death, his relatives reached the spot with two he-goats and sacrificed them in the deceased's name (so that the departed soul might rest in peace).

*Chela* (priest and magic man) is the guide without whose consent people do not even send children to schools. The Gaddis in their everyday life are very religious. Even a literate Gaddi has full confidence in *chelas* or priests.

### The Magic World

Like other tribes, the Gaddis believed in magic which is also a part and parcel of their religion. The magician achieves the desired end by the ritual techniques and not by making any appeal to the spirits. There are *chelas* who act as magic men. They possess some special power, which is either inborn or achieved by training. There are four types of magic:

1. *Vashikaran:* The patients's eyes become as that of an owl's and he cannot utter a single world.
2. *Maran:* Poison is given to person through magic for killing him.
3. *Contagious:* A part of an animal is carried to acquire its characteristics or as a protection against it.
4. *Tantra:* To make anybody a leper or reduce to a skeleton.

## DAYAN OR WITCHCRAFT

The great object of magic can be obtained through rigorous witch rituals.

The *Dayans,* according to the sayings of the tribals, masquerade in the guise of women during the day. As soon as night sets in, they leave their beds and put broom-sticks in their places. Thus, they use a spell on their family members who feel if they are there. The *Dayan rides* on *Garur, lion or mrig* and flies away. All the *Dayans* assemble in a forest and sing and dance throughout the night. They return to their homes before the people wake up at dawn.

If a *Dayan* wants to kill a person, she flies to a *jot or dhar* and brings some herbs with her. Later on, she feeds the same to the man or woman concerned who, if not treated by a *chela* in time, dies of an unknown disease. These *Dayans* are considered very dangerous by the community but they are not as many as in other hill tribes.

The Gaddis, like Santhals of Bihar, believe that the power of witch-craft is not inborn but acquired by training. The *Dayan* herself does not persuade any woman or girl for such training. The learner of her own comes to her to get training in witch-craft.

*Witch Doctor:* Besides the other *chelas* of various gods, there is a witch doctor, who is named as *Gardi chela.*He worships almost every tribal god. He cures those patients who are caught by some black magic. The *dolis* (the patients) gather at his residence for treatment. He starts playing on *dupatra* (an instrument like sitar, made of goat's intestines) to the beat of a drum. Meanwhile he throw a *kauri* towards the *dolis* who fall into trance and start dancing. Consequently, they disclose the name of the *Dayan* who gave them the *booti* (herb).

After this, the *chela* asks the patient to dip is palm and feet into the water already filled in a bucket. Then he waves with a peacock's *muttha* on the patient's body. As a result, some dust, hair, thread etc. come out of the patient's body and fall in the bucket of water. The process goes on for about a week, till the *doli* recovers his health. I collected many instances of such treatment in this area.

*Mani:* Sometimes, a persons buries hair, *trishul, dhoor* of the dead and an effigy of *setisarivan* (turmaric) in the house of his enemy with the help of a magician. Consequently, all the members of the family fall sick and remain so continuously. Then a *chela* is called for their treatment. He brings a *mani* (wooden pot) and keeps it in the centre of the house. Some neighbours gather around it. A *kangana* ( red thread) is tied on hand. The *chela* chants the *mantras* and drops the grains of rice of *Mah.* After this *mani* starts moving and fetches the man to their place where magic has been done. It automatically turns down there. The man is asked to come to his seat and the *chela* rechants the *mantras* for getting the proof again. When the same action is performed three times, the *chela* asks the people to dig the floor, where the *mani* turned down and thus the buried articles are sought and consequently all the family members recover. *Mani* is also used for tracing out stolen goods.

*Chela in Trance:* To induce a *chela* into trance, he is seated cross-legged and incense is burnt before him. The people assemble around him and inspire him by chanting these *mantras* in praise of Manimahesh, Shiva, Burbuhari, etc:

*Olmale Manimaheshwar ki Jai*

" *Shivashakti ki Jai*

" *Chadollawali ki Jai*

" *Burbuhari ki Jai*

" *Kelang Vazir ki Jai*

" *Apshakti ki Jai*

" *Bhattiwali ki Jai*

After a few seconds, the *chela* begins to sway and shake and is seized of religious fervour. Meanwhile, a glass of water is also given to him who turns it down but not a single drop of water falls down. He sprinkles some of the drops on his body and the rest of it is given to the patients. They drink this water and are totally cured. He also throws vermilion around himself and part of it he keeps on his tongue and the rest of it he rubs on his month. At times, he tries to inflict injuries on his naked back with a *haungal* (iron bar) and other sharp pointed instruments.

He is seldom hurt. When he is in a complete frenzied mood and stops playing. It is appropriate time to ask him questions which the devotees do by making cash offering. The *chela* sucks blood of the goat which is sacrificed on this occasion.

## NOMADISM—A BLOT

"We are no more keen to lead the migratory life. Nobody likes to leave his home and hearth and wander hither and thither like nomads for six months of the year, except for the sake of belly."

These are the words of a young Gaddan of Chatrari village whom the author asked of her views on migratory life, 30 years ago. During a public opinion poll, conducted in the Gaddi villages, the author gathered the following interesting data about the causes of their migratory habits:

### Causes of Nomadism

1. Scarcity of fodder for the flocks during the winter season.
2. Unsuitability of snowfall to the sheep and goats.

3. Scarcity of food stuffs as the yield of the crops is not up to the mark.
4. Non-availability of seasonal employment in the region.
5. Cultivation of land by a few in district Kangra for which they have to move.
6. Health-hazard of severe winter.
7. An urge to migrate because of a long-standing habit; and
8. Association of migration with the mythical migration of Lord Shiva from Kailash to Chamba during winter.

Only eight per cent response, in our public opinion polls, were associated with certain conditions regarding their will to lead the migratory life; the remaining 92% respondents felt the migration to be inconvenient. This data is different from what we got from Gadia Lohars a nomadic clan of plain who roam from place to place in the plains and do not want to settle.

## Problems of Adjustment

The author interviewed many persons working as labourers, wood cutters, coolies and domestic servants in Chamba town. On this basis, he came to the conclusion that a Gaddi can adjust himself to any type of circumstances, provided he is humanly treated. Gaddis complain that people, particularly some Government officers, hate them and do not treat sympathetically. The ultimate solution lies neither in isolation of the tribals nor in an indiscriminate and unregulated contact. Dr. Guha thinks that in devising a suitable machinery for the administration of the tribal population, both these factors will have to be taken into consideration.

The solution to this problem is to appoint the officers in this region from amongst the tribals. It is a matter of some satisfaction that there is a number of Gaddi teachers in various primary schools but, unfortunately, suitable candidates from amongst the tribals are not available even for the lower posts.

On the basis of our multifarious study of the Gaddi tribe, it is considered that the following suggestions for their uplift welfare and progress may prove helpful:

**Suggestions**

1. The Gaddis should be induced to give up their habit of leading a migratory life. With this end in view, they should be provided with seasonal employments or remunerative indoor jobs, particularly in winter.
2. An adequate and regular supply of cereals to the tribals may be ensured the year-round.
3. Their complaints against the Forest Department—that the authorities are not sympathetic towards them and of delays in issuing of permits for grazing cattle to them—should be attended to.
4. Some forest cooperative societies should be organised which may arrange collection of the *dhoop* and herbs with medicinal value.
5. Fodder, wood and fuel should be provided to them during the winter season.
6. The landless farmers should be allotted land for cultivation and modern agricultural implements distributed among them. The canals should be dug to facilitate regular and timely irrigation.
7. As this regions is very near to China, our Army must guard there and the civilians should be trained for self-defence.
8. The Khadi Gramodyog Commission can be a more beneficial agency to them, if it increases its work in this area. The craft of weaving and spinning should be encouraged so that the Gaddis need not sell their wool; on the other hand they should prepare cloth from it and then sell them on a good rate.
9. The means of communication need development and the village tracks require reconstruction. Fuller facilities should be provided to the travellers in the rest houses. It has been noticed that in many rest houses even blankets are not available.
10. The Local Administration should not have any prejudiced or biased attitude.
11. Education must be made compulsory and free for them.

12. The Government and private welfare agencies should propagate prohibition, explaining demerits of *sur* and alcohol, so that they may give up this habit after realising its consequences.
13. Animal sacrifices should be stopped with the help of religious agencies. The disciples of Naga Baba can do a lot in this regard.
14. The temples and the historical monuments of Gudiyar region should be repaired or renovated.
15. New breeds of sheep, bulls and cows should be popularized.
16. Medical facilities should be provided in rural area. Family Planning Scheme should be made popular.
17. A.I.R. should relay some more special programmes containing folk-songs, folk-tales and other recreational items for the Gaddis.
18. If a path for travelling by mules is constructed upto Mani Mahesh, which is believed as Kailash, it will help for a happy pilgrimage and also increase the income of this region. To preserve their culture, some cultural associations should be established and aided by the Government.
19. The employees, and particularly the teachers and social workers, who are appointed in this region, should bear a good moral character and they should be sympathetic to the tribals. The heart of the tribals cannot be won by criticising their social customs and traditional ways. The integration and mutual behaviour between the outsiders and the tribals need courtesy and affection both ways. *(There are many social changes now-a-day but hardly any sociologist except Mrs. Puri and Dr. Dharmvir Mahajan, nobody has touched this subject).*

## BRAHMAUR : A GADDI VILLAGE

Brahmaur, a village (now hill town), is the headquarters of the Brahmaur Sub-Tehsil in Chamba district. This had once the distinction of being the seat of government of the old sovereign state of Brahmpura for over 350 years from the 7th to the middle of the 10th century. Then the capital was shifted to the newly laid out town of Champa, which later came to be called Chamba. The beautiful and artistic temples are in a remarkable state preservation and remind one of the golden days that the place had seen. It is a very important village in this part of the land is distinguished by its 1,300 years old temples.

The approach to the village in the past was very hazardous and it will be interesting to read a description of the route from Chamba to Brahmaur as given by Vogel in his *Antiquities of Champa State, part I* which appears as Appendix I. In turbulent times of the day, the place was ideal for defence when every neighbour was a potential enemy. Even now, one has to travel 22 miles on foot or on pony from the nearest bus terminus at Gehra to reach the village.

The road first follows the right bank of the river Ravi and then crosses over to the left side at Bagga—14 miles from Chamba over a rickety suspension bridge–upto Kharamukh. Here it crosses over to the other side of the river and enters Brahamaur valley through a very narrow gorge flanked by almost perpendicular cliffs on either side of the Budhal stream which joints Ravi. Every effort is being made to convert the tract between Gehra and Brahmaur—22 miles—into a jeepable road as early as possible and in fact jeeps are being driven upto Brahmaur, but land slides are the regular problems which damage the track. It is expected that within the next few years it should be possible to reach Brahmaur by a better road.

The Budhal raises in the Kugti pass and flows some 30 miles through the Brahamaur valley commonly known as Budhal valley. The whole valley is roughly the shape of a bottle with an elongated neck ending at Kharamukh. The valley round about the village is fairly open with long terraced fields on the left bank of the nullah reaching far up to the top of the ridge overshadowing the village.

The land is fertile and productive and depends on the rain. The natural water supply is plentiful and small snow-fed streams flow throughout the year to unload their waters into the Budhal. This in turn empties into the Ravi at Kharamukh. The most important of the small nullahs that run near Brahmaur is the Brahmni Nullah. This has enough water to run 40 odd grinding miles of the surrounding villages. The waters of this nullah have further been harnessed to generate hydro-electric power for Brahmaur recently. It is expected that in the very near future the village would have the many benefits of electricity.

Brahmaur lies at a height of about 7,000 in the lap of the Bharmani forest growing on the ridge, famous for the shrine of Bharamani Devi. Goetz compares the scenery to some of the finest sceneries in Switzerland and the climate is salubrious. Just towards the northest of the village, can be seen the peak of Mani Mahesh. This is famous in the surrounding area as smaller Kailash and one of the abodes of Lord Shiva and for this reason also the whole of Budhal valley is called Shiva Bhumi. The landscape affords an interesting contrast on the right bank of the Bhudhal nullah; cliffs, with bush wood here and there, stand perpendicular in their majestic form. These give little or no scope to human hand to display its skills in forming the terraced fields. These clifs are so inaccessible that even the shepherds fell hesitant to scale some portions of them. On the left of the nullah, the valley has *ban* forests at the lower elevation gradually giving place to pine clusters towards the top of the ridge.

Inhabited by Gaddis, the village has a semi-pastoral, semi-agricultural lot of people. The greater portion of their wealth consists of flocks of sheep and goats which they graze during winter in the valley of Kangra and in Suket and Mandi *illaqas*. For the remaining year they drive them across the range into Chamba and Lahaul. The other important occupation is agriculture. They follow it in rather an indifferent and fuitile way on account of their migrations. Spinning, weaving, silver-smithy and black-smithy are other minor trades adopted by some people. The entire Brahmaur sub-tehsil is also called by the name of *Gaderan*—the abode of Gaddis.

There are no remains of old places of kings of Brahmaur. By common belief, their places stood on the *chaugan* which is a small piece of flat land and some 350 yds. long and 50 yds. wide, situated at a little higher elevation towards the North. At the eastern corner of the *madan* some Government offices are being build. An old building known as Kardar Kothi exists just below the temple of Narsinghiji. It is here that the Naib-Tehsildar holds his office. This also served as the office of the Kardar of the *illaqa* in State time. This Kothi was badly damaged in the 1905 earthquake.

The summer is pleasant, the weather remains generally dry, but occasionally, there are a few showers of rain. The average of the last ten years from 1952 to 1961 shows that the average yearly rain and snowfall varies between 22.33"—80.77" and 126"—288." The winters are severe and most of the villagers migrate to low lying areas.

### Configuration

The configuration of the region is given in 'The Revised Working Plan for Upper Ravi Forest':

The two main ridges, which divide the region of Upper Ravi from Kangra on the South and from Range–Lahaul on the North are lofty precipitous, with peaks over 19,000 feet high and from these ranges a series of spurs spread out to the main valleys. At the lower elevations the spurs are broader and the slopes less pronounced. The side valleys between these spurs are 10 to 20 miles long and are often watered by fine streams. The demarcated forests occur in all situations, but rarely extend below 5,000 feet or above 9,500 feet, the greater part of their area being between 6,000 and 8,000 feet. In the higher portions of the main valleys they reach down to the bank of the rivers, and in other places they lie 2 to 3 miles from a stream. The slopes vary greatly and are less than 25 degrees. In average between 40 and 45 and very steep when 45 degrees. The more precipitous forests are often intersected with pretending rocks and cliff and a few are such remote situations that they can only be reached with difficulty. (Source—Range Officer, Brahmaur).

According to the notes on the geology of Chamba, the mountains are formed for the most parts of State rocks of the Silurian age, resting on a central mass of granite or grani-toid gneiss. When the slates are not meta-morphosed by contract with the granite, generally resemble the typical Simla slates. The conglomerates consist of slaty schistose matrix containing pebbles of all sizes and shapes, round to angular. Sometimes veins of white to blue or grey quartz are also common, and in some places massve bands of dark pale blue (weathering buffs) sub-crystalline lime stone and hard greyish green trap are found. The soil is more or less clayey. Sometimes stiff yellow or white clay, but except in these instances the soil is fertile for tree growth.

The only source of drinking water commonly called *panihar* is in the Chaurasi locality. This is fed by the Brahmani pool through pipes. This has saved the botheration of going all the distance to Brahmani pool to fetch water.

**Vanshawali**

According to the records available the village might have been founded in the middle of the 6th century. Maru, the father of the first ruling chief Jaisthambha, settled here. According to a local legend, it is older even than that and is believed according to the common belief to the garden of goddess Brahmani. She used to reside where her shrine now stands on the ridge. This is the source of the Brahmani Nullah, Brahmani Devi was a *Brahmani* whose son was very found of a per *chakor*. The *chakor* was killed by a peasant and the boy died of grief. His mother burnt herself alive along with the dead body of her son and the *chakor* and her spirit started afflicting the people. This legend says that god Shiva with 84 *sidhs* once came to rest in this garden on His way to Mani Mahesh. When goddess Brahmani, the presiding deity of the place, saw the smoke of the fires lit by the *sidhs* rising, she was angry on this unauthorised intrusion and assumed the terrifying giant like body. She came down to the place, ordered Shiva to move out at once. Shiva in all humility begged permission to stay for the night and promised to move out in the morning. The Devi reluctantly agreed to this prayer and retired to her abode on the ridge. When the night weared off, the 84 *sidhs* transformed themselves into 84 *lingas* because Shiva was determined to stay at the place. The place where these 84 *sidhs* stayed and subsequently transformed themselves into *lingas* is known as the Chaurasi. Until today there are 84 big and small temples.

Shiva granted a boon to Brahmani Devi that all persons intending to go on a pilgrimage to Mani Mahesh must have a dip in the Brahmani pool. Failing this their pilgrimage would not be acceptable to Lord Shiva.

Maru, father of first recorded prince Jaisthambha in the Chamba *Vanshawali* was the first to settle at this place. He was a man of religious disposition and belonged to the ruling family of Ayodhya. Leaving his oldest son to look after the affairs of the parent state, he wandered from place to place in quest of peace and came this part of the country. When he reached Kharamukh, he stayed at

Ulansa above Kharamukh on the left bank of Ravi. The people of Brahmaur requested him to establish himself at Brahmaur proper, a better place. They narrate another legend about this. According to this, Jaisthambha was the son of a ruling chief of some un-named place in Rajputana and had fallen out with his father. He was turned out of the domain. Jaisthambha decided to renounce the world and approached a holy man whom he accepted as his *guru*. The holy man advised him to lead the life of Rajput and directed him towards this area where he could establish his principality. When he reached Khramukh with his followers, he was greeted by another saintly person, Agyachari Rishi, who was visited in his dream by Lord Shiva and directed to welcome the prince with the offerings of a *topa, chola* and *dora,* the attire of the god. Anyhow, according to the Chamba *Vanshawali* the first prince who established his principality at Brahmaur was Jaisthambha, son of Maru.

The history of Brahmaur kings beginning from Maru to *Sahila Varman,* has been given in the *History of the Punjab Hill State,* by J. Hutchinson.

The Rajas of Chamba belong to the Surajvansi line of Rajputs; their *Vanshawali* begins from Vishnu or Naryana Rama, the hero of the Ramayana, and is sixty-third in the order of descent; which is continued through Kusa, son of Rama. The original home of the family is said to have been Ayodhya, but they moved out at a very early period of the upper Ganges valley where they settled in Kalpa. The historical position of the *Vanshawali* commences with the name of Maru who was then the head of the family and contains sixty-nine names including that of the present ruling chief.

Maru is said to have been at first a religious devotes whose life was given up to *tapas* or self mortification. But afterwards, he married and got three sons. When they reached manhood, he bestowed a kingdom on each of them. Leaving the eldest in the ancestral home, he traversed the Punjab with the other two and settled one of them in the mountains near Kashmir. Accompanied by Jaistambh, the youngest, he then penetrated to the upper Ravi valley through the outer hills and having conquered that territory from the petty Ranas who held it, he founded the town of Brahmanpur and made it the capital of a new State. This event is believed to have taken place about the middle of the sixth century A.D.

The original state was of very small extent and in all likelihood comprised, at the most, only the present Brahamaur Wazarat, i.e., the valley of the Ravi from below Bara Banghal with its tributaries, the Budhual and the Tundahen, as far down as Chhatrati.

It would appear that the Maru's rule was only nominal, for the chronicles say that, having founded the State, he made it over to his son and returned to Kalpa, where he again became a *sadhu.*

After Maru several Rajas ruled in succession, but only their names are known. They are; Jaistambh, Jalastambh and Mahastambh.

The name of Aditya Varman A.D. 620, appears as Adi Varman in the *Vanashwali* and is of over special interest, for it is twice mentioned in the Brahmaur inscriptions, in which he is referred to as the great-grand-father of Maru Varman, by whose orders they were engraved and he was the first of the Chamba line to assume suffix of Varman.

Following is a list of the rulers of Brahmapur and Chamba principalities;

| *Name of the Ruler* | *Period* |
|---|---|
| Muru, Founder of the State } | Period |
| Jaitsambh | not |
| Jalstambh | known |
| Mahastambh | |
| Aditya Varman | *c.*A.D. 620 |
| Bala Varman | *c.*A.D. 640 |
| Divakara Varman | *c.*A.D. 660 |
| Meru Varman } | *c.*A.D. 680 |
| Mandar Varman | Period |
| Kntar Varman | not |
| Pragalbh Varman | known |
| Ajai Varman | *c.*A.D. 760 |

| | |
|---|---|
| Suvarn Varman | c.A.D. 780 |
| Lakshmi Varman | c.A.D. 800 |
| Kushan Varman | c.A.D. 820 |
| Hans Varman | No record is available |
| Sar Varman | |
| Sen Varman | |
| Sajjan Varman | |
| Mrityanjaya Varman | |
| Vugakar Varman | c.A.D. 940 |
| Vidagdha Varman | c.A.D. 960 |
| Dodka Varman | c.A.D. 980 |
| Sala Vahan Varman | c.A.D. 1040 |
| Soma Varman | c.A.D. 1060 |
| A. Sata Varman | c.A.D. 1080 |
| Jasata Varman | c.A.D. 1105 |
| Dahala Varman | 1118 |
| Udaya Varman | 1120 |
| Lalita Varman | 1143 |
| Vijaya Varman | 1175 |
| Vairasi varman | 1330 |
| Manikya varman | 1370 |
| Bhot Varman | 1397 |
| Sangram Varman | 1442 |
| Anand Varman | 1475 |
| Ganesa Varman | 1512 |
| Pratap Singh Varman | 1559 |
| Vir Vishu | 1586 |
| Balabhadra | 1589 |
| Prithvi Singh | 1641 |
| Chatar Singh | 1664 |
| Udai Singh | 1690 |
| Ugar Singh | 1720 |

| | |
|---|---|
| Dalel Singh | 1735 |
| Umed Singh | 1748 |
| Raj Singh | 1764 |
| Jit Singh | 1794 |
| Charhat Singh | 1808 |
| Sri Singh | 1844 |
| Gopal Singh | 1870 |
| Raja Sham Singh | 1873 |
| Bhuri Singh | 1904 |

On 1st November, the State came under the direct control of the political department of the Government of India.

On 8th December, 1924 the birth of a son Tika Lakshman Singh, the heir apparent afforded much pleasure to Highness.

After independence, Chamba alongwith other States became the part and parcel of the Indian Republic.

A few more facts reproduced below about the history of Brahmpur rulers would prove of added interest to our readers. The highly flamboynts allegorical and mind-curdling description of Sahila Deva is aimed at placing him at par with divine as well as historical personalities of great name and honour. It is to bring out the honour and greatness of the house to which he belonged.

From his residence at the glorious Champaka, the highly devout king (Soma Varman), and ornament of the spotless house of Sahila Deva, who (Sahila) was a fresh rain cloud to extinguish in a moment the mighty blazing fire of the Kira forces; fanned as by the wind by the Lord of Durgara, assisted by the Saumatika; whose army was manifestly crushed by the fearful frown on his brows; whose alliance was humbly sought by the ruler of Trigarta, who was asked the favour of his bestowing royalty in return for services by his kinsman, the Lord of Kuluta, anxious to render him homage, who by the weight of battle had broken, like a wide-spreading tree, the large force of the Rurushka on whom wounds had been inflicted; who bore the fortune name of Karivarsa (elephant rain) on account of the continuous and stable generation of his posterity, joyfully granted by the Lord Bhaskara, who by his unequalled kindness and compassion, combined with unsurpassed bravery, generosity, firmness, and unfathomable profoundness has impaired the fame of heroes like the sons of Jamadagni (Parasurama), Sibi, Karna, Yudhisthira; whose wide-spread greatness, brilliant with matchless and universal effulgence, was renowned like that of Sudarakasvamideva by looking upon whose lovely presence the eyes of the world have been made fruitful who by his fury in setting in array a thousand battles, acquired such names as Sahasanka (marked by rashness), Nissankamalla (dauntless wrestler) and Matamata Sinha (roaring lion).

With one exception all the names in the quotation are fairly well-known and the references are of great historical interest. As regards the Kira, we have seen that they were a people living in the mountains in the vicinity of the Kashmir valley. They conquered Brahmapura in the time of Lakshmi-Varan and they are here represented as having again invaded the State. They were assisted by the Raja of Durgara. Kashmir had from ancient times claimed an intermittent suzerainty over the hill tracts as far east as the Ravi; and the formidable array which is represented as advancing against Sahila-Varman was probably meant to assert and uphold this claim. They doubtless anticipated an easy victory, but a crushing defeat awaited them; for they are spoken of as having been dispersed by the Chamba forces as if by a frown on the Raja's brow.

The next reference is to Trigarta, the ancient name of Kangra, which at that early period also included Jalandhar and a large portion of territory on the Plains, between the Sutlej and the Ravi. We are told that Sahila Varman's alliance was sought by the Trigarta Chief, after a contest in which Chamba was victoriously With such a name for valour we may well believe that Sahila Varman's conquests were not confined to the Ravi Valley; and the war with Trigarta suggests the probability of the Chamba Chief having carried his arms to the south of the Dhaula-Dhar; and annexed the whole southern fringe of that range from the Ravi to Bir-Bangahal. There are said to be many traditions in Kangra pointing to an early occupation of these territories by Chamba. Kuluta is the ancient name of the principality of Kulu and it owed allegiance to Chamba in the time of Sahila Varman, as it had done at an earlier period. The two royal families were also connected by marriage.

The reference to the Turushka is, in some respects, the most interesting of all. This term was applied to all invaders of India from the North-west. Originally used for the Scythians, it came afterwards, to have an exclusive reference to the Muhammedans, who from the middle of the seventh century had begun making their influence felt on the north-west Frontier. The Turki Shahi dynasty, which had ruled Kabul and Peshawar for the centuries was overthrown about A.D. 870 by the Brahman Wazir of the last Turki Shahi dynasty, with its capital at Udabhandapura, now Ohind on the Indus. There this dynasty continued to rule over the kingdom of Gandhara till A.D. 980, and thereafter at Lahore, till finally subdued by Mahmud of Ghazni in A.D. 1021. As we learn from the Rajatarangini, these kings were in alliance with Kashmir; and also doubtless with others States in the Punjab which was for a long time in subjection to them. We may, therefore, conclude that contingents were sent by these states to help oppose the onward advance of the fierce invaders from the west; and most probably in one of these frontier wars Sahila Varman had came into conflict with the Turushka and gained renown for himself by his valiant deeds.

The reference to Kurukshetra is in full accord with ancient custom in India.

Sahila-Varman did no spend the last years of his life in Chamba, probably the home of his early days and greater attractions for him. We may well believe that his reign was a long one in view of all that he accomplished; and when his work was done and old age was creeping upon him, he abdicated in favour of his son, Yugakar and retired to Brahmapura to spend the evening of his life in ;peace. There he dwelt as a sadhu in the company of Charpatnath and the other *Yogis,* many of whose shrines are still pointed out on the small "green" where all the temples stand and which for this reason is called the 'Chaurasi.' For the same reason the Chamba State is believed to have been originally sub-divided into 84 *ilaquas* but they are less numerous.

## THEORY OF MIGRATION

The Gazetteers of Chamba and Kangra and the settlement reports neither give any exact date and year of the migration of Gaddis to their present habitat nor claim their migration from a particular place. The Gazetteers of Rajputana (now Rajasthan), Punjab and Northern Provinces do not give any concrete proof in this regard. It is for the historians to study this problem and find facts in this matter.

General Cunningham believes that the Kolian group who at one time occupied the Western Himalayas, hailed from the same race as the Kols of Central India. There are still many people in western hills who bear the name of Kolis, Halis, Sipis, Meghs and Degis etc. The Degis of Kulu, for example, are called Koli as an alternative name. These tribes must have been of Non-Aryan origin like the other aborginals of India, but a great fusion of race took place in ancient times by inter-marriages and later degradation from the higher castes, a process which is still going on. This, doubtless, led in course of time to many changes in the appearance and characteristics of the people, and to these we may describe the fact that most of them exhibit the features of the Aryan race and use the dialects of the Aryan family languages.

As to the hills, they are believed to have remained to a much later date inhabited only by aboriginal tribes and eventually they were invaded not only by tribes of settlers driving back the old inhabitants, but by military adventures subduing them, much in the way in which Ireland was first invaded from England. Certain peculiarities which are seen in the hills such as the formation of petty principalities, the sole lordship of the chief, the customs of primogeniture in his family, the contempt of plough and business of farming by Rajputs and Brahmans, be explained as the effect of such conquering invasions, and of the military order which the invaders would have to maintain in the constitution of their society in order to keep down a subject race.

Prof. R. Davids has postulated three lines of advance, one along the foot of the Himalayas from Kashmir eastward. The Aryans, being hillsmen, tended to cling to the hills and we learn that there is clear evidence in Sanskrit literature of their presence in the Western

Himalayas at a very early period, probably before the age in which the hymns of the Rig Veda were compiled. We may, therefore, assume that the oldest strata of the Aryan population of Chamba State are of a very ancient origin.

Several theories in connection with their migration are prevalent among the tribals as well as among the historians. Gaddi khatris and Rajputs believe that their ancestors fled from Lahore in the times of Prithvi Singh to escape the persecution of Aurangzeb whereas some of them tell that their fore-fathers came from Rajasthan and Delhi.

When I asked the old Gaddi Brahamans of Brahmaur village about this, they made a different statement. They maintained that their ancestors migrated from Bengal but nobody knew as to why and when they left Bengal to settle down in Himachal Pradesh. However, a few Brahaman Gaddis said that they had migrated from Delhi during the reign of Raja Ajai Varman.

Hutchinson, J. writes in his book "History of the Punjab Hill States."

"It is possible that many of them began to find their way into hills at an early period as priests and religious devotes."

After having a close observation of their cultural and religious life, the author feels inclined to support the following lines.

1. The Gaddi Rajputs are immigrants from Punjab (Lahore).
2. A section of Gaddi Rajputs migrated to this area from Rajasthan.
3. Most of the Gaddi Brahamans came from Delhi.
4. Some of the Gaddis might have come directly from Central Asia.
5. A group among them is aboriginal, most probably the menials, who previously were known as Dravidians and in course of time adopted the customs and religions of the invaders, (see *Vedic India* by Rangozin, Zenaide A., PP. 287-295)
6. A number of Gaddis might have come from U.P., Bengal and other States as cultural aspects are similar to those of the inhabitants of the said States.

As regards the historical basic of Gaddi migration to their present settlements, the references in officials records repeat the same stories as I heard from the Gaddis during my research work and survey of the Gaddi tribe in Himachal Pradesh in 1966-67.

**Marriage**

Marriage is a must amongst the tribals. The unmarried person will die of a dog's death—says a Gaddi of Garola village. The Gaddis are monogamous. The boy and the girl are never consulted and the marriage is arranged by their parents or guardians. The following types of marriages are prevalent among them irrespective of their casts and communities:

1. *Byah (Dharahom Pun):* The regular betrothal takes place with mutual consent of the parents of the boy and the girl. To mature the betrothal, negotiations, take place between the parties and the usual rituals like *Kanya dan* are observed at the time of marriage. This type of marriage is quite rare in Gadiyar region.

2. *Bata Sata or Exchange:* In this form of marriage, a boy gets a wife in exchange for his sister for his wife's brother. This is the most popular form of marriage among the Gaddis.

3. Gudani; This is a widow re-marriage. A widow is married by one of the brothers of the deceased husband. This is allowed among all castes excepts Brahamans. But now this custom is dying out and a widow is free to take on a new husband outside the deceased husband's family.

4. *Kamash or Ghar Jwantri:* This is a typical type of marriage among Gaddis. The boy has to work in the house of his father-in-law, usually for a term of seven years. Though it is on the decline these days, one may see some cases in the interior.

5. *Khewat:* In Himachal Pradesh this marriage is also called *reet* or *lag*. This system permits a woman to take on a new husband if he pays the former husband the amount incurred by him on his marriage. The consent of the former husband is essential.

6. *Bariana:* In this marriage, cash payment is made for the girl. The amount is fixed mutually. Payment in kind is not favoured.

7. *Marriage Burtans.:* The marriage expenses incurred are usually proportionate to the economic position and means of the families involved. There are, however, one or two ways in which such households receive temporary help from their relatives or friends. The most important of these customs is *tambol.* This is prevalent among all the Gaddis. Some cash money is made over to the bridegroom or his parents by friends and relatives who receive a present in return of a little more generally Re. 1 on similar occasion of marriage in their families. Another custom called *saj* is also common where presents are given instead of cash. The presents generally are in the form of clothes, a bit of jewellery and cooking utensils, given to the bride or her parents under the same obligation as in the case of *tambol.*

The third custom is called *chad.* It is sort of loan given in cash and kind to the bride. The portion in kind is composed of *ghee* and flour and other articles which come in use for marriage feast and in this case also a similar return of presents must be made. One could institute a legal suit for recovery of *chad* but not for *tambol* and *saj.*

## Marriage Rituals

All the communities have common rituals but Reharas and Sipis do not observe the sacred thread ceremony. All communities have *purohits* to conduct the marriage. The *purohit* is essentially a Brahman, but he does not accept food cooked by Sipis and Reharas. The marriage are contracted between families belonging to the same caste but of different *gotras* although they have no objection to contract inter-*gotra* marriages also, provided the parties are not of the same blood relations. Efforts are made to contract marriages within a radius of five or seven miles, but sometimes the net is cast wider too.

The average marriageable age for a boy and a girl is 16 to 25 and 12 to 18 respectively.

After the betrothal, an auspicious day is fixed when men from boy's house go to girl's parents with a seer of *ghee* to get a suitable date fixed. If they approve of the proposal, messengers from both sides go to consult the *purohit* who writes the detailed marriage programme which is called *lakhnotri.* For this they pay to the *purohit* in cash, rice and some red thread called *mauli.*

The marriage ceremony starts with *smmhurat* rites by worshipping *Ganpati,* earthen pitcher (Kumbha) and the nine planets (*navagrah*). Batna, a mixture of turmeric powder, barley flour and mustard oil is rubbed on the boy as a cleansing agent and three black woollen threads are tied round his right wrist to protect him from an evil eye. He is then taken out into courtyard by his mother for bath. While taking bath black threads are untied and thrown away and the boy is led back again by his mother.

*The Jogi :* The *purohit* then ties nine red cotton threads round his right wrist and give him *gur* to taste. God *Ganpati, Brahma, Vishnu, Kumbh* and *Navgrahs* are again worshipped and a goat is sacrificed. The blood of the goat is sprinkled on *sandori* and *munjmala* by a Rehara for which he gets Rs. 1.25. The bridegroom then disguises himself as a *jogi.* He is dressed in a *dhoti,* flour *mundras* fashioned out of kneaded flour in his ears, a satchel slung over his shoulders, a black woollen rope round his waist. He also cover his back with a *mrigchhala* or deer's skin, suspends a *fanani* to the black rope and takes a stick in his right hand with the *janeu* tied round his right thumb. Then the *purohit* asks him the reasons for his becoming a *jogi* to which the boy answers: "To receive the *joneu.*" The *purohit* again asks him as to what kind of cord he requires: whether of copper, gold, brass, silver or cotton. The boy requests for the inexpensive cotton cords.

The *purohit* then directs the boy to go for purificatory baths at Badrinath, Triloknath and Mani Mahesh. The boy takes these baths by dipping his hands and feet in water contained in three different vessels.

After this, the *jogi* begs for alms first from his relatives and then from others who give him a piece of bread and promise him goats and cattle. Concluding this ceremony, the priest asks the bridegroom whether he desires to devote himself in *jatera* affairs or in *matera* affairs and he invariably chooses *jatera.* The dress of the mendicant is cast off because the boy has chosen to lead the life of a *grahsthi.*

*Preparations and rituals:* The bridegroom sits on a wicker mat or a sheep skin bag *(khalru)* and a dagger is touched to *munjmala* above his head. Then the boy's nearest kin followed by others offers presents according to their turn, pour drops of oil over his head with grass. They also rub a bit of vermilion on his forehead. The oil and vermilion are contained in bowls held by the bridegroom's uncle. This is called *tel* ceremony. The bridegroom, after taking bath, dresses himself in white *pagri, kuwa* and a red *luncha* specially prepared for wearing on marriage, a white *Patka, a gulabadan suthun* and *loie* thrown over the shoulders.

*Suhag patari* is for the bride. It consists of a *dupata, chandan, chura, kesar, sandhoor, mehandi, supari.* Now nail polish, cream and powder are also added in well-to-do families. There is a *lanchchari, Ghagru, hemodri, ungi, chundi and kanghi,* three pieces of *gur,* some dry fruits, rice and seven *luchis.*

Like other communities of northern India the Gaddi boy wears a *sehra* presented by his maternal uncle. His *Bhabi* puts *kajal* in his eyes. After this he gets up and a *thali* with lighted earthen lamps is waved over his head. This is called *arti* is then sanctified by chanting of *mantras.* The boy's father honours him by presenting a *tambol* of Rs. 1.25, out of which the rupee is retained by the boy and 25 P. go to the *purohit.* Accompanied by his mother, *purohit* and other women he advances to the entrance of the house and stands over his head. *Torans* (thin round poles painted with red and yellow colours) are fixed at the entrance of the house where marriage takes place. A Sipi stands outside the entrance and presents the bridegroom with a *kumbh* filled with water and he puts a coin in it. Then the boy gets into a *Palki.*

Then starts the marriage procession composed of male and female relatives of the groom and friends, dressed in their best and led by local musicians. The head-dress of the relatives of the bridegroom is white *pagri.* To distinguish them from other *barati* golden threads are tied to one side of the *pagri.*

On arrival at the bride's house, the *baratis* are housed in a separate place selected for the purpose. The boy's father and uncle with one or two persons takes a basket full of *luchis* to the bride's parents. This is called *pat-partana.*

In the bride's house, they are given something to eat and in return they put 60 P. in the plate and then they come back to join others. This rite is known as *juthpai.*

*Ceremonies:* The boy's *purohit* then proceeds to the bride's house to deliver the *suhag patri* or *barasuhi.* The *purohit* then comes back to conduct the bridegroom and his followers to the bride's house accompanied by the musicians. The mother-in-law of the bridegroom receives him at the entrance. She performs the *arti* ceremony by waving *arti* seven times over his head with her right hand and holding her left over his turban. Three *chapatis* placed in a *thali* are also thrown outwards the courtyard. The mother-in-law then retires while the father-in-law standing aside with *patka* round his neck washes his son-in-law's feet. The boy's *purohit* places a *duna* containing some rice, a walnut, *drub* and flowers in his hands.

After this the boy follows his father-in-law to the *bedi* where the *purohit* chants vedic mantras. The bride is then brought to the *bedi* and stands face to face with bridegroom. The boy's *purohit* holds the boy's neck with his right and of the girl's with his left, making their shoulders touch each others thrice first pressing the boy's right to the girl's left and so on. This rite is named as *chan par chan.*

Two torches are held on either side of them and seven small twigs are put in the girl's hands. She drops them in boy's hands and he breaks them one by one by placing them under his right foot. This breaking of the twigs is known as *chiri.*

The couple is thereafter made to sit down and the boy's father-in-law offers *sankalap* in which he gives away his daughter to his son-in-law and thereafter washes couple's feet as they sit before him. Certain minor rites called *chichari* are now performed by the bridegroom and his father-in-law. *Ganpati, Brahma, Vishnu, Kumbh, dia* and the nine plants are worshipped.

Thereafter the girls *dopatta* is held out by her brother and the groom dubs it with little red vermillion. Similarly, the girl anoints the boy's *patka.* The girl stretches her hands and the *purohit* puts in it 10 P., a walnut, *drub,* flowers, *til* and rice. The boy now lays his hands over her's. The girl's father performs the *kanyadan* accompanied with the chanting of *mantras.* At the conclusion of this rite, the articles in girl's hand are given to the *purohit* and the couple taste *ghee* and *gur.*

The girl retires, but the boy remains there to go through *manihar* rites. *Arti* is waved over his head. A betel-nut and a red tape are placed near his left toes which the touch with his dagger. After this is done, the *purohit* takes the tape up and throws one end over the boy's head to his mother-in-law and ties the other end round the *pagri* of the groom. This tape is called *manihar.*

The boys is then drawn by the *manihar* by his mother-in-law and led inside the house before a picture of *Kamdeo* (God of Love) fixed in a room. The girl is also brought there by her brother to stand beside the boy. The girl is dressed in clothes given by her in-laws in *suhag patari.* Then seven cord of the *barasuhi* are handed over to the boy by the girls maternal aunt. He places them on the bride's head whereafter the girl's hair are combed and arranged with these cords by her aunt. This ceremony is called *sirgundi. The* groom puts *sindhoor* in between the parted hair of the bride and this is called *mang bharna.*

The bridegroom's shawl and the bride's *dupatta* (kharwas) are then tied together and the bride is escorted by her maternal uncle to *bedi* followed by the bridegroom. The bride's father washes the couple's feet. *Havan* is performed and *Ganpati, Navagrah, Brahma, Vishnu, Kumbh, Saptrishi* and the Vedas and four directions are worshipped to ward off all mishaps. This is followed by placing fried barley in *chhaj.*

*The coming of the bride:* The groom's father and the bride's father sit under the *bedi* and a blade of *drub* is put by the *purohit* into the bride's father's hands. He holds it between the tips of his middle fingers at one end and the other end being similarly held by the boy's father. The bride's father then utters *Asmat Kanya tasmat gotra* meaning "Our girl now goes over to your *gotra.*" At the conclusion, the bridegroom receives *rubar* from his mother-in-law who gives a rupee and twenty five paisa, the others give copper coins only. The bridegroom touches his mother-in-law's feet as a mark of respect. The ceremonies at the bride's house are now over and bride is taken in the *palki* alongwith all the paraphernalia followed by the bridegroom and the *barat* which is now reinforced by the addition of some of the ladies from the bridge's side and her brother. On arrival back at home *arti* is waved over the couple by the bridegroom's mother who also gives the bride a rupee. Then the pair is taken to a room for *Ganpati pujan.*

The couple also takes four rounds of the earthen lamps and *Kumbh* installed in the room. The rite is *athlai.*

After this the *sehra* is removed by the *purohit.* Having done the *athlai the* kangnas of the bridegroom are united by two selected men. At the conclusion, the bridegroom receives *tambol* from relatives and *bradri.* The women gather round the bride and have a look at her face in turn and also give her presents in cash and kind. This is called *munshani.*

The couple after staying there for a day or two leaves for bride's parents house on some aupicious occasion accompanied by the bridegroom's brother and ladies of bride's house who had accompanied the party on its return journey.

The party stays there for a day and is served with the choicest meals. After performing *puja* of Ganesh and *Navgrah* they return to the bridegroom's house. While returning the couple receives presents from the bride's parents. The presents consist of two *gardus* and *luchis* of wheat flour. This ceremony is known as *harphera* and is observed among Brahmans and rich families of Khatris and Rajputs only.

The bride sometimes does not come back with the bridegroom to her in-law. Instead, she stay behind with her parents for a year or two and this period may extend upto five years. On an auspicious day the bridegroom accompanied by two or three of the nearest relatives proceeds to his in-laws where they stay for two days. During their stay the young girls of the house collect around them and crack jokes with the guests. This exchange of jokes is called *galli lagai.* There, they receive *babroos* of wheat flour and the following articles from the bride's parents.

| | |
|---|---|
| 1. Cholu | 2 |
| 2. Luanchari | 2 |
| 3. Ghundu | 10 to 15 |
| 4. Gardu | 4 to 6 |
| 5. Chadars | 1 |

*(This is based on my old study. New social changes are required to be studied).*

## INHERITANCE

There is a peculiar custom among Gaddis that if a widow continues to live in the house of her late husband and gives birth to a child by becoming intimate with another man, the child is called the son or daughter of the late father. In Gaddi dialect, such children are named as *"Hallad"* or *"chakandu."*

In Brahmaur village, Dhakri a widow of Goruba gave birth to a male child after two years of her husband's death. As she continued to put up in her late husband's house, the child was ascribed with the status of Goruba, a dead husband of Dhakri. People call him the son of the deceased Goruba.

Actually *Chakandu* as such, means a child born inside four walls of a house, when a widow becomes intimate with another man implicitly. She should prefer the sibling brothers of her husband or agnates. Still she is free to do so with a condition to remain in the house of her late husband.

Gaddis have their own way of inheritance which is quite different from present Hindu Succession Act. There are two methods by which inheritance goes.

1. *Mundaband,*
2. *Chundaband.*

*Munda* means boy. If the father has one wife, the property is distributed in equal shares among the male children. This is what they call *Maudaban.*

*Chunda* refers to the woman. If the father is leaving behind more than one wife, the property is equally distributed between the wives. For example Panja of Pansei village left two wives and three children, one from first wife and two from second wife, the property was divided into two equal parts and not in three parts. Afterwards each part was sub-divided according to the number of sons from each wife.

### Illegitimate Sons

As regards illegitimate sons, they cannot get any sort of property but the *Chakandu* or *Hallad* sons are entitled to inherit the property.

In case there is no male child in the family, the widow is entitled to it for the whole life. After her death the property goes to the agnates or the nearest collaterals.

The Gaddis of this regions, as a special case, have been exempted by the Government from the purview of the Hindu Succession Act. As a result of this, there is not a single change in their inheritance process, whereas vast changes have been occurring in the Hindu society. When I asked some of the Gaddis as to how would they feel if property were equally distributed among the sons as well as daughters, they replied that the daughter being other's wealth, she would not be given fathers wealth.

On the basis of the public opinion polls conducted in the tribal areas. I come to this conclusion that they are not in favour of allowing their daughter the right of inheritance on movables or immovables.

Makhauli, a Gaddi of Garola, informed me that in the past a custom was prevalent that if the father accepted the child born to someone else, the society recognised him as an illegitimate child and no share from property was given to him.

A Gaddi can be distinguished easily by his peculiar type of dress, which he wears for saving his body from the cold weather. He uses mostly woollen clothes which are characteristic and striking. A few clothes, observed in detail are given below:—

**Chola**

It is a loose coat worn by the men over a cotton shirt to *kurta.* It is prepared from *Pattu* and reaches below knees. Its colour is generally white or grey. It is never washed and is discarded only when smothered to shades. It has deep collars, which hand loose in two lapels in front where one stows away various articles such as foodstuffs, small pots and newly born lambs and kids too. I have seen a Gaddi *Puhal* carrying 3 lambs and 2 kids in his *chola.*

**Dora**

This is a peculiar part of their dress which is worn by every man, woman, boy and girl, young and old. This is a block rope made of sheep's wool and is worn over the *chola* or the *luanchhari* round the waist. This is also named as *Gatri.* We have gathered some interesting data about this rope. Following is a table showing the average measurement and weight of the *dora* according to the different sex and age:

*Details of the Dora*

| *Sex* | *Measurement (length)* | *Weight* |
|---|---|---|
| Man | 180 feet to 200 feet | 2 kilo |
| Woman | 120 feet to 150 feet | 1½ Kilo |
| Children | 30 feet to 80 feet (according to age) | ¼ Kilo to ½ Kilo |

The above table makes it evident that even the children are not spared from wearing this rope. When we asked the people the reason for wearing this *dora,* there were some genuine but interesting answers. These answers can be summarised as under:

1. This rope is very convenient in carrying loads on one's back.
2. If there is no spare rope, they can use it and tie the necks of their sheep and goats together with it.
3. It keeps them alert and is useful in climbing the hills.
4. Flint, sickle, leather pouch, *hukka,* etc. are tied to it.
5. Money bag is also concealed in it.
6. It keeps a person healthy.
7. If they do not wear it, they are likely to suffer from stomachache.
8. It possesses some religious value as well. They say that this rope is a *Sive-ri-Seli (Shiva's* sign) and as *Shiva* is their God, they wear it in His name.
9. Sometimes the luggage is tied with this rope.
10. When they are in migration and sleep at night under a starry sky, this rope used as pillow.

(Based on my old studies, Dora is decreasing even in the villages).

### Death Rites

The tribals cremate their deads. Lepers and those who die of *luhar* (kind of typhus) are first buried but their corpses are exhumed after three months and burnt. The ceremonies are the same as for those who are cremated. The funeral procession is never accompanied by music even if some old person dies, but the mourners keep on chanting *Ram Nam Sat Hai, Jo bole so gat hai* which means God is truth and he who remembers Him, attains *Nirvana.*

The ladies of the bereaved family do not like the urban areas, perform any organised *Siapa* which entails the beating of forehead and breast. Their grief, of course, is expressed in weeping and wailing and ladies of the neighbourhood also gather to offer their consolation. But the melodrama is conspicuous by absence of what? Neither do the ladies accompany the funeral procession nor do they go to the cremation ground.

## FOLKTALES OF THE GADDIS

### 1. Trilochan Mahadev

A *chela* while swimming across the lake Mani Mahesh, disappeared and reached the Piyalpuri, an underground abode of Shiva.

The God asked the *chela* as to what job he knew. The priest replied that he was a tailor master and could do the job very well. Shiva appointed him his personal tailor and gave some cloth to stitch to his *chela.* The *chela* continued to work there for more than six months and then he intended to go back home as the snow was due to fall shortly.

Shiva allowed him to leave Piyalpupri and gave a *Khradu* full of woollen pieces. Shiva enjoined upon him not to disclose any fact regarding his stay in the Nagari and the work he did there otherwise he would become mad.

After receiving the blessing of Lord Shiva, the *chela* came back to the village. All were amazed to see him after a long disappearance from Manimahesh lake. His wife asked the secret which he tried to avoid. But when she insisted on, he disclosed the fact and became insane The woman opened the *Khardu* and saw a lot of gold in it instead of woollen pieces offered by the Shiva.

The mad *Chela* left his house and jumped into the river Ravi. Where his body converted into a rock. A temple in the name of Trilochan Mahadev was built on this rock by the Raja of Chamba, where worship takes place every year in the month of Bhadon or Asuj.

### 2. Manimahesh

Once upon a time a crow, a snake and a Gaddi set out on a pilgrimage to Manimahes. They intended to visit the highest peak of God Manimahesh.

First of all, the crow tried there proudly but the God did not like its attitude and He turned the crow into a stone.

Then the snake strived to approach him with a felling of false vanity which too the God did not favour and the snake was converted into a rock.

Lastly, the Gaddi started to climb the highest peak. He wanted to please the God by sacrificing his lambs at every five steps but with much pride. One by one they all were over and he became a stone as Manimahesh did not like his proud attitude.

Even today one can see the scratches indicating the shapes of a crow, a snake and a Gaddi with his lambs on these rocks.

### 3. Phulmu and Ranju

This is a broken love story of Ranju, son of a well-to-do landlord, with Phulmu, a poor man's daughter.

Ranju and Pulmu both grew up playing together and as they grew up, they fell in love with one another. Ranju's father would not marry his son to a pauper's daughter and so he arranged another bride for Ranju.

When *Batna* was being rubbed on Ranju's body, Phulmu could not hold herself and went to see this from behind the screen. Ranju saw Phulmu and invited her to lend a helping hand instead of peeping through the screen. Phulmu replied that she would not like to apply the *batna* when she was not at all happy at the marriage and that his aunts and other relatives should apply it.

She wanted to know from Ranju as to who had arranged the match for him and who accepted the betrothal. Ranju replied that family priest had arranged the match and his father had accepted the betrothal.

Phulmu then returned to her house broken-hearted and committed suicide by taking poison.

The next morning when Ranju was going at the head of the marriage procession, he saw the funeral procession carrying Phulmu's dead-body to the cremation ground. Ranju could not control his emotions and went to attend the last rites of Phulmu.

He arranged the pyre with his left hand and with right hand he applied fire to it and when the flames roared, it appeared as if they were telling that one should not love immature and faithless strangers.

This tale is the theme of a popular song of Gaddis.

## FOLK SONGS AND DANCES OF THE GADDIS

Song and dance are the most natural traits of a race. They provide an effective yardstick of their temperament and the manners they react to the surrounding joy and beauty.

Of all the uninhabited Himalayan people the Gaddis are easily the most remarkable ones.

With a gorgeous landscape and romantic atmosphere, the Gaddi girls is deeploy in love with the hills of Chamba.

*Gori* is deeply in love
With the hills of Chamba
In every home is a *bindlu*
In every home a *tiklu*
In every home are calm brides
*Gori* is deeply in love
With the hills of Chamba

Manimahesh is covered with perennial snow and is regarded as sacred as Kailash. God Siva is believed to have lived here. There are many temples where Lord Siva is worshipped in a typical form. The land of Shiva has been the theme of songs and are known as *Anchali.* One of the famous Anchalis goes as under:

O Lord Shiva, if you fulfil our desires
We shall give you a *Nuwala*
And we would make an offer
Of eighty goats and eightyfour sheep
O' God, we want your darshan.

A marriage song goes:

Who is that beautiful girl
Sitting with her hair uncombed
Who is sitting with his back turned
Oh, *Gori* is sitting with her hair uncombed
And *Issar* (Shiva) is sitting with his back turned

A Gaddi girl wants to buy some *Bidis* from the market and requests her relations in such a manner that our sympathies are enlisted on hearning the song which goes thus:

In the bazar of town '*Bidis*' are being sold
O my uncle, please purchase it
The cost is so high, how can I buy it?
O my father's younger and elder brother, please buy it
Neither of my father's brothers purchase it
So my pious mother, you please buy it.

*Romantic Songs:* During my study of the Himachal Gaddis, I found that they were leading richer and emotional life than any other tribe of the Himachal Pradesh. The Gaddi is a care-free and happy-go-lucky fellow. When a Gaddi shepherd plays on his flute, Nature nods her head in tune with it, the hill vibrate with joy and the distant hill girl dances in ecstasy. The love-sick shepherdess starts to sing in reply :

1. I miss you terribly my Gaddi
   I miss you very much.

2. This *Patwari* will not write letter for me
   though I beseeched him a thousand times.
   I miss you very much, my beloved Gaddi.
3. I go alone to the spring
   and drink there in seclusion
   And suddenly your memory pierces my heart
   I miss your very much, my beloved Gaddi.
4. With naked feet I climbed the hill
   Hoping to see you when you will return
   But alas! my feet are pierced by sharp thorns
   And of your there was no sign
   I miss you very much, my beloved Gaddi.

Here are a few lines of another famous song which relates to the broken love story of Kunjua and Chanchalo—translated by Dr. Karan Singh:

**Kunjua and Chanchalo**

1. I weep profusely,
   While washing clothes, O Kunjua
   come and speak to me, please
   come and talk with me:
2. In your hand is a silk handkerchief, O Chanchalo,
   and my ring is on your finger,
   as a token of our undying love.
3. My lustrous black eyes, O Kunjua, often admired by you are now filled with tears and sorrow,
   symbols of our hopeless love.
4. On your fair arms
   the red bangles quiver,
   and among them, O Chanchalo,
   is the bracelet I gave you
   in token of my adoration.

5. Do not come to me at midnight O Kunjua,
   there are five loaded rifles in my house,
   itching to fire at your heart.
6. I will surely come at midnight O Chanchalo,
   what harm can five rifles do
   to my immortal love for you.
7. You are going far away, O Kunjua,
   give me a ring as a token of your love.
8. Do not bother about such trifles, O Chanchalo,
   In Chamba there is gold in plenty
   and I will deck you with ornaments.
9. Do not leave tomorrow night, O Kunjua,
   Do no leave me,
   I would sacrifice my very life
   to keep your here.
10. I must go tomorrow night, O Chanchalo,
    I must go for I have pressing work which
    I cannot ignore.

**Stay for to-night**

1. Stay for to-night, my beloved Gaddi,
   stay here for to-night
   I will give you fresh lamb
   and *ghee* to cook it in
   stay till the morrow, my beloved!
2. I will give you soap and oil, bathe in the cool spring
   do not go to-night
   wild beasts visit our fields at night
   and I am alone
   Stay with me to-night my dear Gaddi
   Stay till tomorrow!

Many songs about another shepherd Rupnu have been composed when Rupnu returns to his home, his beloved is waiting for him.

These filksongs are quite simple in composition and are sung with an amazing clarity of expression and each line is repeated a number of tims before switching on to the other line. They are sung in highpitched voice, mostly by women or shepherds while tending their sheep or goats.

## Folk Dances

The folk dance of Gaddis is of a uniform pattern and is performed by a group who move in a circle swaying their bodies half way round at each step in an easy and graceful manner with the arms alternatively raised over the head, hanging down. A dance is always accompanied by songs. The men and women usually dance in separate circles and do not intermingle.

The dance number of the menfolk are vigorous and some times boisterous too. But the women move slowly and gracefully. They clap their hand at regular intervals and after every 2 or 3 steps sit down on their haunches facing each other thereby presenting an attractive sight.

The tempo rises with the notes of the orchestra consisting of *Shenai* and *dholak* (dumdum). The musicians sit outside the circle and play their instruments. The dance is full of verve and aplomb and occasionally reaches a frenzid stage with their costumes flying as the dancers whirl round.

Usually the dancers enter the arena after a drink of *sur* (wine). Dances by individuals are generally timid while collective one starting with graceful steps of a happy contented and peaceful people, lead to a frenzied state. An interesting feature is that Gaddis raise a chord 'ho-ho' at the top of their voice, while women dancers alone sing.

## Social Changes

There are tremendous changes taking place in the community. A large number of Kangra and Chamba Gaddis has joined mainstream. Now many Gaddis live in town and cities including Delhi. Due to reservation as ST, they are in the administration and other services also. (For advanced studies in this area, my book entitled 'Gaddi Tribe of Himachal Pradesh', 'The Nomads of the Himalayas' and research papers/articles are referred)

# 5

# Gujjars: The Pastoral Nomads

THE WHOLE of the Himalayan range is divisible broadly into three major division—Western, Central and Eastern. It has been the abode of several ethnic groups from time immemorial. According to a survey, made in the Western and Central Himalayas, the Ladakese (Bhot or Bodh) and the Muslims of Ladak district of Kashmir, the Lahulese and the Spitians of Lahul and Spiti district, Kinnaurese of Kinnaur district of Himachal Pradesh and the Bhotiyas, the Rajis, the Doms, the Shilpkars, of U.P. Hill districts, are some of the important ethic groups. In the Eastern Himalayas, a large number of ethnic groups reside in Darjeeling district of West Bengal, Mehalaya, Arunachal, Mizorm, Manipur, Nagaland and other places.

Wandering, even today, is strong instinct of man. Nature has attracted him to see its beautiful spots. Man continued his journey for how long and how far who can say. He, perhaps, broke it only when he got sufficient food for is belly. Opportunities for employment also played an important role for migration of man from one place to another.

The nomadic tribes of India were either expelled in their own country due to internal strife or they had to leave their abodes in search of food and employment. Gujjars and one of such tribes who live in jungles, villages or in the valleys for a temporary period and then move to another place in search of grass for their cattle.

Gujjars, mostly postoral, are beautiful tribe of Himachal Pradesh and Jammu and Kashmir. They move from place to place in Jammu-Kashmir, Himachal Pradesh and even the hilly regions of Uttar Pradesh. They, unlike Gaddis, wander in search of grazing pastures for their cattle, throughout the year. Their huts can be seen scattered here and there. They build their *deras* (huts) with the adjacent grass leaves and wood available in the interior jungles. These sheds are temporary and are destroyed or abandoned after they change their grazing tracts.

Cunningham believes that the Gujjars existed even before the birth of Christ. Their homeland is Gujarat. Certain unforeseen reasons forced them to migrate from Gujarat-Kathiawar region to Jammu and Kashmir and later to Himachal Pradesh and Uttar Pradesh, where they settled in the forests on the banks of Ganga. A Gujjar leader came to power and ruled Peshawar, Kabul and even Multan for a considerable period.

In the days of the early Arab travellers, the name of the Jodhpur region of Rajasthan was Gujaratra or Gujarat, a name derived from that of the Gurjara people.

In Huen Tsang's time the trans-Aravalli region, occupying the western slopes of the main Aravalli range, was known as Gurjara.

Cunningham says, "All the early Arab geographers speak of a kingdom named Jurz or Juzr which from its position would appear to be the same as the Kiu-che-lo of Huen Tsang.......Edirisi quoting Ibn Khordadheh, states that Zuzr or Juzr was the hereditary title of the king as well as the name of the country. This statement confirms my identification of Zuzr with Guzr or Gujar, which is a very numerous tribe whose name is attached to many important places in North-West India and the Punjab and more especially to the great Peninsula of Gujarat."

The Gujjar rulers are believed to have founded the city of Gujarat in Akbar's region. Saharanpur district of Uttar Pradesh was also named Gujjar Garh, the abode of Gujjars. They were mostly Hindus but during the reign of Aurangazeb, most of them embraced Islam. Hence, they are mostly Sunnis though their sub-castes, viz., Chandel, Bhatti, Banja, Lodhe, Kasane, Bhensi, Chopra, Chauhan, Chechi, Khatapa, etc., are found even today which smack of Rajput clan.

The Gujjars have not been mentioned in '*Rajatarangini*,' written by Kalhana about the 12th century A.D., although a reference has been made of such communities as Mlechhas, Damsas, Nishadas. Tantris, Nyayaks, Bhuttas, Bhikshas, Khasas, and Dards. However, Drew quotes the Gujjars as an 'Aryan' race.

When the nomads are asked about their migration, they simply say that their ancestors has come from Gujarat. But nobody knows the year in which they migrated from their original abodes. It is also not certain whether they were converted to Islam before they entered the Kashmir Valley as Islam came to Kashmir in the 14th century A.D. and was preached by the Sufi saints in different parts of the valley.

Most of the historians believe that the Gujjars are a Rajput community. The world 'Gujjar' appears to have been derived from 'Gujjar' which means a warrior class of Rajputs. The Gujjars of Chamba had migrated from Jammu and Kashmir long ago.

## THE GUJJARS OF HIMACHAL PRADESH

A Gujjar woman scales the Himalayan peak on foot along-with her children, husband and elder members of the family. She ties a two-months' baby to her lap, puts two to four earthen pots, filled with milk and butter, on her head, and holds only a stick in one hand while covering a painful journey in these valleys. Another woman helps her husband in milking the buffaloes. If during her journey, she has labour pains, with no nurse and medicine available, she does not break her journey, as the journey is automatically broken. After a week's rest, she resumes her journey and does not stop till she reaches her destination.

During such migrations, there have been many cases of delivery among the tribals. In inclement weather, however, such cases may become complicated, resulting in diseases and deaths.

Difficulty arises when the forest authorities do not permit their buffaloes to cross certain ever bridges as the animals weighing 250 kgs or so, may destroy them. As the poor Gujjar cannot forsake his cattle, he takes a longer route.

T.S. Negi's regarding their migrants, are:

"The Hindu Gujjars entered Himachal Pradesh from the neighbouring areas of the plans in isolated and stray migration.

The Muslim Gujjars seem mainly to have first set foot in the then princely States of Chamba and Sirmur and thence spread out gradually to other localities outside these states. Some of them found their way to the Kangra District and the erstwhile Bilaspur State from the adjoining plains of British India."

To the Chamba State the Muslim Gujjars were driven by the growing inadequacy of grazing resources in the neighbouring parts of the Jammu and Kashmir State. That happened some half a dozen generations ago. The history of the "Pilgrim fathers" and their descendants can be traced even now and most of the original 25 families continue to flourish and grow in the Chamba District of Himachal Pradesh.

The traditional version of how the Mohammedan Gujjars were drawn to Sirmur is rather romantic. His Highness Raja Shamsher Prakash of Sirmur visited Punchh for matrimonial purpose. The profuse availability of excellent milk that he noticed at Punch led him to the discovery of the Gujjar tribe and their buffalo herds. He requested the ruler of Punchh for the migration of some Gujjar families to Sirmur and promised liberal grazing facilities. Apart from the matrimonial courtesies on the part of the ruling family of Punchh towards that of Sirmur, the lush prospects of pasturage in Sirmur drew the Gujjars strongly to Maharaja Shamsher Prakash's domains and some nineteen families migrated to Sirmur in the wake of the royal matrimonial ties between Punchh and Sirmur. The immigrant-fore-fathers of these families can be historically located even today through many of their descendants. This nucleus proliferated and dispersed, attracting, in the process, many subsequent and stray migrations. From Sirmur the Gujjars spread out into many of what were in those times known as the Simla Hill States.

In between these above-mentioned three main directions and sources of Gujjar induction into Himachal Pradesh, namely, through Chamba from Jammu and Kashmir, through Sirmur from Punchh and through Kangra and Bilaspur from the neighbouring districts of British India, numerous stray infiltrations went over the generations, till the partition. The historical conflagration of communal hatred and bloodshed which accompanied the birth pangs of Pakistan, drove numerous Gujjars temporarily out of Himachal

Pradesh, though the majority stayed on there. The bulk of the part of Gujjar population which had left for Pakistan returned to Himachal Pradesh and to the old posturing haunts when things cooled down. Pakistan's inhospitable grain prospects drove them back at the first opportunity of communal security in these parts of India.

As the subject of the British Raj of the Indian Rajas, before Independence in the areas now comprised in Himachal Pradesh, the Gujjar had no political handicap. His ability to serve those in authority with milk and products kept him generally on the right side of authority. The general appreciation of his contribution to the economy of the place with dairy articles, and to the State coffers with taxes, also stood him in a good stead. Thus, though a stranger to the soil in autocratic times, he never felt any political pinch, as such.

According to Negi, the Gujjar has consciously been treated one of the favourites of the national care for the backward, after independence. However, his nomadic mode of existence, coupled, with his own past indifference to his franchise, has deprived him seriously of his exercise of the right to vote as an ordinary citizen of Himachal Pradesh. In the first place, the majority of the Gujjars are believed to miss the very entry in the list of voters. Then, even amongst those who do get listed only very few get to the ballot boxes.

Exact statistics of the percentage listed and of that actually voting shall have to be ascertained and ways and means to improve the situation devised.

### Milkmen

The Gujjars in Himachal Pradesh are mainly a pastoral people. They rear buffaloes in large numbers and cows, too. Some Gujjars have sheep and goats like their fellow nomads of the valley. They sell milk and ghee to the villagers. They are known as honest milkmen, they claim that the milk products sold by them are cent per cent pure. They are god-fearing people and do not adulterate the commodities, they sell. But due to social contacts with the outside world, their values of life are also being eroded and nobody knows when they will break their-age-old traditions.

Among the Gujjars, there is no specialisation of jobs, as such every adult can be employed for any work, viz., rearing domestic animals, milking, weaving and selling the products, etc. Each member of the family has to bear his joint responsibility. If a member of a family is sick, another will perform the duty automatically. In fact, the joint family system has unified them so much that there is nothing but their spirit which maintains their daily life.

The animals of the Gujjars are as notoriously destructive to the growth and conservancy of forests as the migratory flocks are. The damage done to the vegetation by the buffaloes is universally known and acknowledged. The buffaloes are very much more exacting than the cows. Their greater demand for fodder leads to serious decrease in gross production. With their heavy hoofs they trample down the ground and on step slopes cause sheet erosion and give rise to ravines. Herds of these buffaloes are taken to the alpine ranges in summer and are brought down in winter. Not only do they graze in the alpine pastures, but throughout the high lying undermarcated forests they cause much damage, both by the lopping and heavy grazing. The damage done by these herds is responsible for the appalling conditions in which the forests of Chamba's low hills in particular, and other parts of Himachal Pradesh in general, are present.

The Gujjars migrate to the Dhars (high mountains) during summer and wander down in winter. The men graze cattle, whereas the women-folk cook, milk the animals and prepare ghee.

The census returns of 1961 and 1971 disclose the following district wise Gujjar population in Himachal Pradesh:—

**Year 1961**

| *Name of District* | *Males* | *Females* | *Total* |
|---|---|---|---|
| 1. Chamba | 2532 | 2304 | 4356 |
| 2. Kangra | — | — | — |
| 3. Mandi | 1832 | 1692 | 3524 |
| 4. Kulu | — | — | — |
| 5. Lahaul-Spiti | — | — | — |

| | | | |
|---|---|---|---|
| 6. Bilaspur | 2138 | 1954 | 4092 |
| 7. Mahasu | 938 | 862 | 1800 |
| 8. Simla | — | — | — |
| 9. Sirmur | 1414 | 1221 | 2633 |
| 10. Kinnaur | — | — | — |

1. The blanks against Kangra, Kulu and Simla are misleading. The Gujjar not being a Scheduled Tribe in the undivided Punjab, these districts, inherited from the Punjab, have continued even in 1971 to be treated as in 1961 for this purpose. In fact, the position is that all there districts contain considerable Gujjar population

2. Till 1951, the Gujjar Tribe had not been declared as a Scheduled Tribe.

**Year 1971**

| *Name of District* | *Males* | *Females* | *Total* |
|---|---|---|---|
| 1. Chamba | 3400 | 3104 | 6504 |
| 2. Kangra | — | — | — |
| 3. Mandi | 2279 | 2281 | 4560 |
| 4. Kulu | — | — | — |
| 5. Lahaul-Spiti | — | — | — |
| 6. Bilaspur | 2435 | 2476 | 4911 |
| 7. Mahasu | 1174 | 977 | 2151 |
| 8. Simla | — | — | — |
| 9. Sirmur | 1337 | 1169 | 2506 |
| 10. Kinnaur | — | 2 | 2 |

*The exact figures are not available in the new censuses as many Gujjars have shifted to U.P. and Uttranchal, and some educated Gujjars are living in towns. Hindu Gujjars are economically well off and many are employed in Govt. jobs. They are well placed, but educationally very backward. A Sociological Study of Hindu Gujjars is required.*

It has yet to be ascertained how many of these people, exactly, are still leading nomadic existence and how many have settled down and what their religionwise composition is.

**Social Life**

The Gujjars, like Gaddis are simple, sturdy, hard-working and virtuous. They are peace-loving, polite, social and hospitable. They love their cattle, their jungles, their huts and the tracks they cover.

Gujjars can be recognised by their typical beard and dress. They wear on their heads a special type of turban, which resembles Rajput the head dress. The women wear *kurta* and *vhuridar payjama* like the Mohammedan women of Kashmir but do not strictly follow the *purdah* system or wear *burka* which is a common practice among the Muslim women.

The Gujjars' staple diet is simple but nourishing. It consists of maize, milk and ghee. It is surprising that the vast majority neither use any beverage nor any stimulant. I have met about a dozen centenarians among Gujjars who never touched wine. Whether they pass the snow-covered tracks of cross the deep forest, they never feel the necessity of any beverage.

The birth of a child is considered a gift of Allah (the God). A son is welcomed with great joy. The news of birth of a son is given to the neighbours late to avoid evil eye. A husband cannot enter the room where his wife gives birth to a child. Children are brought up in traditional ways but with great affection.

Gujjars do not believe in contraceptives and considered them as anti-social. None should break the laws of God. Family planning is not known to these people. Abortion is never practised.

Being the followers of Islam, the circumcision ceremony is observed when boys are five-years old. The operation is performed by a barber and the ceremony is attended by animal sacrifice. A feast is held for the relative and friends.

The Gujjars are monogamous and patrilineal. Though believing in purity of the blood ties in the partilineal line, they neither have any localised clans, nor posses any tendency towards local exogamy or endogamy. In this sense, the tribe can be described as agamous (Murdock, G.P.—"World Ethnographic Sample").

The prohibition against clan endogamy, a special feature of clan customs is lacking these days. This may, to some degree, be attributable to the Islamization of the Gujjars. Islam, in fact, permits marriage between cousins of all shades and degrees.

There are some Hindu Gujjars also who reside in Mandi. They comprise of the following clans:—

| | |
|---|---|
| Khatana | Chohan |
| Gursi | Didhar |
| Bhumphal | Katarya |
| Parswal Malheria | Koli |
| Kantiya | Motle |
| Chaichi | Bhunch |
| Bargat | Kalas |
| Chhore | Ladi Chai |
| Bajar | Badhana |

According to Dr. Y.S. Parmar, "The economic conditions of the Gujjars cannot be judged by their appearance or ornaments. The sight of a family of Gujjars, moving up or down the hill, gives the impression that theirs must be a precarious existence and incredibly uncomfortable one. But it has got to be remembered that these are the only people who sell milk and ghee on a commercial scale. It is not possible to ascertain correctly as to how much profit a Gujjar makes from the trade after paying the grazing dues, satisfying the requirements of petty officials and village dignitaries and getting the financial relief obtained by manuring private fields during transit. For all intents and purposes, it cannot be incompatible with his hard work particularly when the dues paid are low and grazing availed of enormous. My own impression is that, on the whole they are better off than the Zamindars with whom they live in symbiosis though some of them received a set-back during the disturbances of 1947 from which they have not wholly recovered."

## THE FAMILY

In Gujjar family, the father and son live together for the whole lifetime or for the best part it. Brothers seldom stay together long after marriage.

A nomadic family would follow the same pattern, or less, though the numbers of members, as also of Buffaloes are likely to be found more among the nomads than among the settled ones.

The settled families enjoy facilities of education, medical treatment, stable markets, convenient living, membership of Panchayats, exercise of franchise, etc., but they have to husband their fodder resources and other feeds wisely with human ingenuity more than depending upon the bounties of Nature.

The following details of the composition of some Hindu Gujjar families, settled for numerous generations, in the Paonta Tehsil of the Sirmur District along with the broad details of the family properties will afford a comparison with the newly settled families mentioned earlier and with the nomadic families generally:-

There are quite a large number of Mohammedan Gujjar families partly nomadic and partly settled.

### Inheritance

As regards the inheritance of property, it goes from father to sons, who equally share the same. If there is no child in the family the property goes to the widow but in case she re-marries, she loses her right to property and then the same is equally distributed among the brothers of the deceased.

The daughter in a Gujjar family gets a nominal dowry at the time of marriage. Bride price is a common practice. It is very difficult to get a wife unless one pays a heavy amount to the bride's kinsmen. This may be between Rs. 500 and 1000 or even more. Ornaments and clothes are presented to the bride before marriage.

Adoption is not so popular among the Gujjars, who believe in joint family system. A family is simple as well as compound. The main authority is vested in the eldest member of the family but the old woman of the house controls the domestic affairs.

## Marriage

The parents normally select the bride for their sons. There is no choice of selection of a spouse by the boy or a girl. Cases of elopement for marriage are not known among the tribals. *Bata-Sata* or marriage by exchange is also common. It may be parallel or triangular. For example, Zahur Baksh can marry Rahman's sister in exchange of his sister, who marries Rahman. This parallel system of marriage is by exchange. In a triangular system 'A' marries 'B's' sister, 'B' marries 'C's' sister and 'C' marries 'A's' sister. This custom was also prevalent among certain clans of Rajputs in Rajasthan and Gujarat in the good old days.

A man may crack jokes with his wife's sisters. During marriage ceremony, the bride-groom is invited by the bride's sisters. They offer him a seat and crack some jokes. They may also tease the groom's sisters. They apply *kajal* to his eyes and what is more interesting, is that the girls sit on his knees. They leave the groom only when they receive cash presents.

Child marriages among Gujjars are common. There are cases of betrothal even before the birth of a child. Bride wealth is paid by the husband and after divorce the new husband has to pay the same amount to the divorced husband. Marriages in exchange are popular. Only wealthy tribals have two or more wives, otherwise monogamy is the general rule.

## Religion

Gujjars, like other Muslims believe in *Dozakh* (hell) and *Zannat* (heaven). They believe that the deads rest in their graves and appear in the land of the deads on the doom's day, when they will be rewarded or punished according to their past deeds.

The corpse is buried according to Islamic laws and there is weeping and wailing in the family for three days. The bereaved family do not cook food during this period. The neighbours offer food to them. On the fourth day non-vegetarian food is prepared in the house and served to the neighbours in the name of the deceased. On the tenth day, a stone is put on the grave and pudding is distributed among the children in the neighbourhood. After a gap of 40 days, the neighbours and relatives gather at the grave and offer prayers *(Fateha)*.

Their God is Allah or Khudah who created this world. He stays in the seventh sky, sleeping and watching all. Though it is believed that prayer (*Namaz*) should be performed five times a day very few people follow this strictly.

Every Gujjar remembers God and invokes *Allah* before taking his meals. Feasts are offered to the relatives at various religious ceremonies.

## No Change

A Gujjar travels from place to place, from one dhar to another hill and from one State to another. He has no fear of wild animals but the foresters who tax him at every step. He has to pay various taxes to State Governments.

Modernity has its own role in changing the tribal culture, but it has not touched them despite the seasonal exodus which brings them into contact with the civilisation. Their aloofness has brought them backwardness and their own type of happiness. Hence, their life is an admixture of pain and joy.

## Tribal Welfare

The Himachal Pradesh Gujjar Welfare Committee was established by an eminent social worker, Pt. Dharm Dev Shastri. In the beginning, some schools for children of the Gujjar tribes, were opened. Adim Jati Sevak Sangh Parvatiya Adim Jati Sewak Sangh and other Govt. NGOs have launched many welfare schemes for the nomadic Gujjars.

The Gujjars cannot stick to one place for a longer span. Hence, welfare schemes launched for them have normally failed. Nomadism, is a blot on the part of a nation; it requires a systematic change. Unless their institution are diverted and land is allotted to them, no substantial results can emerge.

When we plan a welfare scheme one more question arises, and it is, whether the tribals should be allotted land for their permanent settlements or should they be allowed to live a nomadic life. What the present writer thinks of the immediate requirements for them, are as below :–

1. They should be allotted land for their permanent settlement.
2. They should be provided with grazing fields for their cattle.
3. If dairy experts are detailed to guide them properly, more milk can be obtained. They should be encouraged to establish more milk dairies. A silent revolution can be brought about on cooperative basis.
4. Schools and boarding houses should be opened for educating their children properly.
5. Adim Jati Sewak Sangh, Parvatiya Adim Jati Sewak Sangh and other social and tribal agencies should be asked to increase their areas of activities.
6. Medical facilities should be provided in their *Deras.*
7. The authorities should be sympathetic to their requirements.
8. Liberal financial assistance should be made available for building their houses.
9. Since they can prove good soldiers, they should be recruited in the Army for defending our borders, which they know better than others.

*Since the Muslim Gujjars have similar Gotras as that of Hindus, a comparative study should be conducted by social scientists to study both the sects.*

## The Sarvodaya and the Gujjars

As a result of continuous efforts of Pt. Dharm Dev Shastri, the then Secretary of Adim Jati Sewa Sangh, a 'Gujjar Sammelan' was held on 14 October, 1959, in Draman village of Himachal Pradesh, the Chief Guest was Vinobaji Raja Bajrang Bahadur, the Lt. Governor of Himachal Pradesh presided over the function. Mr. Jayaprakash Narayan was also present.

Hundreds of Gujjars were present on this occasion. We are giving here a free translation of Vinobaji's speech to find some solutions of the various problems confronting these nomadic people in their everyday life. He said :–

"Dear Gujjar brothers,

While listening to the speech of your Lt. Governor, I learnt some new facts about you. I am happy to know that the Government is taking interest in your welfare. I believe that the nomadic life of the Gujjars must end now. Since you do not have house to live in, your children cannot get proper education at present.

"In my opinion, all the Gujjars should not settle down at a particular place as this will not be practicable from economic point of view. Some families can be settled at Chamba, others, at Pathpankot or Nurpur, so that they may sell their milk and ghee easily. I will advise you that you should sell the ghee but not the curd; it should be consumed in your families. If your want to sell milk, please do have some share for your sons too."

"Now the time has come when the Gujjars and other tribals should not be restricted to their own bands but they should mix with other people too. They should change their age-old tradition of staying with their clans only. I would also suggest that those who can reside near some small to big cities, they should do so. Others can live in the villages."

"I do not favour separatist tendencies in the tribe or caste."

**Resolutions**

The following resolutions were passed by the Tribal Conference on this occasion:

1. The nomadic life should end. Nomads should settle down here and there according to their choice and convenience.
2. Rahdari tax should be erased. Permits may be given only for exact number of cattle that they bring with them.
3. The tents built on Dhars should not be taken over from them.
4. They should be allowed to grow plants around their tents.
5. All neighbouring States should be asked to help in their settlement.
6. Cows should be exempted from taxes.

7. Those, who have settled down in Chamba, should be given facilities like other Jamidars.
8. The bridges should be repaired by the Forest Department so that they may take their cows and buffaloes without any obstruction.
9. The sheep rearing occupations should be encouraged.

The following Resolutions were passed on the occasion of the Nomadic Tribes', Day Conference, held on 25 February, 1960, under the Presidentship of Mr. U.N. Dhebar;

**Resolution No. 1**

This Nomadic Tribes Conference strongly recommends to the Government of India for allocation of substantial funds for the rehabilitation of the Nomadic and Denotified communities so that they stay at a place, build their own houses and subsist as a good citizen of the community. Such a course will also wean them away from criminal tendencies if and where they exist consequent on the nature of their unsettled lives. Such a provision should also include the opening of a considerable number of schools for them, both elementary and vocational, so that the allurements of an honest livelihood may stand against their lust for wandering.

**Resolution No. 2**

This Nomadic Tribes' Conference strongly recommends to the Government of India to formulate rules under which the Nomadic and Denotified Tribes can conveniently secure financial help in the shape of grants and loans for the improvements in their skill and profession. The experience of social welfare institutions connected with them has it that some of them are artisans of a high class in blacksmithy, carpentry and other professions practised by them and some have a high degree of skill in rope-dancing, taming of animals, jugglery, etc. Such a facility incorporated in the rules will very much improve their economic conditions and be an encouragement towards a settled life.

**Resolution No. 3**

This Nomadic Tribes' Conference strongly recommends to the Government of India to make special efforts to include the Nomadic and Denotified Tribes in the Census enumeration of 1971 to draw up a comprehensive State-wise and Union territory-wise list of Nomadic Tribes and Denotified Tribes.

**Resolution No. 4**

This Nomadic Tribes' Conference strongly recommends to the Government of India to allocate separate funds for the social welfare of the Nomadic and other backward tribes. At present they are receiving a very half-hearted attention in this regard. The insignificant allocation of funds for their welfare is only out of savings and left over from other backward communities. The Conference earnestly feels that substantial and distinct allocations of funds for these communities should be provided in the Five Years Plan.

**Resolution No. 5**

The Nomadic Tribes' Conference strongly recommends to the Government of India for amending the Constitution as to include the Nomadic and Denotified Tribes as well in list of backward communities for whom social welfare provisions exist in the Constitution. The Conference has also noticed that in some State these communities have been included in the Scheduled Tribes but they do not have a uniform recognition in the Constitution on the whole.

The Ex-Commissioner for Scheduled Castes, Scheduled Tribes and Backward Classes was constrained to write : "I cannot help quoting here what Lokur Committee has to say about Nomadic Tribes and Denotified Tribes as I completely agree with their views so authoritatively expressed in their report" which says :

"We suggest that the present anomalous position regarding the Denotified and Nomadic Tribes who could more properly be identified as communities rather than Tribes should be rectified as soon as possible after detailed investigation."

The Commissioner further reports:

Even since I took over charge of the office of the Commissioner for Scheduled Castes and Scheduled Tribes in the year 1950. I have been hard at solving the problem of finding the definition of what constitutes a Tribe Article 338 of the Constitution. Thereafter, when the occasion arose for the revision of the list of Scheduled Castes and Scheduled Tribes under Articles 341 and 342, I have been propagating for the following suggestion to be accepted by the Government:

That in order to have the revision of the lists in a rational and scientific manner, a High-Power Commission be appointed of the following, among others—

1. Anthropologist (representative of the Anthropological Survey of India),
2. Sociologist (of a University),
3. Officer from the Department of Social Welfare (Ministry of Law, etc.),
4. One of the judges (of social service inclination),
5. Two members of Parliament; one from the Rajya Sabha (Scheduled Tribes) and one from Lok Sabha (Scheduled Castes),
6. Social workers, one from Tribal Welfare field and one from Scheduled Caste Welfare field,
7. Director General, Census Office,
8. Member Secretary.

The Commission should keep the following constantly in view when finalising the list:—

1. National integration.
2. Backwardness has a tendency to perpetuate itself (an extract from my Annual Report 1956-57 as the Commissioner for Scheduled Castes and Scheduled Tribes).

Five very well attended Gujjar Tribal Conferences have been held from 1952. The last one was held in 1965:

1. On April 5th, 1952, at Pathankote in the Punjab, inaugurated by the then Chief Minister of Jammu and Kashmir, late, Mr. Bakshi Ghulam Mohamad.
2. On the 26th and the 27th May, 1956, at Chamba, Himachal Pradesh, inaugurated by late Mr. B.N. Datar, the then Minister of State in the Ministry of Home Affairs, Government of India.
3. On November 20th, 1959, again at Pathankot, inaugurated by the then President of India, late Dr. Rajendra Prashad.
4. On the 24th to 26th November, 1961 at Vikas Nagar, Chuharpur, District Dehra Dun, inaugurated by late Pt. Jawahar Lal Nehru, Prime Minister of India.
5. On February 20th, 1965, at New Delhi, presided over by Mrs. Indira Gandhi, who was, at that time Minister, for Information and Broadcasting.

Our National Government policy for the tribal development and modernisation follows the intermediate path between the policy of isolation and de-tribalisation. It is true that the policy of isolation is no longer today and radical approach of de-tribalisation is not favoured by the national Government. According to Dr. Verrier Elwin, the Government of India is determined to help the Tribal people to grow according to their genius and anything to impose on their traditions is not the intention.

The Commissioner for Scheduled Castes and Scheduled Tribes in his 1972-73 report presented to Parliament on 28th August, 9174 has stated that the tribal people have special problems of their own. The typical environmental conditions in which they live, the geographical distances of their habitats and their own traditional way of life, have kept them away from the mainstream of the national life and activity. The tribal people, innocent as they are, had been living a peaceful and comparatively happier life in older times without any outside interference. But with the enforcement of forest laws without much consideration to the human life in these forest areas, land restrictions and alienation of their lands, the indifference shown towards the human problems of the tribal communities by the planners of the industrial projects in the tribal areas, their dependence on and exploitation by the money-lenders, landlords and other unscrupulous elements, like liquor contractors have greatly disturbed their way of life.

No doubt, since independence efforts have been made to ameliorate their economic and social conditions and steps have been taken by the concerned State Governments for their development. It is, however, unfortunate that in spite of specific safeguards provided in the Constitution for their protection and advancement, most of the tribals have not only remained neglected but an exploited lot. In order to raise their social, educational and economic standards, special programmes and development schemes are required to be designed suiting the prevailing conditions and keeping in view the natural resources available in the respective areas.

In the Fifth Year Plan, the Planning Commission has adopted a new strategy and a new approach for the development of the Scheduled Tribes. However, in order to ensure the success of these schemes, apart from the systematic and scientific planning, it is highly essential to tone up the administrative machinery responsible for implementing these programmes. It is also desirable to provide suitable incentive to the officials working in the remotest tribal areas. Actually, development schemes concerning the Scheduled Tribes could be more successfully implemented by enlisting cooperation of voluntary agencies devoted to this cause. Such voluntary agencies and institutions which are already working effectively and with dedication in that field, and those which might come forward for this cause, should be whole-heartedly encouraged and supported by Government financially or otherwise.

## THE GUJJARS OF KASHMIR

The Gujjars of Kashmir according to Dr. Sarojini Bisaria are an exciting, strong, hardy and ubiquitous folk. Their habitat, the tough life therein and their occupation of generally exploiting the surface of the land has always evinced a keen interest in the visitors to Kashmir. The Gujjar women have caught the imagination of all those who come across them for their exceptional physical charms, combined with their hardy and tough bearing.

The whole stock of Gujjars of Kashmir consists of two types of people. The Baniharas are sheep rearers, the Bakarwalas, besides having sheep, are basically buffalo rearers. Both of them have a very small percentage of theirs which engages in agriculture as well. A small number has settled down with some land. They tame animals as well. They have their own way of social life, despite their having been in the area long since, and their religion puts on a pastoral gown, irrespective of all them being Islamic people. Their habitat and its pastoralism have determined their economy and social life which is very much different from that of their own kith and kin, left behind in the plains of the five rivers, or even beyond that.

According to Punjab Ethnography, it is, however, possible that Jats were the camel Graziers, perhaps husbandmen, the Gujjars the cowherds of the hills and the Ahirs the cowherd of the plains. So, whatever be the possible thesis, this much is clear that right since Babar wrote and Jahangir emphasised, in all written accounts, the community has lived upon exploitation of the surface of the soil. The Census of India, 1921 recognized the fact by laying down a figure of 795.4 in each 1,000 of the Gujjars whose occupations was reckoned as exploitation of the surface of the soil. Thus, the natural habitat of a Gujjar is pasture land.

In Kashmir, the land is in abundance on mountain slopes and in snow-bound valleys, popularly known as 'murg,' which are rendered uninhabitable during severe winter days. The slopes of mountains are both green and dry. From the side, that is dry, the grazing Gujjar has to march to the green side: for example, from Hammur and Reasi, Poonch climbs towards Jhelum and Sind valleys which get lush green during the hot summer days of this side. The habitat of a Gujjar, therefore, undergoes a change through variation and he does not have to face the extremes of hot areas to the colder ones during summer and vice-versa during the winters. The race map of Jammu and Kashmir State, Census of India 1921, and the foot note for it show that the population of Gujjars used to be thumping in Samba, Ranbir Singh Pora, Jammu, Reasi, Poonch and Mirpur. The Emperor, Jahangir has written about the habitat of the Gujjars that Gulmarg is not permanently inhabited but is frequented by the Gujjars of Kashmir during summers. There is internal immigration of the Gujjars and it has always been so. While describing internal immigration, the Census Commission reported in 1931 that the large number of immigrants found in Udhampur (8000) and (12,000) in Reasi consisted chiefly of the hordes of Gujjars and other pastoral nomads who descended from higher hills to winter in the warmer regions of the lower altitudes.

It is not difficult to recognize a Gujjar, by appearance in Kashmir. He is very much different from the Kashmiri, and is not at all a Mongoloid.

**A Glance**

For his appearance, Drew writes, "the race is Aryan but their countenance cannot be called high Aryan; their forehead is narrow; they want in the well-formed brow of the finer races. The lower of the face is narrow too; but the nose has always something of the curve as is often seen in the Aryan Nations. Some I met with had lighter eyes than are common among other surly in disposition, having that kind of independence which consists in liking to be left alone, and to have, as little as possible, to do with other races. When, however, one does come in contact with them they are not bad to deal with" This account brings out following features in the general appearance of a Gujjar of Kashmir to which a few may be added by the observations of a scholar Dr. Bisaria who in the course of the survey met nearly 2,500 Gujjars:

1. Narrow forehead,
2. Thick eyebrows,
3. Curved high nose,
4. Lighter eyes,
5. Strong, protruding teeth,
6. Scanty beard,
7. Tall figure,
8. Thin of a pinched appearance,
9. Not a very fair complexion,
10. A graceful feminine body,

11. Smart bearing of women.

Ibbetson opines "Gujjar is a fine, stalwart fellow of precisely the same physical type as that of Jat, and the theory of aboriginal descent which has sometimes been propounded is to my mind conclusively negatived by his cast of countenance. The proverb says, 'The Jat, The Gujjar, The Ahir and Gola are all for hail fellows well met'."

Dr. Dowson and Elliot, say that Gujjars as a tribe have always been noted for their turbulence and habit of cattle-stealing. Babar in his Memoirs describes how the commander of the rear guard captured a few Gujjar ruffians was followed the camp, decapitated them and sent them after beheading to the Emperor. The Gujjars of Pali and Pahal became exceedingly audacious while Sher Shah was fortifying Delhi, so he marched to the hills and expelled them so that "not a vestige of their habitations was left." Babar observes, "every time I entered Hindostan, the jats and Gujjars have regularly poured down in prodigious numbers from hills and wilds and really inflicted the chief hardship and were guilty of the chief oppression in the country". Jahangir remarks, that the Gujjars live chiefly on milk and curds and seldom cultivate land. They maintained their old reputation during the freedom struggle, when they perpetrated numerous outrages and seriously impeded the operations of the British Army.

The Gujjars of Kashmir even today remember those days of bravery against foreigners. But surprisingly enough, it appears so inapplicable to the Gujjars of Kashmir, as they are extremely peace loving and not turbulent at all. Padma Shri Mohammad Din of Gulmarg and Padman Shri Ghulan Din of Poonch who reported the infiltration from across the Cease Fire Line have characterised it to have been done with a view to save the city of Srinagar from a battle. In their view this infiltration and love for Srinagar are only embodiments of the community sentiment for peaceful life and quiet pursuits of these people.

**The Difference**

In Rajasthan, the general characteristics of a Gujjar are that he is more a man of flocks and herds than the Jat, who is one of the most industrious and skilled cultivators in the areas. They are known for drinking spirits, and eating mutton, pork and fowls. They can, in most places, eat, drink and smoke with the Ahirs and Jats. In Bhartpur the Khare Gujjars are inferior to Laur, being principally engaged in making butter and ghee, which their women sell, and which is considered derogatory by others. They have curious custom of making a cow of cow dung, covering it with cotton and going through the process of killing it—a custom for sacrifice to gain better fertility, which seems to show that the reverence for the cow which they now profess may be of comparatively modern growth.

Three sayings have been recorded from various sources which hardly supply any characteristics applicable to the Gujjars of Kashmir. There is exaggeration of facts based on rulers observations.

"The dog and the cat, the Gujjar and the Ranghar, if these four were out of the world a man might sleep with his doors open."

"When the Dom made friends with the Gujjar he was robbed of house and home."

"Pine, tobacco, courtesan, the Gujjar and the Jat are all alike, they are like the rice of Jagannath's temple which all castes may eat together."

Here again according to Dr. Bisaria also, amongst the Kashmiri Gujjars contrary to their counterparts, addiction to drinking alcohol is not found. He is generally a vegetarian. He is quite found of smoking. Women too smoke as freely as the men folk. He is generally a vegetarian, although by religious ritualistic convention he takes meat, but never pork. He does not mind his women going out for selling commodities in the markets and the community as a whole is at harmony in this way of thinking. Gujjars have been reckoned as an Artisan Community of the State engaged in making milk products, butter and ghee.

The Musalman Gujjars living in Agra and the Meerut Divisions were apparently converted to Islam at various times; but their tradition in Agra attributes this to the compulsion of Timur. They are mostly Sunnis and a Sunni will not inter-marry with a Shia family. In spite of their conversion, it is said, they retain a number of their tribal practices of 'parchana,' 'deoghar' and the worship of the guardian deities of the families.

## Ethnography

While talking about their ethnography, it is said that Jats and Gujjars are all of one and the same ethnic stock, based on caste system. Gujjar and the Bargujjar tribes are often found together and suggest that the latter may be to the Gujjars what the Khanzadas are to the Meos and what most Rajputs are to the Jats.

Drew writes that they are seemingly Aryans but there is some difference alright. Looking to the Ethnography of India in general, it is not possible to call and stock a pure racial stock, This much is certain that there is some mixture of other stock than that of pure Aryans.

## Language

The language of a Gujjar of Kashmir has always been, and continues to be, the most revealing factor about his affinity, is original stock and possible accretions to the same. Grierson discusses the question of Gujjars and their language in Part IX of his exhaustive report. According to it, the Gujjars of the Punjab plains have lost their language and adopted that of their neighbours, those of the hills north of Punjab, who are not Gujjars but Gujjars speak a language closely allied to Rajasthani. The language of the Gujjars of Kashmir accordingly, closely resembles that of Hazara and Swat. The main differences are really matters of spelling. The borrowed forms come from Kashmiri and some of them are instructive. He maintains that there is a Pisacha tendency to dis-aspirate soft aspirate consonants and then to harden them. Drew concludes that all Gujjars do not speak the same language, and that it depends on the country they are settled in not that which they come to in their summer wanderings.

The anthropologists do not agree with it because a larger number speak Gojri and Bhadwarwahi, Kishtwari where their usual summer haunt is. The conclusion of Drew about their language being a type of Pahari is also not very palatable to the Census of India, 1911.

After the Account of Drew, Gujari was classified under Pahari, but it is doubtful if this is more correct than its previous classification under Rajasthani. The families of this nomadic race, which have permanently settled down in various parts of Jammu and some of Kashmir and taken to agriculture, may have adopted local languages, but the wandering groups, who from the largest majority, have absolutely no dealings with the natives of country, and leading the isolated life that they do, far removed from the largest majority, have absolutely no dealings with the natives of country, and leading the isolated life that they do, far removed from the villages and in the pastures and woods of the land, they have managed to retain their original tongues; and their language continues to be a kin to Rajasthani than Pahari.

Berrman believes that there is general agreement in the relationship between the Pahari and Rajasthani languages and it is attributable to the movements of peoples, notably the Gujjars between these two areas.

As to the explanation of Gujjars picking up Rajasthani, Grierson is of the opinion that Khasas are the first to settle in the Pahari tract, and then Gurjaras settled down after 6th century and occupied Sapadlaksha. At that time they (like the Khans) spoke an Aryan, but not necessarily an Indo-Aryan language. Of these Gurjaras, the bulk followed the pastoral pursuit and became merged in and identified with the proceeding Khasa population. Others were fighting men and were identified by the Brahmans with Kashatriyas In this guise they invaded eastern Rajputana from sapadlaksha and possibly western Rajputana from Sindh and founded as Rajputs, the great Rajpjut States of Rajasthan.

## RELIGION

Frederic Drew wrote of them in 1875, "As to religion, all I have met—all who live within these territories—are Mussulman. The belief is in 'NOORALIAH' more than in God Himself and rituals, all Islamic, have been superposed by modes of propitiating so many pirs and religous leaders from their Abode of Rest that the whole religious structure is a complete picture of pastoral co-existence of man with spirit-Divine."

Folk Prayer of the Gujjars of Kashmir:

Aidi in Karada banoor Ho<br>
Paalan haara Janaab<br>
Jeda Paalada asisa banoor ho paalada<br>
Phir Lakh Darud puncha Nabi Paak Sar par NOOR<br>
Jeda Asma be bu Khuda Nabi Paak Sakhar NOOR

The Gujjars recite this as for Ram Dhun. The prayer reminds them of the fact that the Almighty is in the Sky, but He has sent 'NOOR' through the Nabi for help of the Human-Beings.

**Beliefs and Practices**

The Gujjar is a staunch believer in The *Allah, Al Rahman Al Rahim* and is a Momin. He knows that everything is to be read, recited, spoken, written and delivered in the name of the same who will protect him and the non-believer alike till *Qayamat. He* thinks that this High God is an enormous Light and lives behind the seven skies where according to the theme of *Miraj Nama* the Prophet visited Him when the Prophet was of fifty two years of age.

"Saal bavanja umr nabi dee aahi us dehare

Hoya jadoo Miraj Nabi no ditthe arsh minare"

"Mohammed dedda nam us Noor da

Kita yun zuhoor apne Manzoor da."

**In Trans-humance**

The Banihara Gujjars and, to some extent, the Bakkarwals, as well, subsist on stock of sheep, goats and animals and migrate from lower altitudes to higher ones (between differing ranges of 1000 feet to 13000 feet at times) in search of pastures during the summers. They have to take another migrating journey back from the pastures to their winter resorts where they live till spring comes back to higher valleys and pastures. It is, therefore, their individual need, as householders, to form groups for the purpose of this movements, in which they leave bag and baggage—women and children all—motivated to keep the flock and other animals intact and feeling thrived at the prospect of a comfortable stay after the arduous journey, both ways. They take half for rest, for grass, for replenishing food supply and due to uncertain bad weather. If the grass at the halt is enough, the group decides to stay there longer than the schedule; generally they try to maintain a schedule whererby they reach their final pasture by the second week of May, leaving their winter resort about *Aaoroz,* the last week of March.

Thus, trans-humance for the Gujjars is this alternating movement, seasonal, of live-stock and shepherds between areas of permanent and temporary settlement situated at different elevations and having appreciably different situated at different elevations and having appreciably different climatic conditions. This is a type of pastoral economy, based on these oscillatory settlements which was perhaps much the same as of Neolithic man in the mountainous and semiarid regions. The whole community of a locality moves in the case of these Gujjars—Baniharas and the Vleche Trans-humants of the Balkan Peninsula are one of the same type. According to Dr. Bisaria, the Bakkarwals are more of the Swiss and Norwegian types from amongst whom only a few members of the community move like that. So far as the question of the number of component villages which constitute the settlement is concerned is concerned, these folks have been mostly found to have only one well defined village, which too, they abandon completely for summers and the second place where they had during this season is a congregation of few crude huts and tents. Some Italians, Tasmanians and Vaccarians do it like this. The third basis of looking at their trans-humance in the length of orbit, and the Gujjars, have both the long distance trans-humance like those of Spanish and Iranian migrations and the short distance ones of the Swiss and Blackwood Creek type. The first is the Banihara Trans-humance and the second is followed by cattle rearers, who have generally some agriculture also with them and keep small radii..

Generally the Gujjar women of Kashmir have not to stand the strain of polygamy. It seems that the Gujjars are not fond of it. May be that it is difficult for them to find one woman for themselves. The community knows the religious and communal laws about polygamy yet nowhere polygamous structure was found except where the previous wife was sick or had delivered no children.

## THE GUJJAR SONGS

The Gujjars sing the folk songs in groups but hardly dance like Gaddis and other tribals. Dr. Bisaria has collected a number of Gujjar songs and we are inserting a few representative samples here. A Saharfi, a Rubai, Balo Maiya, Baisakhi, Marital song, Jogiya, Menhdi, and Dhol besides are beings produced below.

### Seharfi Song

This is known as Seharfi. In this there are the beginnings of each couplet with *Alif* and continues upto *yay* the last consonant of

Persian script. In Kashmir only Gujjar sings it. The tune is very easy and it is a slow moving rhythm. "Paharan ten gulzaran andar rende Gojor Baai Abdal Satara sakhat pari Jinnan naal lagaai" and thus goes on the song after substituting *Meem, Daal, Swaad, Zwaad, Fay, Hay, Abdal* in the second line of the song."

**Rubai Song**

Rubai is that type of song in which first two couplets are equal. The song produced below means that we planted the mango saplings and people took the mangoes; pepper likewise was also planted and nurtured by watering similarly with the help of dew and moisture. All our labour went a waste. O' fellow beings of the same soil do not harass us, God is our only Provider.

> *"Amban dan way bootao of asan pari lala paleaa ke amb*
> *Khande Asan suka jalan jalea kiamb khade lokan*
> *Hari Dave bootao osan pari dede paaliaa ke hari khadi lokan*
> *Asan Suka jaalan faalea ki hariyan khadiyan lokan*
> *Ona mar desan waleo pardesiyan da allaa-O."*

**Balo and Maiya Songs**

Balo and Maiya songs are sung in the Punjab and also by the Gujjars of Kashmir in Gojri but with the same tempo.

**Balo**

> *"Do Boota chinaaran da sonokay dukhray channan*
> *Eil phatan paharan de son key dukhare channan"*
> *Baagan bich as maaiya bicharya muttan ke ya*
> *Le gal naal laa maiya bichriya mutta daya*
> *Koi dakhan din ras maiya dil na bisariyon channa*
> *Paaven kabal bas maiyan dil no bisariyon channa.*

**Maiya**

> *"Koi gari kiyan ko lairan jddo jind yaad pavay*
> *Chatt bay kay ro lenran jaddo jind yaad hore."*

## Baisakhi Song

This song is sung in the honour of Baisakh (April). It is sung by women. It presents a description of Kashmir on the occasion of Baisakhi.

*"Chadya baisakh alla huiay baisakhi te khill gayi her dali*
*Aaya you mosam potjharwala ronwan bagan de mali*
*Hai hai kardi vay daee hay julekha te okok duniya way phani*
*Charay wa cheeza hai na aawan maan pay husan jawani*
*Apsos hay absassa kaira zulom kamaya."*

## Wedding Song

This is a song sung by women at the time of a wedding.

*"Too ten mili Bichoriya Sajna way too te mil meinoo*
*Charkha Katan te mal mari ringay*
*Mere Watne da ra lama peenga*
*dame dame tursa mel mainoo."*

## Jogiya Song

Jogiya song is sung by women generally. It is sung with variations all over Northern India.

*"Jogi te chala deewana leemaya khooye te jogita da*
*Padan sudaujaw kar aiyar leemay khoody te dera joguja do."*

## Mehndi song

'Mehndi' song is sung in praise of the Mehndi. Mehndi is applied on hands and feet to tint scarlet red. Mehndi tinted hands embellished with ornaments enhance the beauty of a woman.

*"Mendi da rang ujla te chogla mendi laval see apna mawala mendi rang lee ay*
*Mendi do rang oriya maroriya pin te munachan hon maroriya mendi rang lee ay*
*Mendi da rang okhra thokara mendi lowalsi apna phophra mendi rang lee ay.*

## Dhol Song

This is a song for the Dhol, i.e., the Drum
*"Dhol lala kari raar julan te kari parva*
*tere jore keeta chenkar ve suti di jagaliyan to-lala*
*To-lala paro aawen te athay wich baarman og*
*Lage daniyan diya sharman Sayan a Janya to-Illa."*

## Routes

Some of the routes followed by Trans-humant Gujjars during their migratory periods are given below :

1. Starts from Navashahr and closes are Nayi Basti. Takes following halts on way—Satvari, Nagrota, Bantala, Chejjerkotli, Tekri Gadi, Udhampur, Batote, Asserbagar, Doda, Palano Bhadarwah and reaches Tar (Pasture).
2. Starts from Chakroi. Takes road upto Sonmarg Via Banihal on Jammu, Srinagar Road.
3. Starting and closing point, Navashahr. Takes following halts on way—Satvari, Nagrota, Udhampur, Batote, Ramban, Ramsu, Deogol, Banihal, Qaziagund, Islamabad, Inshan, reaches Wadwan top (pasture).
4. Starts from Navashahr, Choalla and closes at Choalla takes the same route—Satvari, Nagrota, Bandtalaw, Chaja, Tekeri, Khalyani, Udhampur, Batote, Asserbager, a Parano, Daranja Badarwa, Jaie (posture).
5. Starting and closing point Nawahaahr Chakroi. Follows the same route as Group No. 4. Pasture is Kanser Top.
6. Starting and closing point Kathau-Gatti. Takes following halts at the following places: Dhani, Galma, Ramkot, Ramnagar, Mansadevi, Sudmadevi, Gorigund, Patnitop, Batote, Chanderkote, Ramban Ramsu, Deogol, Banihal, Quzigund, Verinag, Sarigali, Gali, Choky, Nabug, Khaddi, and Wadwan (pasture).
7. Starting and closing point is Chak Sakta. Takes following route: Barnoti, Lakhanpur, Behani, Parthanwala bela, Basoli, Jateer, Lari, Poond, Bani Chandal, Long, Sarthal (pasture).
8. Startingand closing point is Nangal in Kathua. Takes the following halts enroute : Channi, Bengab, Galkh, Nagrota, Samnibanj, Kaitha, Razal, Bangodi, Farma, Doda, Chell, Savetar (pasture).

9. Starting and closing point is Gatti, Kathua. Takes following haltson route : Shahpur, Kayar, Nalagesh, Mdi, Shahpur, Balhoogi Chamba, Keyar (pasture).
10. Starting and closing point is Leter, Reasi. Takes following halts on route : Trete, Mal, Bodal, Golchane, Ramsu, Banihal, Qazigund, Verinag, Kukernag, Nabki, Inshan (pasture).
11. Starting and closing point is Thandapani, Reasi. Takes the following enroute : Nalaharanas, Budal, Golchane, Ramsu, Banihal, Qazigund, Verinag, Kukernag, Nabki, Inshan (pasture).
12. Starting and closing point is Numheri, Rajori. Takes the following route : Sealsui, Kassrgalla, Goder, Sararo, Thanamang Meelrujal, Parhote, Thanna, Rattanshah, Galichak, Chandimar, Dugger, Poshiana, Alyabad Serai, Sathri, Dubjan, Oder, Sangrama, Pampur, Shalamar, Khember, Ganderbal, Wantat, Naranag, Gangabal Chornar, Jabdor (pasture). The old Mughal Route.
13. Starting and closing point is Dharmsala. Takes the following route: Jalari, Ban nu, Sangri, Leengalli, Kangdori, Pirpanjal, Nunakhal, Lamarbridge, Anantnag, Phalgam, Baltal, Machoi.
14. Starting and closing point Sorankot, Poohch. Takes the following route : Bafleyaz, Chanaban, Chandimar, Dogran, Poshiana, Pirpanjal (pasture).
15. Starting point Khanna and closing point Khanna. Takes the following route : Khanna, Basantpura, Theni, Basoli, Jatiyar, Pond, Bani kamleyada, Kharoda, Sarthal, Badarwah, Kansar.
16. Starting and closing point Gatti. Takes the following route: Gatti, Shahpur, Keyar, Nalagash, Modi, Shahpura, Dalhoji, chamba, Khyar.
17. Starting from chaksakta village in Kathua, Takes the route following by No. 8. upto Wadwan (pasture).
18. Starting and closing point Gatti. Takes the following halts enroute: Dani, Porth, alma, Galakh, Ramkot, Khoon, rathiyal, Salu, Dahari, Ramnagar, Mansadevi, Chiki, Keer, Sudmadevi, Gorigund, Patnitop, Batote, Ramban, Banihal, Verinag, Sonf, Nubug, Inshan.

**Clans' names of the Gujjars**

1. Awan
2. Akla
3. Bani
4. Bijar
5. Bigyal
6. Bhatti
7. Chowhan
8. Chachi
9. Char
10. Chechar
11. Dader
12. Fomla
13. Fomra
14. Gagale
15. Gagi
16. Gorsi
17. Jangoa
18. Jagal
19. Khatana
20. Khan
21. Kasana
22. Kalase
23. Kalookheil
24. Khari
25. Konshi
26. Koli
27. Kataria
28. Lone
29. Loda
30. Moner
31. Monam
32. Mota
33. Mota
34. Mir
35. Manass
36. Malik
37. Nathiyal
38. Nali
39. Pathan
40. Pujwal
41. Padana
42. Paswall
43. Palaser
44. Qureshi
45. Rathor
46. Shah
47. Saiyad
48. Sheikh
49. Tadua
50. Turk
51. Tenda
52. Tendaa
53. Thikri
54. Thikiyal

## Social Change

Like Gaddi of Himalayas, many Gujjar clans have joined mainstream now-a-days. The Hindu Gujjars already occupy the higher status in the society. There are separate studies on Hindu Gujjars who are in the OBC list of reserve communities.

*(For further studies, read my books 'Nomads of the Himalayas', 'A Socio-History of Ex-Criminal Communities OBCs in India' and my research papers/articles on the subject).*

# 6

# Bhotiyas : The Trader Nomads

Bhotiyas, the nomadic tribe, are basically traders and move from place to place in Garhwal, Uttarkashi, Dehradun and other districts of Uttaranchal. They had their business with the Tibetans before the Chinese invasion in 1962 and used to visit their villages frequently.

Garhwal is bounded on the north by Tibet; on the east by Kumaon; on the south by Bijnor, and on the west by Tihri and Dehra Dun. It lies between north latitude 29-26'-15" and 31-5'-30", and between the east longitude 78-18'-34" and 80-8'-0", with an area of 5,500 square miles.

To the north, the water-parting forms the boundary with Hundes. To the east, the boundary is somewhat arbitrarily fixed by an irregular line drawn from the southern peak of Trisul to Pindar river abut twenty miles from its source, thence in a south eastern direction along the Badhan to Ramganga river near Mehalchauri, crossing it, to where it again meets the river in the Patli Dun. It skirts the southern base of the hills by the Ramnagar and Ganges road to Gorighat on the Ganges. On the west the boundary follows the Ganges river to Deoprayag, thence the Alaknanda to Rudraprayag and after the at the Mandakini river to Agastmuni. An irregular line above the right bank of that stream to the snowy range to the west of Kedarnath temple completes the circuit. The Greatest breath is 55 miles, the least is 30 miles and, the mean about 42 miles. The estimated area is 3,520,00 acres or 5,500 square miles. But owing to the difficulty in measuring the snowy wastes the area in acres cannot be correctly given. The natural divisions are mountain ranges and narrow valleys which, as a rule, are little more than ravines. That of Srinagar is the largest in the district, but it is hardly half a mile wide and has an elevation of only 1,500 feet above sea level. To these may be added the narrow strips of waterless forest at the foot of the hills called the Bhabar, about two to three miles in breadth, where it adjoins the plains.

## Topography

The shape of Garhwal on a map is not unlike that of hourglass, broad at the north and south and narrowing to about one-half in the middle. The Alaknanda and its tributaries drain the entire district and form the valleys, which are, as a rule, much narrower and contain less arable lands than those of Kumaon. Mr . Batten's description may be quoted here:

"Vast tracts are composed of bare rocks or are covered with forests; in some parts such features are confined to the upper parts of the mountains whose sides and base are endowed with the richest fertility; whilst in other parts, the fairest slopes or the finest valleys are succeeded by continuous miles of river glen where precipices and woods extend to the lowest depths. Sometimes the jungle is above the cultivated parts; sometimes below. In one place, individual village or sets of villages are separated from their neighbours, by almost impervious forests or impassible crags and rivers; in another, villages having little barren waste are mutually divided by a small corpse or ravine, or by the natural boundary of a stream flowing between their fields; so various are the features of the country, throughout which the hamlets are inter-separated. However, notorious, one sub-division may be for its plenty and another for its poverty, no opinion in either case can be formed of the natural capabilities of one village in one of its neighbour, in even the smallest sub-division of a tract."

River Alaknanda marks the great central line of the lowest elevation, receiving rivers on either side which in turn receive minor streams, and these again rills and rivulets until the great dividing ridge is met which forms the watershed between the head waters of the Kali or Sarda river on the east and the Ganges system on the west. The entire drainage of Garhwal flows into the Ganges. With the exception of paraganas Barahayun and Chaudkot, which are almost entirely bare of arboreal vegetation, the entire district is thickly covered with forest forming in many places an almost impenetrable jungle.

## The Himalayan Ranges

To the north the mountains form a portion of the great Himalayan chain of which the principal peaks in the district are West Trisul, 23,381 feet above the sea level; East Trisul, 23,982 feet; the third peak, 22,231 feet; Nanda Devi, 25,661 feet the Nandakna peaks, 20,771, 20,773, 22,093 feet, Kamet, 25,373 feet; Nilikanta, 21,661 feet; Badrinath, 23,210 feet, and Kedarnath, 22,790 feet. From the main range to the north-west the slope in lines to the elevated plains of Tibet, and the Vishnuganga river which gradually comes down to 6,200 feet at its confluence with the Alaknanda is up to 18,000 feet at its source in the glacier adjoining the Mana Pass into Tibet. Between the valley and the upper course of the Alaknanda, here called the Dhauli or 'white river' is a ridge of great height, ending on the south in a peak, having an elevation of 22,073 feet and in Kamet on the north. The Dhauli valley comes next and leads to the Niti Pass into Tibet, which is described in the article Bhotiya Mahals. To the south of the main range of hills we find numerous spurs running from it generally in a direction from north-east to south-west and parallel to each other with cross spurs at intervals and occasional ridges of greater elevation, such as Tungnath or Chandrasila (12,071 feet), Duda-ki-Toli (10,188 feet) and Dhubrri (9,862 feet). South of the river Nyar, however, the ranges run more parallel to the plains and are seldom more than 7,500 feet above the sea level. Most of the hills are rugged and densely wooden upto between ten and eleven thousand feet- steep towards the ridges somewhat flatter about the middle and end in abrupt slopes towards the valleys. Along the larger rivers, the hills present gradual slopes at the base and end in a succession of narrow terraces of flats, which are all dry and are, as a rule, also cultivated. The soil varies greatly in different valleys. That of the Alaknanda is somewhat sandy; of the Pindar, Ramganga, and Mandakini is reddish clay and that of the Nyar is clay mixed with shingle. The soil in the smaller valleys is usually very rich, being composed of the washings for the hill sides. The strip of Bhabar from Kotdwara to Siwalik range, which is crossed by numerous passes, some of which are practicable for wheeled carriage. The remainder of the southern boundary is wholly open to the plains.

**The Sacred Alaknanda**

The Alaknanda with its tributaries marks the distinguishing physical features of the district and shows the direction of the lines of lowest elevation. This river is one of the sacred streams of India and each of the places where it meets a considerable affluent called (Prayaga or confluence) is esteemed holy, and forms a station in the pilgrimage which all devout Hindus make to Himachal. The first confluence is at Vishnuprayga, where the waters of the Dhuli from the Niti Pass unite with the waters of the Saraswati or Vishnuganga from the Mana Pass and thence onwards to Deoprayag, the stream is known as the Laaknanda. At Nandlprayag, the Nadak stream joins the Alaknanda on the left bank, and brings with it the drainage from the Nandakna peaks and the western slopes of Tirsul.

At Karnprayag, on the same bank, is received the Pindar, which drains the southern and eastern slopes of the Trisul group. The Mandakini falls in on the right bank at Rudraprayag and brings with it the surplus waters of the entire tract along the southern slopes of the Badrinath and Kedarnath Peaks. At Deoprayag the Bhagirathi from Gangotri joins the Alaknanda, and henceforward the united stream is known as the Ganges. The Bhagirathi rises in Tihri from the Gangotri peak, and though popularly considered the chief branch of the Ganges, is inferior in importance and volume to Alaknanda. The only other important tributaries are the Nyar and Hinual Streams, which join the Ganges on the left bank below Deoprayag. The only river of any size in Garhwal, which dies not join the Ganges within the limits of the district, is the upper water of western Ramganga. This river takes its rise in Lohba and flowing through Kumaon for a considerable distance, re-enters Garhwal in the Patili Dun, where it receives the Mandhal, Plain and Sona streams on the right bank and brusting its way through the Siwaliks, reaches the Ganges in the Hardoi district of Oudh. All these rivers, owing to their great velocity and the existence of rocks, boulders, shoals and rapids are useless for navigation though several are used for rafting timber.

Wherever culturable land occur near their beds, they are used for irrigation and are also made available for giving power to mills for grinding corn. The beds of all the rivers consist of hard rock and gravel with a little sand and little erosion takes place. Diluvion, owing to sudden floods, occasionally takes place, but alluvion in the sense it is used in the plains van never occur. As a rule the banks of all the streams in the hills are abrupt and high.

Srinagar, the only place in the district approaching a town, is built on the right bank of the Alaknanda, well above the stream, but still before the conquest one-half of the town was swept away by a flood and again in 1868 and 1880 great losses occurred through a sudden rise in the same river. Rapids and eddies occur in all the rivers at short distances apart. The usual appearance is a succession of short, sharp rapids, sometimes having a considerable fall with a long and deep pool. Occasionally, the bed becomes very narrow and runs between gorges with high impassible cliffs on either banks. Such phenomena are most frequent on the Alaknanda and Pindar. None of the rivers flow through subterranean channels, through the Alaknanda some 25 miles above Joshimath appears to do so owing to rocks having fallen in and completely hidden the water. There are a few small ferries on the Alaknanda, the boat being a canoe formed from a hollowed log. Fords are rare on the rivers in the snowy range, but all the others are fordable even in the rainy season, except where there has been a fall of rain sufficient to cause a heavy flood. All the hill streams are liable to floods and occasionally to some of considerable volume. In 1968, water that had been dammed up by a landslip burst the barriers and coming down by the Alaknanda, caused very great damage and loss of life. Two larger bridges were swept away with some seventy pilgrims who sleeping on the river bank Chamoli, twenty feet above the ordinary flood level. When such floods happen to flow over any cultivable land they usually, by covering it with rocks and gravel, render it useless for a number of hears until the debris is cleared away. Floods had damaged the area in the recent past too.

There are no lakes of any importance in Garhwal. The largest is Diuri Tal (q.v.) in Kalighat, which is about 400 yards long and 250 yards wide. It is oval in shape and is mainly interesting from the panoramic view of the snowy range above Kedarnath which is seen reflected on its surface. There are a few small lakes situation on the tops of some of the high hills, such as Doe Tal near the Mana Pass, Gadyar tal in Painkhanda Talla and Bhairon Tal in Dasoli Talli.

## Hot Springs

There are several hot springs in Garhwal. Those at Gauri Kund on the road to the temple of Kedarnath are situated above the right bank of the Mandakini river. On the 6th October, at 5 p.m. when the temperature of the air was $64^0$ Fahrenheit and that of the river was $52^0$ F. the temperature in one of the springs war $74^0$ F. and in another $128^0$ F. The water is collected in an artificial reservoir built for the purpose of bathing, as all pilgrims are required to bathe here before proceeding to Kedarnath, a procedure full of physical as well as spiritual benefit.

There is another spring of a similar description at Badrinath called the Tapt Kund. It runs under the temple and is also collected in a large reservoir for bathing purposes. The temperature was noted at $128^0$ Fahrenheit, when that of the river close-by was only $38^0$ F. Cold water is let into the reservoir in order to allow the pilgrims to bathe into it. There are four separate hoot springs at Tapuban, two about a mile and two about one-quarter of a mile, from the village of that name and all close to the Niti road. The tow most distant well up into artificial reservoirs and are used as bathing-places, their temperature being $127^0$ F. and $123^0$ F. respectively. The other two are springs and not used for bathing, their temperature being $99^0$ and $109^0$ F. The water of the first two is of a dirty colour and leaves a whitish sediment, but does not seem to have any sulphur in it, while that of the latter two is clear and somewhat aerated though tasteless. The spring of Bhauri lies near the villages of Amola in latitude $30^0$-3' and longitude $78^0$-2'. It has a somewhat saline taste and the stones are discoloured by a reddish sediment. The elevation of this spring is between 3,500 and 4,000 feet. It rises in a small *sal* forest and has a temperature of $94^0$ F. There are also two other springs considered by the natives to be warm. One occurs at Kulsari on the left bank of the Pindar river and the other on the river Palain in Badalopur Patti. The water is rather less cold than ordinary hill water, but not even slightly hot.

## The People

Bhotias are a loosely knit tribal community, numbering about 35,000 to 40,000 people and having their permanent abodes in the seven river valley in the inner Himalayas which sprawl across Uttaranchal. This division was not earlier an administratively integrated unit and conceptualized for purposes of formulation and implementation of development plans. This consists of three districts; Uttrakashi, Chamoli and Dehradun. Uttarkashi originally belonged to Tehri state and Chamoli to British Garhwal. Pithoragarh was a sub-division of the Almorah district. Now there are eight districts in newly constituted state.

A triangular region is formed in the northern part of Uttaranchal, with its longest side forming the traditional international frontiers between India and Tibet. The continental division formed by the high Himalayan ranges giving rise to two distinct watershed systems—one flowing northwards in Tibet and the other flowing southwards in Indian territory, constitutes the actual border between India and Tibet. The right side of the triangle is formed by the river Kali which makes a natural border between India and Nepal. Its apex and the lower most point at Jauljibi to Thanga Pass, near the tri-junction between Himachal Pradesh, Uttaranchal and Tibet completes the triangular Bhot Pradesh, containing the Seven river valleys, which have been the homeland of the Bhotiya communities from time immemorial.

The seven river valleys are : Bhagirathi-Jahanavi Gangs in Uttarkashi district; Alaknanda and Dhauli Ganga in Chamoli district, Gori Ganga, Darma or Eastern Dhauli; Kali and Kuti Yankti in Pithoragarh district.

### Tibetan Mandis

The original and permanent settlements of the Bhotiyas of these seven valleys are situated within a short distance from the mountain pass leading to Tibetan *mandies* (business centres). Thus, Neelad and Jadung on Jahanavie Ganga comprises the *maits* or original settlement of Jad Bhotiyas. These people had to evacuate Neelang and Judung, and resettled at Bagori near Harsil or Bhagirathi, some 20 miles south of Mana Pass leading to Tibet. It is situated on Alakananda, only 3.5 km. north of the famous Badrinath shrine.

All along Dhauli Ganga, from Suraithotha up stream upto Jhelum are villages inhabited by Tolcha group of Bhotiyas, Malari, Farkiya, Bampa, Gamshali and Niti Villages in Khauli are inhabited be the Marchha group of Bhotiyas. They are related to the Gori Ganga is called Johar. The last village on this side is Millam and the last inhabited village in the Darma valley is Go. The lower reached of the Kali river, from Khela to Malpa is called Chaudans. The upper reaches of Kali, from Budhi upto Gunmji, where the Kuti Yankti rivers meets it, the valley along Kuti comprises the Byans Patti. Each valley has one or more mountain passes leading to Tibetan *Mandies.*

The Bhotiyas have their residences in the villages situated in the upper reaches of the river valleys. The move to their permanent abodes at lower altitudes on the same river, or on other rivers, in Garhwal and Kumaon. They have been carrying on trade with Tibetan businessmen for a long time. They would buy products from Indian *mandis* which had ready demand in Tibetan markets, such as: foodgrains, *gur,* textiles, tobacco and manufactured goods; in turn they would import wool, salt, borax, hides and skins animals from Tibet. Trade in Tibetan *mandis* had brought financial affluence to the Bhotiya community. But due to long range changes in the world trade carried on by the Botiyas had started dwindling from the middle of twenties and thirties. Further significant drop took place during the fifties with the advent of the Chinese in Tibet. All trade came to an abrupt and complete stop with the sealing of the indo-Tibetan border since Bhotiya occupy the frontiers which have strategic importance for the defence and security of the country, their state of national integration assume considerable political-administrative and defence implications in 1962. The economy of the Bhotiya people based upon trade is with Tibetans through rearing of a large number of animals, like sheeps, goats, jibbus, ponies, mules etc. staggered under this blow and has not made any substantial recovery since then.

## SOCIAL STRUCTURE

Bhotiyas, today, by and large, claim to be Kshatriyas, and attach the caste appellation of *Singh* to their names. Those who do not attach such an appellation may be Brahmans, or untouchables belonging to Scheduled Castes. Kolis in Jads are Schedules Caste people. Srivastava holds that same caste groups exist in Johar, Karma and Chudans, Byans valleys are populated by Doms. This generalization also appear to suffer from simplistic attitude. The structure among the Bhotiya community is delineated by Srivastava as follows:

1. Different groups of Bhotiyas named after the river valley;
2. The local village group; surnames often derived from the name of the village;
3. Sometimes it may be the same as the local group, when an entire village is inhabited by the member of one clan (Gorkha);
4. Based on lineage *(Ranth);*
5. Based on family traditions.

**The Family**

The caste hierarchy among the Bhotiyas of Johar valley is as follows: Khasiya Brahmans, who are the priests of the Johari Bhotiyas; followed by Johari Bhotiyas who are Kshatriyas; next come Nitwals and Khasiya Rajputs. The difference among these levels is slight. A sharp cleavage occurs then, with Kunkiya servants, followed by Doms, Hurkiyas and Mirasis coming last. Doms and Hurkiyas and Mirasis are untouchables. In Johar, Nitwals are supposed to have immigrated from Niti and mana, but they claim to be Brahamans, and yet are at a lower level than the Kshatriyas of Loharis. The Nitwals act as *pujaris* (priests), cooks and occasionally they work as servants of the Bhotiyas.

This overall structural arrangement provides a good framework for understanding the present situation in the different valleys. The jads asserted that there is no caste differences among them. The Kolis are treated as Harijans, and, therefore, untouchables. But there are a number of *ranths* among them, representing different lineages weighing the same villages. The different *ranths* in Bagori among the Kolis, (Kabirpanthis and Sanpals are to be found. The evidence is not clear whether the Kolis of Bagoris also can be appropriated) *ranths* like those of the Jad Bhotiyas. Likewise, whether 'Raj' is a *Rath* of the Jadsor Kolis, is also not clear.

When we move to Mana, we find that these people belong to the clan called Marchha. Among the Mana Marchhas there are also a number of sub groups of *ranths*. These are : Kherash, Pankholari, Parmar, Badwal, Jitwan, Kalkholi, Dalia, Khola, etc.

Among the Tolchhas and Marchhas of the Dhauli Valley, similar *ranths* are to be found, though the names are different and may be linked to a particular village to which they belong. Among Tolchhas, following old caste groups are named : Kilia, Buda, Nilora, Khana Pati, Ganiya, Bulia, Bongcha, Thtowals, Dharkwal.

Since Marchhas are found at both Mana and Niti valleys, some of the *ranths* are identical. For example, in village Gams Hali, one of the four main villages of the Niti valley the *ranths* are Rana, Rawat, Kunwar, Virat, Phonia, Badwal, Chauhan, besides Harijans. Rawats, Kunwars and Phonia are most numerous and also prominent. In Bampal, Pals and Bampals predominate. In Niti village, the *ranths* are Rana, Khati, Badwal, Phonia and Gania, the first two Rana and Khati forming larger numbers.

**Sub-casters of Bhotiyas**

1. Rawat, Pangti, Darmshaktu
2. Nikhurpa, Nitwal, Sayana
3. Brijuwal
4. Burphal, Jangpangy
5. Tolia
6. Sumdyal
7. Khinchal
8. Panchpal
9. Mapwal
10. Martolia
11. Rilkotia
12. Laspal or Dhapwal
13. Darmawala
14. Ralmal
15. Patyal
16. Harkotia
17. Papra
18. Bogti
19. Imlali
20. Joshal
21. Bothal
22. Chulkotia
23. Ringwal
24. Tomikal
25. Namkial

Garbiyalis consists of several *ranths,* grouped into sets of 3 each, with one *malgujar* (revenue collector at the village level). In Gargiyang, the following groups may be seen:

1. Langu ranth, Ringin ranth, Chhamil ranth–one malgujar;
2. Kharwanchhim ranth, Rangchim ranth, Nuchim ranth—one malgujar;
3. Buta ranth, Nimphai ranth, Chhindu ranth—one malgujar.

## Marriage

Marriage customs among Bhotiyas of all the seven valleys have undergone a lot of change, though the extent and quality of change are different in various valleys. The marriage customs in the seven valleys have been described by Dr. B. Chatterjee as under; It is surprising to observe that no other social institution has got so much changed and complicated as is the case with marriage customs among the Bhotiyas.

Marriage among Jads takes place at the residence of the bridegroom. After completion of the ceremony, *pooja* is offered to God Satya Narayan. The system of dowry exists among Jads, but it is not compulsory. The *Gandharva vivaha* or marriage by courtship and choice of brides and bridegrooms, is not found here. Widow remarriage and divorce and separation are not recommended; in fact, these are frowned upon. If some marries a widow, she does not receive the same level of acceptance or prestige as a virgin bride would be entitled to. During the marriage ceremony, *sindur* (vermillion) is applied by the *pandit* (priest).

*Marriage among Mana Bhotiyas* :The marriage is settled according to compatibility among the lineages of the brides and the bridegrooms. Match making is the sole prerogative of the parents of the bride and the bridegroom. The father of the boy, who bears all the expenses of marriage, settles the marriage of his son with the father of the girl. The bride's father only gives the girl to the other side. He also gifts cattle. Sheep and goats, etc. as dowry to the bridegroom, as much as his means would permit, but there is no compulsion.

Marriage takes place in the house of the bridegroom. The *pandit* recites hymns, and makes the bride and the bridegroom go round the sacred fire kindled for *Havan* in the *Yanga-Kund;* usually 7 or 9 rounds are made (in most Hindu sacramental marriages, the marriage is completed only when bride and bridegroom both have performed the *Sapta-padi gama* i.e. taking 'seven steps together, which is vedic ritual).'

There is a lot of gay festivity of the day of marriage. Two dances, *doon-kudi* and *pauna* are staged and these are very popular in which members of both the sexes take part. People drink *chhang* and wine to their hearts content. (*Chhang* is a locally brewed, in almost all families.) The festivity of *Chopdi* is held on the day of marriage, which is well, known as *Bhotiya-Chopdi.* On the second day of the marriage *pooja* is offered to God Satya Narayan, literally meaning gifting the daughter away. This ceremony is performed in the bride's home, and then the marriage is celebrated at the residence of the bridegrooms.

Contrary to what we have recorded before, marriages occasionally take place, where the bride and bridegroom choose each other. However, remarriage of widows, and divorce have no social sanction among Marchhas of Mana. Marriages are restricted among ones owns community only.

*Marriages among Talchhas and Marchhas:* Marriage customs here have similarity with those of Mana, with some local variations. Marriage is held according to vedic traditions and the match-making is done through negotiations between the parents of both the parties—of the bride and the bridegroom. Entire expenses of the marriage have to be borne by the parents of the bridegroom, as the bride here has greater importance. However, whatever money is taken by the bride's parents is meant for spending on the marriage only. If the bride's parents are poor, they sent the girl to bridegroom's party for marriage ceremony which takes place at the residence of the bridegroom. On the other hand, affluent parents of a bride would perform the marriage ceremony at their own house and would not accept any money for expenses from the bridegroom's parents. Only a few cases were found where a boy and a girl married according to their choice.

Marriage ceremony is performed by a *pandit*. The sacred fire is kindled, vedic hymns chanted, when marriage is performed. The sacred fire is the witness to the marriage. The bridegroom, followed by the bride, makes seven rounds of the *yagn-kunda*. When marriage takes place in the house of the bride's parents, the bridegroom comes to the place riding a horse, along with a procession. There is a big feast in which wine flows liberally and *pauna* dance is also held. On the next day the bride accompanies the bridegroom in a *doli* (palanquin) to go to her father-in-law's place. Thus, the marriage ceremony is completed, according to vedic traditions. The occasion is for great festivity and merry-making, accompanied by songs and dances, specially the *doon kudi* dances. The whole night is spent in gaiety and consuming wine drunk in copious quantities. There is a friendly competition in singing—males sing in chorus, and women reply them back singing. It creates a sense of repertee, which continues for a long time. Boys and girls form two separate groups and dance together. This dance is called *Bhotiya Chaukad*. After marriage *pooja* of God Satya Narayan is a must. Here too, widow remarriage and divorce have not received social acceptance though it may be tolerated.

*Marriage customs in the Johar Valley* : Marrchhas of Mana and Niti valleys had marriage relations with Johar valley, with the result that there is a good deal of similarity in marriage customs between these three valleys.

*Marriage customs in Darma Valley* : Marriages here are settled by negotiations held among parents and other relatives of both the parties. Here the bridegroom arrives at the bride's house in a *doli* (palanquin). The *fera,* that is the bridegroom going round the bride, take place here, and then the *bridal* (parting) ceremony takes place and the bride is taken to the bridegroom's place. All the expenses are met by the bridegroom's party.

*Marriage customs in Chaudans and Byans Pattis* : The institution *rang-bang* had been very common here to specially in the selection of the life partner of one's choice. But it is now dying out slowly. Instead, marriages are held according to vedic rites, with the help of a Brahaman *pandit.*

Now-a-days, the marriages are held according to traditional Hindu methods. Horoscopes are matched, and auspicious dates are decided upon, by Brahman *pandits*. The parents of the bridegroom have to do a lot of pleadings before any marriage is agree upon by the parents of the bride—the final say is with the bride's party.

It is interesting enough that the Bhotiya people are conservative in developing social intimacy where the question of marriage within the family is involved. They do not prefer a marriage with a member of a non-Bhotiya community, like Garhwali, Maidani, Nepali, etc. Leaving aside marriage outside one's own community, the Bhotiyas are very liberal and do not discriminate between other communities with whom they have to come into contact. The fact that the Bhotiya communities are liberal may be vouched by other evidences also. Their proverbial hospitality, their unstinted help rendered to tourists, pilgrims, *sadhus* and mendicants—are legendary.

### Child birth

As in the case of marriage, considerable extent of Hinduization has gone through in customs and rituals connected with the birth of a child and death in the family. Some interesting informations collected on this subject have been described below :

Among the Jads there is the ceremony of *mundan* (shaving of head-hair) but this is confined only to the male child. This ceremony takes place when the child is 3 year's old.

### Ram-Bang or Rang-Band

This was a type of dormitory or club which was found only among the Darma, Byans and Chaudan Bhotiyas. Joharis do not agree that it existed in their valley. Jads Marchhas and Tolchhas of Mana and Niti valley also do not know about it.

Promodo Chatoopadhyaya, has given a very detailed and lively picture of the *rang-band* of his time, nearly ninety years ago. He has described the institution in detail giving interesting account.

"It was customary for girl to get married after adolescence is passed," he writes, but the process of marriage is a sort of combination between *rashash* and *gandharva* styles. It is based upon courtship or pre-martial acquaintance and love. There is a secluded room within the village called *rang-bang,* where young men and women congregate after sun-set. All adolescents, near post-adolescents, and fully post-adolescents, unmarried men and women, put on their best dress, and assemble there to spend the night in drinking, singing and dancing. This may be to lead a healthy community life. The mothers after sun-set, would dress up their unmarried daughters and would send them to the *ran bang*. In these people's marriage, there was no priest, no hymns, no *shaligram* stone, no *bedi* (raised platform for performing yajna), no registration. Whoever falls in love with another becomes his or her bride or bridegroom. Only the chosen bridegroom gifts some amount to the bride to get one ring made. She informs her parents about it. Then on some convenient night he absconds with the girl to his own house. Later, there is a feast, where a couple of goats or sheep may be sacrificed. The family life starts then. However, exceptions have started in certain places. Some people are in favour of marrying after obtaining consent of their parents. Just as among Hindu society, these people want to recast their society according."

Pant mentions four types of fine dances that are performed in these clubs—Dandyala, Chamfuli, Dhusha and Dhurang.

Even with the institution of *rang-band* is on its way out, there was also an incipient movement in Byana to revive it, or atleast sustain it. This was a part of the revivalist movement which was favoured by certain Bhotiya young men, who exercise some leadership functions. The underlying idea is that *rang-band* was a typical Bhotiya indigenous institution. The Bhotiyas should take pride in their own indigenous social institutions, which have been serving a social purpose for ages. The research scholars found that at Gunji the *rang-band* was thriving well.

Even in *rang-bang* courtship is conducted so as not to violate any taboo, such as breaking the prohibition of co-sanguinarity. Dabral says, "Marriage among *sama-gotras* is prohibited. Men cannot marry daughters of father's brother or mother's sister. For girls, marrying maternal uncle's son, or paternal aunt's son is desirable."

As this system is changing, it is clear that attitude towards pre-marital sexual relationship is also stiffening, coming closer to that of the orthodox Hindu society. The Jad at Bagori were asserting that they did not favour pre-marital sexual relationship in their community.

Dabral has described a very interesting procedure by which a divorce is carried out.

"Divorce usually takes place under two circumstances, when the husband takes another wife, or when the wife falls in love with another man and absconds with him, under such circumstances, the first husband, after obtaining a separation tax *(patni-shulka* wife-tax), 'cuts off the string.' He picks two blades of grass or two strings of straw and asks the new husband to pull off one of these two. When the new husband pulls off one of the strings, the divorce seems to have become finalised".

Dr. Chatterjee reports that the question of polygamy and polyandry may be settled here quickly. Among the Bhotiyas, neither polygamy nor polyandry exists. Because of the dearth of girls, the question of polygamy does not arise but polyandry has also no place among the Bhotiyas—which is found among the Jaunsar-Bawar tribes of Chakrata in Dehra Dun district and also among certain sections of Tibetans. Even remarriage of a widow with the younger brother of the husband is a rare phenomenon; if it occurs, it is just tolerated, but never receives social approval or recognition as the marriage of an unmarried girl would normally receive. There is an idea among some people that polygamy and polyandry are found among Bhotiyas. This is palpably incorrect.

## RELIGION

In most texts there is some mention about the religious beliefs and customs of the Bhotiyas. Here two aspects about religious practices, beliefs, and traditions, particularly of tribal people, have to be kept in mind. The tribal people have no written records or other forms of permanent records, like rock edicts, copper inscriptions from which one may construct the conditions that existed in the past. Thus so far as tribal people are concerned, the past has to be carefully distinguished from the present. What the past was is largely a matter of speculation. The present is something which can be observed and accurately described. The present study will take primary notice of the present state of affairs, and will not try to establish the truth or otherwise of what the state of affairs was in the past. But it has to be described briefly to provide the backdrop for the present.

Dabral has devoted an entire chapter on the religious and social life of the Bhotiyas. His description can be summarized here to make this study more authentic and complete.

Because the Bhotiyas spend a lot of time with animals, their standard of cleanliness may be much lower than many others and the world *Marchhya* used for these Bhotiyas is derived from the Sanskrit world—Mlechha. This is not tenable. Dabral has fallen into such phonetic traps many times. For example he writes: "Among these 17 villages, inhabitants of 4 villages—Nabi, Nepalcho, Garbyang and Budi—have their *gunshas* within the boundary of Nepal. Here the name of a village is Nepalcho. From this, is evident that here the boundary between Nepal and Kumaon had ben shifting and inhabitants of Nepal have come to settle on this side of Kali also." According to the latest studies the whole statement is full of errors. The *gunshas* of these villages are not in Nepal, but Byans Bhotiyas have their *maite* in two villages well inside Nepal, viz. Chhangru and Tinkar. These two villages are at so high an altitude that they cannot be sued as *gunshas* for spending winter. Dharchula is used as *gunshas* by the Byans Bhotiyas. There is one place called Deothala which is inside Nepal and is reached by crossing Kali at Dharchula, which is used as a *gunshas* by Garbyang Bhotiyas, who own land there. Nepalese also own land on this side of Kali. But that does not mean that the boundary between India and Nepal had been shifting.

According to linguistics the error that Darbral commits is due to his going by the similarity of sounds, rather than meanings about the world *Nepalcho.* This is village on the right side of Kuti Yankti, almost facing Gunji. Its correct spelling will be Napalcho. Here the word 'Nepal' is a form of wheat *(buck-what)* which is grown extensively in this region. In any case there are no inhabitants of Nepalese origin here.

Ram Rahul believes that the Bhotiya religion is mixture of animism, Buddhism and Hinduism. The eastern Bhotiyas still follow their traditionally folk-religion based on belief in and worship of spirits. They offer, sacrifice to ward off the evil influence of spirits.

The present trend among the western Bhotiyas, who are partly Hinduized, is to become Hindu to achieve better social status.

This description of the religion of Bhotiyas is very faulty and extremely naive, more, so as it has been written as recently as 1970. Ram Rahul seems to give the impression that the Bhotiyas religion is a mixture of equal proportion of animism, Buddhism and Hinduism. Further, he makes out that the eastern Bhotiyas still follow their traditional folk-religion based on belief in and worship of spirits. They offer sacrifices to ward off the evil influence of spirits. The questions arise: "Do the Hindus not offer such sacrifices to deities? Are not local deities and spirits worshipped by Hindus?"

Dabral also states that Bhotiyas are extremely credulous. They are fatalists, in constant fear of many gods and goddesses, spirits and demons etc." Perhaps, Darbral thinks that this fear is the fear of the unknown and is fostered by the extreme solitariness of the upper Himalayas. Nature is here sombre, threatening and cruel. Dwelling upon this question, Dickinson clearly states:

"Bhotiyas.... live in the wildest surroundings, where the awful solitude overwhelms the mind and fantastic forms and eerie sounds seem to speak of an ever-present spirit world which compel men to see the supernatural in every bush and rock and avalanche. Every rock and rivulet is dedicated to some saint or deity and has its appropriate legend."

According to Shering : "In these lovely valleys there is still romance and poetry of life: each tree has its god, each bush its spirit; precautions are taken to exclude malevolent ghosts from the house by turning a basket upside down and sticking twings in it and leaning it on the outer wall."

Sacrificial offers of goats and sheep are made to propitiate gods, goddesses and spirits for obtaining relief from some illness or difficulty.

About the Jads, Dabral is categorical, that they are Buddhists: "Even though the Jads are Buddhists, go round Chortens, bow down before gombas, turn mani wheels and erect 'lungta' flag mast, they", he writes, "like Marccha-Tolchha are full of blind faith and are constantly afraid of ghosts and spirits."

Pant writes:

"Such is the awe-inspired by the great snows that at every prominent place on the wayside whence a full view of red and white cloth has been offered and may be seen tied to some bush or tree. As soon as the Bhotiyas reaches these spots he bows with folded hands to the range which is to him the abode of the mighty deity and hums a short prayer."

It so happens, that when a spot is reached by a steep ascent and then a descent starts, the spot is dedicated to wayside goddess called Kathburiya and every passer-by adds either a stone or a pine cone to the heap, as thanks—giving, offering for the ascent to that point.

Sometime it may so happen, that a small temple or a chorten may also be erected there. In course of time, the temple may acquire a Hindus name and the deity, usually of a stone, start symbolizing the 'lingam' of Shiva. Such a temple can be seen at Kala Muni Top (8,900 ft.) on your way to Munshiyari; Unnamed Top (10,000 ft.) between Sirkha and Simkhola—Bongbond and at Chhialok height (11,000 ft.) between Buddhi and Garbyang in Byans Patti. A beautiful but small temple is to be found near Nabi, which is the next village after Gunji on way to Kuti, on the Kuti Yankti river. A very small temple was seen beyond the village of Kuti on Kuti Yankti river. Whatever the original deity might have been, now they have become Hindu temples with stone deities symbolizing Lord Shiva or Gauri, his consort.

It is said that Manibhadra was a Yaksha and so was Kuber, who are the patron gods of Mana. The local god, Chantakarna is also worshipped here, for whom there being a fairly big temple at Mana.

This proliferation, of local deities and rituals connected with faith in spirits and ghosts, has been responsible for the naive acceptance of an assumption that Bhotiyas were or Buddhists and are being Hinduized. This is highly conjectural and the evidence adduced is meagre, if not wholly untenable. The influx of some Buddhistic influences need not be assimilation has taken place all over India. But to say that the original structure itself is Buddhistic and simplistic has little basis of any empirical validity.

Pant mentions the preponderance of 'mountain, river and wayside gods,' and 'weather deity.' But he never makes them out to be Buddhistic in character. The universal and most popular rain-god is *Gobla,* who is worshipped with offerings of goats and cakes. After a long persist of drought, the god Dharmua is worshipped thus : "Two poles are thrust into the ground. On the top of one of them is tied a yask-tail and an iron trident and on the top of the other an image of the human form. Music is played and a goat sacrificed. In the Darma valley, above Bogdwar, the rain-god Dharmua is worshipped, but below Bogdwar, the name of the rain-god is Hardyal. In Darma the rain-god is Kungr. Unlike Kharmua, Kungr brings rain as well as stops it. When he is asked to stop the train he is offered dry flour and when the people want rain wet flour is offered."

Such worshipping of rain-god still continues. It is observed in the village of Kuti, on the Kuti Tanki river, which is the last village in Byans. A long, tried tree—a local variety of poplar—or maybe juniper, was stuck into the ground, and a coloured flag was unfurled atop the makes like tree-stem. Old men and young congregated below the tree for worship and the ritual took some time. The team could not wait to see if a sacrificial animal was offered or not.

Pant writes about the two Shepherd-gods—Runiya and Sain, "Like his nomad worshippers, Runiya is always wandering from village to village and has steeds which he rides by night in order to find lost flocks." When animals are sick, "the shepherds worship the Gods Sidhua and Bidhuwa," two brothers who are supposed to come to rescue "ailing beats."

"Besides these gods, each village has its own appropriate deity, who deals with its peculiar problems. The temples are mere worship poles with branches and are decorated with dangling strips of cloth and Yak-tails."

Another interesting ritual is the 'sara' or 'raglosha' which is driven, while going from 'mait' to 'gunsa' or vice versa, to prevent ghosts and spirits accompanying the peripatetic party.

However, all these local and tribal rituals are fitted into an overall dominating structure of Hinduism—which is a fact, fully recognised by Pant who made his investigations in 1928-32, by Darbal who made his research around 1956-58, and by R.P. Srivastava, whose investigations were carried out a little later around the sixties. The following extract from Pant will suffice to bring out the dominant Hindu theme of the religion of Bhotiyas:

"Among the gods worshipped by the Bhotiyas, the highest Himalayan peak—the abode of the mountain god Mahadeva—are the best known. In Johar Nanda Devi and Hansling and in Darma Panchachuli figure as the most prominent deities. Kailash, Mansarowar and Badri-Kedar are also worshipped. At Martoli at a height of 11, 080 feet above the sea-level on a silent, solitary and impressive spot, Whence a marvellous view is obtained, a temple has been erected to the consort of Mahadeva—who is supposed to reside on the peak."

He mentions of an annual fair held there in the second week of September in which nearly al the families of the fifteen highest villages of the valley are assembled and ten buffaloes and more than three hundred goats are sacrificed. In Darma Valley the Panchachuli group is known as Miyua.

Obviously, the majority of gods of the Bhotiyas are the majestic forces of nature.......They worship Kailash Parvat, Dronagiri, Hathi Parvat and Nanda Devi, Peak as gods and goddesses.

Throughout Bhotiya land, on majority of high pro-monotories i.e., *Chandas* or from where either Nanda Devi peak or other high peaks of higher Himalayas are visible, temples of Nanda are to be found. There are many folk-songs related to Nanda Devi. Nandaghunti peak is the *ghunghat* or veil of Nanda Devi; Nandakit peak is the '*kot*' or fort of Nanda Devi; Nanda-Khat is the bed of Nanda Devi and Trisul peak is the trident in the hand of Nanda Devi.

According to local folklore, Panchachuli peaks are five *chulhis* or evens erected by Kunti, mother of the five Pandava brothers of Mahabharata, for cooking food. A hillock dedicated to Kunti is to be found just above Kuti village also in Byana Patti. The situation in Johar in the sixties has ben delineated by Srivastava. He writes:

"Most of the regional gods and goddesses have been worshipped in Johar. Nanda Devi is worshipped with special fervour and Nanda Ashtami, the festival when this goddess is worshipped, is the most important annual event in Johar. *Gita* and *Ramayana* are recited on ceremonial occasions. Most of the rituals include the sacrificing of sheep or goats to the various deities. These Bhotiyas, like the immigrant Rajputs, also have pictures of Rama and Krishna in their homes. The temples in Johar are extremely crude and built on ridges. There is usually a trident (Shiva's symbol), a round stone representing the *linga* and a statue whose frame is made of twings and later covered with clothes and jewellery to represent Nanda. Other regional deities worshipped in Johar are Thatiyal-Bhumiyal, the god of fields and rain and Runkya, the shepherd god. There are also a number of purely local deities which are individually worshipped in different villages."

The situation in the eastern Bhotiya villages is not very different either. The extensive influence of Vyas Rishi, with numerous temples dedicated to him can be observed in this region.

**Rooma Devi**

Pradmode Chattopadhyaya's description of Rooma Devi, a pious Bhotiya lady of Garbyang, who used to help Hindu Pilgrims to Kailash-Mansarowar and who founded the Ashram called Tapovan just north of Darchula and later spent her life with Anandamayee Mata, is very revealing:

"Rooma's house has two storeys. It is amountain house, made of wood, clay and stone like all other houses built in this part. In the room, in the second floor, in the front is the window in three sections. The room she left to us is her bedroom as well as room for worshipping also. Wall is made of clay; on all the four walls are pictures of gods and goddesses—Radha-Krishna, Mahaveer (Hanuman), Ramachandra, Shiva."

This is what Chattopadhyaya saw in 1918 in a typical pious Bhotiya lady's house—not very different from what was seen recently in the room of Shanti Devi, at Kuti. Only here the walls of the room were not covered with paintings. Framed pictures were on one wall. There were small deities of stone—and metal below those pictures, which were not of great antiquity. A photograph of Rooma Devi was also there, who happened to be the aunt of Shanti Devi—her father's cousin sister.

The gods, goddesses and local deities are worshipped in a formal manner and religious scriptures like *Ramayana* are read. In Johar the remnant of Tibetan contact is to be found only in the worship of the rain god Dhurmadevta and of the fertility god Lhamsaldevta or in some folk-tales. Characteristics of other Huniya gods have been appropriated by Hindu village deities. The custom of giving Tibetan names to men and women have been stopped since last 2-3 generations.

About the essentially Hindu character of the religion of Bhotiyas, the following passages from Sherring is interesting:

"It speaks volumes of their national character that although they have been for centuries in constant touch with Tibet for business purposes, they have never absorbed into their own simple religion the extravagance and demonology of Lamaism."

But Dabral's own conclusions are fairly definitive:

"They (Bhotiyas), when in trouble would make offering to Tibetan gods—Phaila, Dharma, Lhamsal and seek amulets of protection (Yantra and Tabiz) from Tibetan Lamas."

Still they are Hindus and have deep commitment to Hindu religion. It is a testimony to their character that despite their contact with Tibetans over centuries and despite being under the rule of Tibetans, they have been observing their Hindu traditions with steadfastness. They did no accept the Buddhism and the Lamaism of Tibet. Neither they turn Mani wheels nor do they recite the Mani Hymn. Nor they keep pictures of Buddha or Bodhisattva."

Coming back to the religion of the Bhotiyas of the three remaining valleys viz., Darma, Chaudans and Byans we may say, that the essentially Hindu core of their religion has been maintained despite absorption of some characteristics of the neighbouring lands and evolution of local variations.

## ECONOMIC ASPECTS

The amount of land that can be used for cultivation and raising of stable crops is awfully meagre in all the Bhotiya valleys, considering their populations. At certain places a river may widen up, creating what is called a *Bangar* on one or both banks which is usable for cultivation. But such *Bangars* are rare; the area is not extensive and some of it has been taken up for building dwelling houses.

The unit of land measure among the Bhotiyas is the *nali* which is 240 square yard or 1/20th of an acre. Average landholding may be as low as 2-3 *nalis* and it may go up to 25-30 or in rare cases, 50 nalis, i.e., 2½ acres. How much of crop can be raised in such small areas can be easily guessed.

**Trade**

The main commodities the Bhotiyas used to sell to Tibetans were food grains, *gur,* utensils, clothings and small instruments and ornaments and fancy things. They would bring in exchange, usually through barter, salt, wool, borax musk and similar exotic material found only in Tibet. It is doubtful if gold and precious stones would be available in Tibet.

Goats are extensively used by Bhotiyas for pack purpose, as well as for meat, but most probably not for wool.

**Trade Hazards**

Trade with Tibetan Dokpa businessmen involved several types of hazards. One was the hardship of travel and transport over steep, narrow, hazardous climbs, braving snow, ice, blizzards animals, privation. Secondly, in Tibet there would be the raids by Khampa dacoits. These dacoits would raid in group. They would ride on Tibetan horses and use swords and very old fashioned country-made shot-guns. They would never attack any party which is armed with modern weapons. They would extort money and if demand not conceded to they kill main or would.

Before Tibet was fully occupied by the Chinese, the Khampas were terror and the weak administration of the Tibetan Government could do little for protection of Bhotiya or Tibetan traders. Of course it is said, that in case a Khampa robber would be captured, he too stop the Khampa menace or reduce it terror. Thirdly, the Tibetan Government officials were very feudal, unpredictable and uncertain and indulged in extorionate practices now and then against Bhotiyas traders.

**Changing Trends**

We have the similar view as have been described by Dr. Chatterjee in his report. The major findings are:

Certain amount of modernization in the social customs, traditions and modes of the Bhotiya communities has taken place. But by and large this process is slow. Hinduization is taking place quite rapidly. The traditional death rite Dudung in Darma, Byana and Chaudans, Pattis is on its way out, being increasingly replaced by Hindu forms of *Shraddha* rites. Marriages are becoming more Hinduized. Occasionally, Tibetan names used to be given to children but this is not done any longer. The women folk particularly those who have received education in schools and colleges, are increasingly taking to dress style of the plains; the same applies to ornaments. Food drinking habits are changing rather slowly. Bhotiyas are addicted to drinking of country made liquors. They do not appears to be giving up this addiction.

With the closure of the border, profound economic changes have taken place among the Bhotiyas. Most of them have become impoverished. They had very little land for purposes of growing food grains. A portion of that meagre land has been occupied by the army or has been damaged. Animals of all kinds have been reduced drastically. Bhotiyas are traditional spinners and weavers of wool. This business has been seriously affected. Imported wool is costly and in short supply. Profound structural changes in the occupational pattern of the Bhotiyas have taken place within the last decade. Many of them have become daily labourers in road gangs. Some of them are engaged in transporting of goods required by army, police, civilians etc. Some have shifted to contractor's job. But the general impoverishment of the economic standard of the Bhotiyas is a near-universal phenomenon. There is a fast assimilation and acculturation too, among the Bhotiyas due to their frequent interactions with the outside world.

*(My book 'Nomads of the Himalayas' and articles are referred for further studies. There are some authentic works on Bhotiya culture by Dr. Pangati and other which are also referred for Hindi readers).*

# 7

# The Khampas

Eternal snows, lush green forests, singing streams, dancing birds, lovely lakes, verdant vales, emerald meadows, smiling glaciers and gay girls—this is the picture of Himachal Pradesh and Uttaranchal which sprawls in the north-western lap of the Himalayas: Abode of eternal peace, it is for lovers of nature—a veritable paradise. Its lowering mountains, colourful valleys and charming people cast a spell on all, particularly the geographers, the anthropologists, the social workers and the tourists.

Before Tibet was fully occupied by the Chinese, the Khampas were being governed by a weak administration which did little for the protection of these Tibetan traders. It is said that once they had been rulers but later some turned to be robbers. They were considered as brave fighters who get trained in fighting with sword. Whenever they were captured, they were given a cruel punishment. This, however, did little to stop the Khampa menace. The Tibet Government officials were very unfavourable and uncertain in dealing with the evil practices every now and then against Khampa traders.

The word 'Khampa' means nomadic people in their language. They used to travel from Tibet to India for selling various cosmetic commodities. Pt. Dharam Dev Shastri, a great social worker of Himalayan region, observed that those persons who came from Tibet to India and who are still leading a nomadic life, are known as Khampas. Rahul Sankrityayan says that once Khasha were leaving their families under emergency. The Khampa brought persons to Yudhistra to show their loyalty to the King. Perhaps some of the Khasha may have intermingled with Khampas in course of time. The Khampas now-a-days address themselves as Thakur also.

Many Khampas in the past used to live in tents and do export and import business particularly between India and Tibet. They carried their belongings on the back of their ponies.

We can divide the Khampas into four main groups—1. Petti Khampas—those who live in Spiti but are nomads, 2. Garja Khampa—those who left Tibet for visiting religious places and are now leading a nomadic life. 3. They are also called as Shayar Khampa. Many of them were known as dacoits also and 4. Khunu Khampa—those who live in Rampur Bushar, are called Khunu Khampa.

Besides the above categorisation we find that there are a considerable number of Jads who also claim to be a part of Khampa tribe whereas many Khampas do not recognise them as their own community people. The Khampas and Jads are scattered in Himachal Pradesh and Uttaranchal. Some Khampas and Jads go to Patna, Delhi, Calcutta, Asansol, Tata Nagar, Baroda, Rajkot and Mussoorie for selling their cosmetic and woollen garments. In the past, they used to sell horses also. Now-a-days they have no trade with Tibetans and have settled in various placed in India. Their women folk sell combs, jambo and asafoetida.

*Present day life* : After Dalai Lama left Tibet and settle in India, large number of Khampas also migrated to India and settled in various places like Chamba, Kulu Kinaur District, Uttar Kashi, Nainital, and in others. Now-a-days these tribals are known with the places they belong viz. Chamba Khampa, Harshi Khampa, Manali Khampa, Danda Khampa, etc.

Being the nomadic community, the exact number of Khampa people is not available. According to the available data there are about 10 families in Chamba, 16 in Kulu, 55 in Dunda, Uttar Kashi, about 35 in Nainital, 50 families in Sarhan, Narkanda and Kotgarh of Himachal Pradesh, 10 families in Ranikhet, four in Lansdowne and 15 in Chamoli District. These families do not include the Jads who may be called as lower caste of Khampas. Jad Khampas live mostly in Chamba, Tehsil and Hangrang areas of Himachal Pradesh. They speak Tibetan language which is different from local language of Kinaur. Jads migrated to India long ago as refugees from Tibet. They used to eat flesh of yak and cow. But the King of Rampur Bushar asked them to give up this food habit, otherwise they would not be allowed to stay in his State. The Jads of Hangrang area of Himachal Pradesh consider themselves superior to Tibetans. There is a category of Jads as Bhairon Jads who inhabit in Lahaul Spit of

Himachal Pradesh and Nelang areas of Tehrwal. Thus the number of Jads Khampa and Bhairon may be around 30,00. It is worth mentioning that they left Tibet earliest in the 5th or 6th century B.C.

The menfolk wear coat and churidar pyjama whereas the women folk wear full length skirts. Women usually do not cover their heads except in winter when mufflers or scarfs are used. They garland on their necks with ornaments. Mala spread over their chests, rings on the fingers and tops on the ears. The ornaments are made of sliver and other metals. They wear woollen clothes most of the time.

The menfolk while in migration need no personal decoration, they seldom take baths and clean their teeth but even then they have pleasing personality and lead a care-free life.

*History :* The Khampas are a well-built race of Mangoloid origin. They are short structured. Their complexion is fair or copper like. Their eyes are small, typical cheeks and nose of medium type i.e. neither sharp not flat.

Khampas are monogamous and their marriages are mostly arranged. Polygamy is observed among Jad Khampas only. Both sororate and leverate type of marriages can also be seen. They consider two pedigrees, not fit for marriage also while seeking a relation. In the past, boys and girls who loved each other used to elope from their houses. They would meet Lamas who conducted their marriages.

Jads and Khampas do not inter-marry. The usual tradition of engagement is that boy's father approaches girl's father with a bottle of wine. If the girl's father accepts the present, it is treated as confirmation of engagement. The marriages are performed with the Buddhist rites. There is no dowry system. The cases of divorce are rare. Widow marriage are also hardly seen among them. Marital age for boys is 25 and for girls 18. Many women do not marry and become *jamo.* They get their heads clean shaven and follow the sermons of Lāma. They work for their parents.

Among Jads where polyandry system is prevalent, the women are very hard-working. This tradition is like that of Kinner tribe and not the way of polyandry prevalent in Janusar Babar.

They burn their dead and observe the condolences for more than week. In the past they used to offer the dead body to the kites. The dead body would first cut into pieces by a non-Khampa and mantras were chanted and then put into open place for kites and animals. Now this practice is no more.

Khampas are mostly traders. Earlier they used to sell to Tibetan *gur*, food, clothing, ornaments and fancy things. They would exchange through barter salt, wool, boroax, musk and similar antiques material found in Tibet. Horses and goats were extensively used by them for pack purposes. Now-a-days in the cities they sell antiquities, pearls and ornaments and at times perfume also. But this does not apply to poor Jads. In Kulu, they grow apples and in Tehri Garwal, some of the families are agriculturist also. In Himachal Pradesh many lead a life of cowherds and shepherds. The people of Jad sub-group of this community are very poor. Some of them are even beggars.

Tribals have their own Panchayats in which they solve their problems. The individual cases are discussed and decided then and there. Some cases of elopement may be found in the community but not of rape and theft as such, etc.

*Religion* : The Khampas follow Buddhism. Their day-to-day life is guided by their religious leaders, the Lamas who perform various rituals. The Lama chants mantras *Om Maan Ni Pai Me Hoons* in performing various rituals. The Khampas believe in evil spirit and try to avoid it by putting flag in various places. Another mantra *Om Bhane Padme Hom* which means pray to God for saving the tribals from evil spirit is chanted on special occasions. They unfurl flag of five colours i.e. blue, white, red, green and yellow to remove the fear of evil spirit.

They celebrate various festivals like Loasar i.e. New Year's Day on 25th February, Buddha is worshipped on Buddhpurnima and other festive occasions. It is interesting to know the sect of Khampas also worships Guru Nanak and the Lama perfomes the *puja* to Guru Nanak. On this occasion, roasted grams are distributed among the tribal children. They drink chhung (a native wine), prepare meat and relish it on festive occasions as well as in their daily life. There is no Gotra or Caste system prevalent among the tribals. However, their interaction with Hindus has Hinduised them. The young educated people are now giving up their age old traditions.

*Language* : Khampas speak Tibetan language, Khampa language, Hamasket and Hindi too. Khampa is a dialect as well as language in itself. A few words of kinship terminology are given below:

| *English* | *Hindi* | *Khampa* |
|---|---|---|
| Mother | Amaa | Amala |
| Father | Pita | Pala |
| Uncle | Chacha | Aso |
| Uncle | Tau | Au |
| Grand-father, Grand-maternal father | Dada Nana | Mame |
| Grand-mother | Dadi | Ewi |
| Grand-maternal mother | Nani | Ewi |
| Elder brother | Bara Bhai | Aso |
| Younger brother | Chota Bhai | No |
| Elder sister | Bari Bahen | Ejji |
| Younger sister | Choti Bahen | Nomo |
| Maternal uncle | Mama | Asang |
| Maternal aunt | Mami | Aani |

Representative names of Khampas are given below:

Male : Darjo, Medang, Arigyal, Rigvih, Yoma, Cyachche and Shaltu.

Female : Tashi, Paljam, Yagshim, Dunuku, Devanpati, etc.

The women know weaving and embroidery, work etc. For treatment, they go to the Lama who worships on their behalf for recovery from the disease.

The Khampa used to perform folk dances and folk songs in the past, but now-a-days only women sing songs or particular party of menfolk sing on the occasion of marriages or festivals. Earlier on festive occasions, they used to drink *Chhung* but now-a-days some of them have given it up and become teetotaller and vegetarian.

In the past there was an oral tradition of folk tales, but now-a-days hardly anybody remembers the old stories.

Since the Khampas have been included in the list of Scheduled Tribes, they are entitled to get scholarship in schools and reservation for jobs but they are not coming up to avail that like other tribal communities. Having nomadic habits, they are still not settling down. They prefer to sell their cosmetics like vendor. Many Jads and Bairon Jads are below the poverty line. The progress is very slow them. Now-a-days many Khampas live in various towns of the country and they are engaged in business and jobs also.

*(My book entitled 'Himachal Nature's Peaceful Paradise' is referred for further studies. Scholars should undertake sociological research of Bhotiyas living all over the country.)*

# 8

# The Banjaras

'Banjara' is a common term used for travellers in general and trader nomads in particular. They are known as lamana, laban, Lambadi, Vanjari in India and Roma Gypsy in Europe and America. We are giving here two view points by Banjara scholar and social Activist Mr. Ranjit Naik and another renowned Roma scholars Dr. Ian Hancock about the community who has been included in different categories of SC, ST and OBC in different states without any anthropological consideration.

## Laman or Laban

The origin of term 'Laman' was given by historians of the Muslim and the British rule in India. The Sanskrit word 'Lavan' means salt. Obviously, people who were transporting salt on pack bullocks to far–off places in olden days, were called the 'Lamans.'

Due to the development of other languages in South after Sanskrit, the term 'Laman' came to be pronounced in the southern accent as 'Lambadi" Lambada,' etc. Similarly, with the influence of regional languages in some parts of Northern, Eastern, and Western India, the terms 'Laban' or 'Labhan,' became common. As a matter of fact, the original root of all these terms, i.e. 'Laman,' 'Lamani,' 'Lambadi,' Lambada, Labana, Labhan' 'Labhani' 'Labhana,' can be ascertained since they convey the same meaning as the original Sanskrit word 'Lavan.'

## Laman Marg

The Historian Shri S. R. Kanitkar, the author of the book called *History of India* written in the year 1934 has made references of transportation by Lamans. While describing the conditions of the people during the period between 600 B.C. to 350 B.C., Kanitkar has made reference to the means of transportation of the period. At that time he has stated that, Laman people were transporting merchandise on the back of the bullocks and the camels. From this, it can be said that this information supports the information contained in the note describing the position of Laman Marg in the Map.

1. Most of the coastal towns from Bharukach and upto Nelcynda are taken from Periplus of the Erythryean Sea, a Greek work dated about 180 A.D.
2. The coastal tract on the coromandal coast i.e., eastern coast is adopted from Ptolemy's Geography.
3. In Northern India, the routes in the Gangetic Valley are known from the Buddhists Jatakas dated about 1st century A.D. to 4th Century A.D.
4. The tract in Central Maharashtra is adopted from Satavahana inscriptions in the Deccan between 200 B.C. to 150 A.C.
5. On North West province the routes are taken from Alexandra's Route (about 723 B.C.) and later Kushan inscriptions about 220 A.D.
6. In general, the places and the routes fall within the time log between 200 B.C. to 400 A.D.

**Banjara**

The derivation of the term 'Banjara' itself was a subject of great discussion among the Muslim and English historians during this period. It can be stated without any prejudice to the views expressed by these historians, that the meaning attributed to it by them, is inadequate to express the full implication of the term 'Banjara.'

It is our considered opinion that the word 'Banjara' is derived from the original Sanskrit word 'Vanijyam,' the meaning of which is trade. The Banjaras were ancient carriers of foodgrains on animal backs, but they were not the trading community which was generally known to the community and people. After the development of regional languages, such as Gujarati, Rajasthani, Urdu, Hindi and Marathi, the Sanskrit word 'Vanijya' was pronounced in Gujarati as 'Vanajara,' in Rajasthani as Banajara, in Urdu as Banjare, in Hindi 'Banzara,' in Marathi 'Banjari.' The term 'Banjara' does not indicate any particular caste or race. It denotes a profession of transporting foodgrains. There is still a practice prevailing in this country of naming the people by their prfessin. For example, those who do the craftsmanship of Gold (Sona) are called Sonars (Goldsmiths); those who take to iron and steel (Loha) are called 'Lohar' (Blacksmith), and those who do washing are called 'Dhobi' (Washerman). Similarly, since the Banjaras took up the profession of transporting foodgrains from place to place, they were called 'Banjaras.'

In the olden days, there were no other means of transport except animals (bullocks, etc.) to carry daily necessities of life from one place to another. Those who did successful transportation of goods on animals and withstood the hazards of long distances were called 'Banjaras' by the society they served, the Government they helped, the army they fed, the Banjaras also on their part accepted this terms honourably.

E. Thurston, in his book—*'Castes and Tribes of India,'* Vol. IV, has given a vivid description of the Banjaras in the following words of Moor: "Banjaras associate chiefly together, seldom or never mixing with other Tribes. They seem to have no home, no character but that of merchants, in which capacity they travel great distances to whatever parts are most in want of Merchandise, which is the greatest part of corn."

In support of this contention about the origin of the Banjaras we can quote Sir H.M. Illiat who, from his research has found that a reference to the Banjaras has been made is a Sanskrit Book called '*Dasakumar Charitam*' written in 11th and 12th centuries A.D. On the basis of this references, H.M. Illiat has described the 'Banjaras as nothing but the same ancient tribes which were in existence during 4th century B.C. The tribes were reported to be residing in small tents and hiring out their bullocks for transport of foodgrains.

The Banjaras as a main group popularly address each other throughout the country as *'Gor.'* The term *'Gor'* is not used either by any historian or the general public, anywhere in India. They were also addressed by other synonyms and sub-names as detailed below in a separate heading called, 'Synonyms and Sub-groups of Banjara.'

In the course of our survey throughout the country, we have learnt that the Banjaras are referred to by different Synonyms and Sub-groups in different States. According to our information they are known at least by 27 Synonyms and as 17 Sub-group as detailed below. We have discussed the various names by which these people are known in different states.

## (A) SYNONYMS OF BANJARAS

1. Banjara
2. Banjara (n, as in Pran)
3. Vanajara
4. Banjare
5. Banjari
6. Brinjari
7. Brujawasi
8. Laman
9. Lamani or Lambani
10. Lambada
11. Lambadi
12. Laban or Labana
13. Labhan
14. Labhani
15. Labhana or Lobhana
16. Baladia
17. Ladenia
18. Sugali
19. Gwar or Gavuria
20. Gwaria
21. Gavaria or Gamalia
22. Gavara
23. Kangi or Kangashiya
24. Phanada
25. Shirkiband
26. Shirkiwala
27. Shingade Vanjari (not the Vanjaris of Maharashtra).

## (B) SUB-GROUPS OF BANJARA PEOPLE

1. Gor
2. Mathura or Mathure
3. Dhadi
4. Sanar
5. Navi
6. Dhalia
7. Bagora
8. Digora or Gigora
9. Charan
10. Badi
11. Bajigar
12. Jogi or Bharava

13. Shingadya
14. Maru
15. Bamania
16. Rohidas
17. Dhan-Kute

According to our survey, we have come to the conclusion that these synonyms and sub-groups or tribes referred to above have come to be associated with the main Banjara community on three grounds: They include: (1) The influence of local languages on the terms 'Banjara' and 'Laman,' (2) Varied professions taken up by Banjaras on account of the set-back they received to their age-old profession of transportation, with the introduction of railways and road transport and (3) Strict observance of the 'Tanda' administration in which the Banjarars have their own professionals like Navi, Dhadi, Sanar, etc.

**Banjara Dress**

If we make an attempt to write all the details on banjara dresses it may turn into a thesis which will be unwieldy and out of place here. We, therefore, restrict our description of Banjara apparels to the barest minimum which we consider essential for the purpose of this report.

If we make a careful study of different patterns of dresses the people have evolved in different parts of the world it would clear that they are designed to suit the climataic conditions or customs prevailing in different nations or continents. One can generally see the difference in patterns of dresses from continent to continent, from nation to nation. And in big nation like India, we see that patterns of dresses vary from State to State. But the dresses of Banjaras are a unique case. It is identical throughout the country. The colour schemes and designs and the models of their dresses are all almost same in every state. Because of this unique feature, a Banjara can be easily recognised in any part of the country. The fabrics used for the Banjara dress might be woollen silk or cotton, but the designs adopted have a common national pattern. The dress-making is never given to tailors. Women at home do their own stitching with their needle and embroidery skill they make their own dresses, lending and artistic blend to them during their spare time. They use glass pieces, small sea shells (Kodis), lead ornaments or worn-out coins to decorate their dresses. The dresses are predominantly red but other colours are used, but less in proportion. The Banjaras do not have any seasonal changes but wear only one type of clothing in all seasons. The Banjara men also have their own patterns unlike others.

The Banjara men and women wear ornaments of their own specification. In his study on the tribal people. E. Thurston has given an interesting description about the dress and ornaments of Banjara women in the following words:

"Their dress is peculiar, and their ornaments are singularly chosen. We have, seen women who have had eight to ten pounds weight in metal or ivory round their arms and legs. They pay little attention to cleanliness, their hair once piainted is not combed or opened perhaps for a month, their bodies or clothes are seldom washed, their arms are indeed so encased with ivory that it would be not easy matter to clean them."

We reproduce here some statements by an American Roma scholar Dr. Ian Hancok from his article *'The Gypsies: Forgotten Children of India'* to compare Banjara life and language with Roma and Romani.

Passes, though recent linguistic evidence suggests a more northerly route out of India, perhaps through the Shandur and Baroghil Passes. Moving westward, they became, we can surmise, embroiled in a succession of Middle Eastern confrontations with Islam. It has been suggested that the impetus for this migration was their defeat at the Battle of Tehrain in 1192, but this would have allowed only a century or less for the population to make its way to Europe, which, while conceivable, is argued against by the extent of Iranic and, particularly, Byzantine Greek, linguistic influence which, some argue, would have required a much longer and more intimate period of contact. As they became more and more remote from their homeland, they shared Indian identity, we may hypothesize, overcame whatever newly-acquired jati or caste distinction might have divided them socially; and in time, the population became one. This also provides an acceptable account and in time, the population became one. This also provides acceptable account for the character of the Romani language, which demonstrates both Central Indian (Paisaci) linguistic characteristics. A 1987 medical report, in the August 15th issue of the prestigious medical journal *The Lancet,* determined that "analysis of blood groups, haptoglobin phenotypes, and HLA types establishes the [European and American] Gypsies as a distinct racial group with origins in the Punjab region of India. Also supporting this is the worldwide Gypsy language Romani, which is quite similar to Hindi."

The Banjara, who call themselves Gorwat or Gormati, claim descent from the Rajputs, and believe that they represent the descendants of the Roma who never left India. They maintain contact with Romani groups in Europe and America, and support a periodical called Banjara Roma. Grierson, mentioned earlier, says that the Banjara "are originally Dravidian," becoming Aryanized at a comparatively early date, and philosophical consideration point to the conclusion that this occurred somewhere in Rajaputana. Consideration of the Dravidian element in Romani ancestry is nothing new: as early as 1882, the German scholar Richard Pischel discussed this in the journal *Deutsche Rundschau* (63: 353-375); *but the dual racial heritage of the Roma,* i.e. Dravidian and Pratihara, was not discussed until 1968; when the Romani linguist Vanya de Gila Kochanowski proposed it in his seminal article "*Black Gypsies, White Gypsies*" in Diogences (63: 27-47).

The prominent 19th century Romanologist Alexander Paspati said that the key to Gypsy history is to be sought in the study of the Romani language, and this is quite true. Romani is, metaphorically speaking, like an onion, because it is built up layer upon layer. Its heart is first of all Central and Northwestern Indian, then there is a layer of Cardiac; it is because of the latter, and because there are elements from Burushaski, spoken in the Hunza, that we must locate them are through which the Roma left India in the extreme north of the Hindu Kush. The next layers are of Persian and Kurdish words, there are over seventy of them, but there are hardly any from Arabic, thus we can posit a migration westward along the southern shore of the Caspian Sea which then followed its western littoral up into the eastern Caucasus. Because there are Georgian, Ossetic and especially Armenian words (about 45) in the language, its speakers must have gone along the northern coast of Turkey;

and because of the massive influence from Medieval Greek (over 200 words), a considerable amount of time must have been spent in the Byzantine Empire.

When we examine these layers, we can also get some idea of the social situations of the Roma; the words for "horse" and "cart" were picked up in the eastern Byzantine Empire, and the word for "road" further west; the words for nearly all the metals, as well as for "forge," "melt" "nail," "horseshoe," "hammer," were also acquire in the Byzantine Empire, from Greek and Armenian. Nevertheless, three quarters of the basic vocabulary is Indian: eat, drink, run, jump, sit, sleep, big, hungry, thirsty, silver, gold, girl, water, milk, knife, there, one, two, three, four, five, are all Indian words (xa-, pi, prasta uxti-, besh, sov-, baro, bokhalo, trushal, rup, sumnakai, raklli, pani, churi, anth, onth, uekh, dui, trin, shtar, panj).

Besides the language, specifically Indian retention among European, Australian, American, Canadian, Brazilian and other Roma throughout the world are found in all areas of the culture as well. The maintenance among some groups of the Indian Bhairava musical scale, as well as the type of mouth music known as bole, which consists of nonsense syllables imitating the rhythm of the table drum. The tribunal where internal disputes are settled, called the Kris, in Romani, while a Greek word, is identifiable with the Indian panchayat and has the same form and function. The pilivani wrestling matches with oiled bodies, and the stick dancing ( called rovliako khelipen in Romani) are both still found amongst some populations, the ritual suicide of the widow (called lustering among the British Gypsies, though now an obsolete practice), had striking parallels with sati. The worship of the goddess Sati-Sara, who is Saint Sarah, the Romani Goddess of Fate, which forms part of the yearly pilgrimage to La Camarague at Stes. Maries de la Mer in the south of France is of particular significance; Sati-sara is the consort of the god Siva, and is known by many names, Kali, Bhadeakali, Uma, Durga, and Syama among them. Siva's trident, called trisula in Sanskrit, changed its role from Hindu symbol to Christian symbol and has become the Romani word for "cross" (trisul). This probably happened in the 11th or 12th Century, when the migrating Roma reached Armenia: in the Gypsy language spoken there, t(e)rusul means both "church" and "priest."

Furthermore, the Romani word for "Easter," Patradiji, is an Armenian word, so this is probably where the Roma first encountered Christianity. Although Hinduism as a cohesive faith has not been retained, Rome today practising a great number of religion adopted because of a historical need to survive, nevertheless they strongly maintain many Hindu-based cultural beliefs. These similarities have been discussed in a number of works by Indian authors themselves, among them Rishi, Bhattacharya, Lal, Shashi and Singhal.

Although eating habits and the techniques of food preparation among the various populations throughout northern India have much in common, it is from Rajhasthan and the Punjab that the Roma originated, and it is among the modern-day Banjara that the strongest parallels should be sought. Notions of ritual pollution, central to Romani belief, existed in the varna system and continue to exist today; thus members of the same jati may eat together without risk of contamination, for example, but will be polluted if they eat with members of other jati; and because the jati affiliation of one's associates might not always be known, contact between the mouth and the various utensils shared with others at a meal is avoided. In conservative Romani culture (called Romanipen), liquids are poured into the mouth from a container held away from the lips, so that the rim of the vessel (the kerlo is not touched); smoke from a shared tobacco pipe is drawn (in the Romani language pilo or "drunk", rather and "sucked") through the fist clenched around its stem, again to avoid contact by the mouth. The surest way to avoid contact with utensils used by others is to eat with the fingers, and all of these habits are to be found among Roma today. Like the Rajputs, the Roma divide goods into "ordinary" and "beneficial" or "lucky" (baxtalo) categories (the Rajputs call them "cold" and "hot" foods, though this has nothing to do with temperature or pepper). Similarly, and again like the Rajputs, Roma divides illnesses into those which are natural to the group, such as heart conditions or irritability, and those which are the result of over-familiarity with the gadje or outsiders. Those in the latter category include, for example, all sexually-transmitted diseases. For such affliction, a non-Gypsy physician must be consulted; but for "romani afflictions", traditional cures are provided by a drabarni or female healer. This is the same as the Rajput siana. The root of the word "Drabarni" is drab which means "medicine" (from Sanskrit dravya "medication," compared Hindi darb). It is also the root of the verb drabar-which is usually translated in English "to tell fortunes," but which from the Romani perspective means "making well." When speaking English, Roma prefer to call his skill brought from India "advising" rather than "fortune telling," or which another verb, duriker-exists.

It is in the area of spiritual and physical well-being that the Indian origin of the Romani people is most clearly seen. In the preparation of food, and in one's personal hygiene and department, it is absolutely essential that a separation between "pure" (vujo) and "polluted" (mekhardo or pokhelime) states be maintained. A pure state is achieved by maintaining balance (kintala) in one's life; maintaining balance or harmony please the spirits of the ancestors (the mule), and they are there to guard one and help and do it, but if they are displeased, they will mete out punishment by way of retribution (prizaka). The penalty for extreme pollution is banishment, or becoming outcast, and an out cast, from the community, for which the Romani words are marume and gonime. Prozaka brings bad luck (bibaxt) and illness (nasvalipen), and it can be attracted every by socializing with people who are not vujo. This includes all non-Romani people or gadje (singular gadjo, from Prakit gajjha which means "domestic" or "civilian"), and this is why the Roma have so successfully kept their separateness-and as a result their identity-for so long, and why they will continue to do so.

In recent years, and especially since the collapse of Communism, the Romani population in Europe has faced hostility, both for being different and because they have no country, consequently being regarded everywhere as intruders. Now between nine and twelve million strong throughout the world outside of Asia, a sense of solidarity and common origin more important than ever. The awareness of our Indian roots is growing. Roma are visiting India and Indian scholars are attending Romani congress in Europe. Thanks to the support from the Indian government, the International Romani gained admission to the United Nations Economic and Social Council in 1979. India helped finance the First World Romani Congress in Britain in 1971, and shorty after that, the Indian Institute of Romani Studies was established under the directorship of Padmashri Weer R. Rishi in Chandigarh. The knowledge of having descended form a proud warrior caste and having retained so much of its Indian heritage across the centuries, has become vital to Romani identify and the growing spirit of reunification. Links with the ancestral homeland, Amaro Baro Them, can only become stronger in the years ahead.

Comparative Wordlists in Banjara (Indian Gypsy, or Lamani) and Romani (European Gypsy) Languages)

| *Lamani* | *(Banjara Gor Boli)* | *Romani* | |
|---|---|---|---|
| acho | "good" | lacho | "good" |
| anga | "before" | angla | "before" |
| angar | "fire" | angar | "coal" |
| ata | "here" | athe | "here" |
| bakra | "goat" | bakro | "sheep" |
| ban | "sister" | phen | "sister" |
| bes- | "sit" | besh- | "sit" |
| bhand- | "tie" | phand- | "tie" |
| bhar- | "fill" | pher | "fill" |
| bhari | "heavy" | pharo | "heavy" |
| bhas | "straw" | phus | "straw" |
| bhuk | "hunger" | bokh | "hunger" |
| bori | "daughter-in-law" | bori | "daughter in law" |
| char | "four" | shtar | "four" |
| dant | "tooth" | dand | "tooth" |
| dar | "fear" | dar | "fear" |
| das | "ten" | desh | "ten" |
| de- | "give" | d- | "give" |
| dek- | "see" | dikh | "see" |
| dev | "good" | devel | "god" |
| di- | "two" | dui | "two" |
| dora | "thread" | dori | "thread" |

| *Lamani (Banjara Gor Boli)* | | *Romani* | |
|---|---|---|---|
| dud | "milk" | thud | "milk" |
| duk- | "pain" | dukh- | "pain" |
| dur | "far" | dur | "far" |
| busman | "enemy" | dushman | "enemy" |
| ek | "one" | ek, yekh | "one" |
| gan- | "count" | gin- | "count" |
| gam | "town" | gav | "town" |
| ghar | "house" | kher | "house" |
| ghas- | "rub" | knos- | "rub" |
| ghi | "butter" | khil | "butter" |
| gid | "song" | gili | "song" |
| gol | "sugar" | gulo | "sweet" |
| ham | "we" | ame | "we" |
| hamaro | "our" | amaro | "call" |
| hankar- | "call" | akhar | "call" |
| has- | "laugh" | as- | "laugh" |
| hava | "yes" | ava | "yes" |
| chanda | "moon" | chon | "moon" |
| chhink- | "sneeze" | chik- | "sneeze" |
| chor | "thief" | chor | "thief" |
| chum | "kiss" | chumid- | "kiss" |
| jang | "thigh" | chang | "knee" |
| jhal- | "go" | ja- | "go" |
| kalo | "black" | kalo | "blac" |
| kaichi | "scissors" | katsi | "scissors" |
| kan | "ear" | kan | "ear" |
| kana | "when" | kana | "when " |
| kangsi | "comb" | kangli | "comb" |
| kar- | "make, do" | ker- | "make, do." |

| *Lamani* | *(Banjara Gor Boli)* | *Romani* | |
|---|---|---|---|
| kha- | "eat" | xa- | "eat" |
| khas- | "cough" | xas- | "cough" |
| koni | "no" | konik | "no one" |
| kun | "who" | kon | "who" |
| kuni | "elbow" | kuni | "elbow" |
| laj | "shame" | lajav | "shame" |
| le- | "take" | I | "take" |
| ma | "I" | me | "I" |
| maki | "a fly" | makh | "a fly" |
| manas | "man" | manush | "man" |
| mang- | "beg" | mang- | "beg" |
| mar- | "beat to death" | mar- | "beat" |
| marda | "dead person" | merdo | "dead person" |
| maro | "my" | miro | "my" |
| mat | "don't" | ma | "don't" |
| mut- | "urinate" | muter- | "urinate" |
| naga | "naked" | nango | "naked" |
| nak | "nose" | nakh | "nose" |
| navo | "new" | nevo | "new" |
| nind | "sleep" | lindri | "sleep" |
| nun | "salt" | lon | "salt" |
| pad- | "fall" | per- | "fall" |
| pako | "ripe" | pako | "ripe" |
| pani | "water" | pani | "water" |
| panch | "five" | panj | "five" |
| pet | "abdomen" | per | "abdomen" |
| phangori | "pimple" | phugni | "pimple" |
| pharena | "walk" | phir- | "walk" |

| *Lamani* | *(Banjara Gor Boli)* | | *Romani* |
|---|---|---|---|
| phul | "bridge" | phurt | "bridge" |
| pi- | "drink" | pi- | "drink" |
| pindi | "foreleg" | pindro | "leg" |
| puch- | "ask" | puch- | "ask" |
| raja | "king" | rai | "lord" |
| rani | "queen" | rani | "lady" |
| rat | "night" | rat | "night" |
| ro- | "cry" | rov- | "cry" |
| rup | "silvery" | rup | "silver" |
| sabu | "soap" | sapui | "soap" |
| sai | "go ahead" | shai | "able" |

### Social Change

Banjara are ST in Andhra Pradesh SC and OBCs in other states of India. Many of them are in mainstream. They are Doctors, Engineers and Administrative Officials. There are Parliamentarian and Ministers also from Banjara community.

*(For advanced studies, my project Report on Banjara Community submitted to ICHR is also referred.)*

# 9

# Gaduliya Lohars—The Descent of Maharana Pratap

Sociological studies of the Gaduliya or Gadia Lohars have been conducted by Dr. S.P. Malhotra and Dr. S.P. Ruhela. These people even today lead nomadic life and roam about in various villages and towns. Their *gotras* prove that they are from Kshatriya clans of Maharana Pratap of Rajasthan. Here are some details about the Gadia Lohars who are like the black smiths. Dr. S.P. Malhotra says—

"In India, nomads are largely concentrated in the arid and semi-arid zones of Rajasthan where the source of livelihood and the way of life of the people have been conditioned by disturbances in ecological balance due to severity of arid climate, continuous deterioration of soil, dwindling natural resources, occasional droughts, invasions, poor means of communication and consequent social and economic uncertainties.

The chief groups of nomads operating in this region are pastoral nomads (livestock breeders), artisan nomads (*Gaduliya Lohars)* and trading nomads *(Banjaras).* They are not a separate ethnic group and do not have separate territory with exclusive rights and economic framework. They have in general a symbiotic relationship with the settled population, and function as an ancillary to its economic pursuits. The nomads were found in a combined form since the time when the numerous flowing rivers like the Sarasvati river, the Drishadvati river, the Niamal river, the Nara, etc., disappeared and others shifted westward preferably in the second millennium. B.C Krader (1959) stated that nomadic pastoralism in the arid parts of the Old World was the result of coalescence of two components, nomadism and pastoralism. It appeared long after the neolithic period with domestication of plants and animals.

*Pastoral Nomads*

The pastoral nomadic population of the Indian arid zone is concentrated along its western boundary. It is contiguous to the pastoral nomads of Pakistan. Out of the nomadic groups of arid zone of interior Asia, South-West Africa and North Africa, the pastoral nomads form the highest percentage. The cause responsible for the appearance of those pastoral nomads are also applicable to the pastoral nomads of this region. It is believed on the basis of the archaeological evidences that this region was once well-watered and fertile. There were several rivers flowing through this part during the Mohenjodaro and Harappa civilization some 5000 year ago. But due to the onset of extreme arid condition, the land became dry and desolate. The vegetative cover deteriorated. The people were compelled to roam with their stocks in search of water and pasture, and thus, gradually the settled peasants turned into semi-pastoral nomads depending mainly on animal husbandry.)

The livestock breeders have recently been facing great difficulties for food and water for their livestock. Due to improved means of transport the local sedentary population does not depend upon the livestock breeders for livestock and livestock produce. Their visits are generally not liked by the villagers, since their animals exhaust the water and grazing land of the village. The construction of the proposed Rajasthan canal may also turn the grazing lands into crop land.

*Artisan Nomads*

The nomadic blacksmiths are locally called Gaduliya Lohars. They are one of the artisan nomads in the States of Rajasthan, Haryana and Madhya Pradesh. Their territorial extension is even in semi-arid and humid environments. Their nomadism is traced back to the conquest of the fort of Chittor by the Mughals. History has it that consequent upon this conquest the *Gaduliya Lohars* took a vow that they would not have a settled home, would not eat in a plate and would not sleep on cot till the fort is reconquered (Malhotra *et. al.* 1966). The defeated ruler of Chittor fort needed blacksmiths to make weapons for war. The ruler had gone into the forest for seclusion and war-preparation and was moving from place to place so that the enemies might not trace them. This required the settled blacksmiths also to live a nomadic life like their ruler and since then they have become nomads.

The traditional occupation of the *Gaduliya Lohars* is smithy and trade in cattle. Their movements to different places are dependent upon the availability of smithy-work and prospects of trade in cattle. They have developed a symbiotic relationship with the sedentary farmers for supplying them with agricultural tools and implemeans. They also sell utensils for farmers households. These materials are supplied to the rural population on cash or exchange basis. The technology of manufacturing the tools, implements and utensils of iron is indigenous and involves hard work and large amount of labour. Almost all the members of each family remain engaged in this occupation. On an average a household earns about one thousand rupees annually from this occupation. Uncertainty of availability of work and risk in earnings have created feelings of fraternity and mutual give-and-take in the society. Unlike other nomadic groups, generally, they do not take loan from the money lenders. They are economically and culturally very backward. Their children are not sent to schools, and as such, illiteracy is very common.

They move about in small kinship bands in their bullock carts with their full family. The nature of movement of different bands of these artisan nomads follow a regular cycle with regular monthly intervals. They own their allegiance to a definite demarcated area. In one band the number varies from one to twelve families. During movements they split themselves into smaller constituents which group and regroup at different places depending upon their social and economic needs. Their movements are limited only to those places which are connected by roads or tracks in which their bullocks carts can go. Due to recent changes in economic and political set up and the increasing means of communication the *Gaduliya Lohars* are not as welcome in the villages now as about 15 years ago. About one-fourth of the *Gaduliya Lohars* stated that there has been a definite decrease in their getting work of blacksmithy or cattle trade in recent years. Ninety-five per cent of the households surveyed, therefore, desired to divorce nomadic life, and lead a sedentary or semi-sedentary life leading finally to sedentarization.

Efforts have been made by the State Government of Rajasthan to sedentarize *Gaduliya Lohars* in colonies consisting of many households at one place but such sedentarization has achieved only a partial success.

The present investigations revealed that most of the *Gaduliya Lohars* desired to sedentarize in small kinship groups consisting of mostly agnatic (blood relations) and affinal (relations through marriage) relations. The present kinship composition and the area of movements of the nomadic *Gaduliya Lohars* of Jaipur District of Rajasthan has been demarcated. The nomadic *Gaduliyas Lohars* desired sedentarization in scattered fashion at a central place within the present area of their movement locally known as *Chokla* (Malhotra, 1966).

*(Dr. S.P. Ruhela's book on Gadulia Lohars is referred for higher learning on this subject.)*

# 10

# The Nomadic Shepherds

During my sociological survey on the Kuruba, Kurumba, Gond and other shepherd and cattle rearing communities of India, I wrote number of articles for Indian and foreign press. My book entitled *'Shepherds of India'* was the first of its own kind which was published in 1971 from Delhi. I have already written books in Hindi on this subject entitled *'Hamara Samaj' 'Bharat Ki Pashupalak Jatiyan'*, *'Veerangna 'Ahilya Bai Holkar* Aur *Hamare Rajvansh'* etc. which were acclaimed as the authentic studies by the sociologists and anthropologists of India and abroad. My studies were based on not only the participant and non-participant observations but there was a mission and commitment which I adopted from my young age when I began my research journey to study the Gaddi nomads of the Himalayas since 1966.

I have proved in my books that these communities belong to martial clans who were forced to lead a nomadic life due to defeat in wars and to save their religion.

There are seventy five per cent *gotras* of Kshatriya Varna and the rest from Indian tribes and castes found in shepherd communities of India. They depended on forest and grazing grounds but later on settled in villages and towns. The Dhangar shepherds in Maharashtra had their army which succeeded in founding the Holkar State under the leadership of Sub-Malhar Rao Holkar. Indore State is known for its great woman ruler Devi Ahilya Bai Holkar. Similarly Vijai Nagar State in Karnataka was founded by the great warriors Hukka Bukka belonging to Kuruba shepherd Community. Rani Durgawati, the ruler of Gondwara was from Kuruba Gond community. Before I quote from my book *'The Shepherds of India*, I would like to reproduce from the Anthropological studies conducted by Dr. Daxayani K. Metry Head, Tribal studies Kannada University, Hampi Vidyaranya where in

2004 I delivered my lectures on nomads of the world and visited some Kuraba Gond shepherd families who even today live in jungles and lead a nomadic life. It is surprising to observe that the Kurubas of Karnatka do not get any benefit reservation as scheduled tribe like Kadu Kuruba, Jenn Kuruba and Gond Kuruba. In fact, once all the sheep and cattle rearing communities of India used to live in forests and lead a tribal life where they built-up their forts and Gurukulas also.

Dr. D. K. Metry Writes in his Article entitled *'Identity of Rajgond Tribe'*—

"India is basically a land of tribes. Kol, Gond and Munda are the aboriginal tribes. Gonds are the largest in number among the Indian tribes. An off-shoot of this tribe are the Rajgonds. They first lived in Gondwana forest. Their language Gondi came from the Dravidian language family. Because of their political background they were called Rajgonds.

**Background:** Long ago, the Gonds of central India organised themselves into small kingdoms. They have a glorious history of having built 52 forts and reigned over this land. Gond kings are called as Rajgonds. As the heritage of the kings continued, those associated with the kith and kin of the rulers were identified as Rajgonds. Earlier, they used to live by hunting, animal rearing and agriculture. They established kingdoms. They continued to practise their old tasks. There people were very intimate with the secrets of nature. They worshipped nature.

They had deep knowledge about the medicinal values of herbs in nature. Later, they emerged as native doctors or ayurvedic curers. They became Ayurvedic doctors to the kings and royal families of Gonds and were called Raj-Vaidyas (Vaidya-Doctor). When the kings lost their kingdom by the invasion of Muslims, these Raj-vidyas became obsolete. So they turned to common people for medicinal services. In course of time these people were called Rajgonds by all.

## Early Studies

Studies undertaken so far made in India regarding the Rajgonds are innumerable. Among them are: Bhoomia Gonds of Eastern Mandla (1960) by Puch ; Gonds of Central Indian Highlands (1984) by B H Mehta; Customary laws among Gonds of M P (1985) by M L Patel; Among the Gonds of Adilabad by Sethu Madhav Rao Pagadi; The Rajgonds of Adilabad (1948) by Further Haimend of Von; Castes and Tribes of H E H Nizam's Dominions (1989) by Siraj Ul Hassan; Gond Samskriti by Jamir Ulla Sharif; Gond Tribes in Bindar District: A Sociological Study (1994) by Dr. K M Metry, A Study of Gond - Kurubas in Bidar Dist (1995) by Dr. Bandeppa Kalagi; and The Scheduled Tribes (1994) by K S Singh etc. give invaluable information about these tribes. Along with this Man in India; Anthropological study of India and Census records also carry important results of studies on Gods. Gondavana Darshan, a monthly magazine about the Gonds is being published from Nagpur.

## Nomadic Rajgonds

The Rajgonds who lost the patronage of their kings were forced to migrate to different parts of India for bread. Later they came and settled in the following areas : Phulenagar in Takkar Maidan in Maharastra, Hivarkhed, Kajaleshwar, Mrithjapur at Akol taluk in Amaravathi dist, Malegaon and Upanagar of Dhuliya dist, Shrirampur of Ahmednagar dist, Vadala (Dadar) in Mumbai, Pachor Railway station of Jalagaon Dist, Vikasnagar of Latur dist, Shivajinagar in Pune, Kakandi of Vijayavada dist, Kukatpalli and Anantapur in Andhra Pradesh, Sudhampuri, Bhopal and Ujjain of Khandva dist in M P, Coimbatore in Tamil Nadu, Ajmir in Rajasthan, Keshod and Ahmedabad of Bhavanagar dist in Gujarat, Bevas in UP and Delhi. In Karnataka, Halladakeri on the outskirts of Bidar, Belludi in Harihar taluk, Maruthi Sevanagar in Bangalore have given shelter to them. In India there are about 2000 families and 10,000 population of Rajgonds.

Those families that have settled on the outskirts of Bidar keep moving between Bidar and Hyderabad, Nizambad, Bongir, Adilabad, Udgir, Nanded, Chandrapur, Nagpur, Latur, Pune, Parali, Parabhani, Gulburga etc. for their business of Ayurvedic medicines. Rajgonds of Belludi in Harilal migrate to Chitradurga, Hoskote, Gangavati, Harapanahalli, Bellary, Davanagere, Chikkamagalore, Bijapur, Bagalkit, Dharwad, Mangalore, Hasan, Goa etc. and those of Maruthi Sevanagar in Bangalore migrate towards Kerala and Tamilnadu for the same.

Generally the Rajgonds migrate along the paths of railway tracks. The reason is that they can easily transport their belongings along with the tents by railways and also it is convenient to use the water in the stations. It suits their economic conditions. They migrate along with their families and stay months together in villages for their business of Ayurvedic medicine.

## Social Structure of Rajgonds

Social structure of Rajgonds consists of septs of clans. The whole population of Rajgonds can be divided into four groups. They call these groups *deva*. They are *Shardev* (those worshipping four deities), Panchadev (worshipping five deities), Sader (worshipping six deities), Statedev (those worshipping seven deities). Devas have been identified as the original link for their population. At first there were twelve such devas. Later they were reduced to only four according to the book "*Gondi Dharma Darshana*."

Thus, there were four men in Chardev, five men in Pachadev, six men in Sadev and seven in Satadev. They were the aboriginal men perpetuated as deities. The men of this race are the Rajgonds, because even today they identify themselves, their relatives and kith and kin with their Devas and septs.

In Karnataka the septs belonging to all the four Devas can be found. According to the survey made in 2000, there are 169 Sadev families, 32 Chardev families, 20 Statdev, families and four Panchadev families. The reason for increased number of Sadev families is that there are more number or septs and families in this sept. The names of septs in sadev are Rayaseedam or Jamkar (73), Uika (79),. Tadasam (6), Vadakade (7), Atram (7) and Gadam (1). In Satadev the septs are Pusnake (14), Mashram (2), Vadaviya (3) and Dhurve (1), Panchadev has one sept named Ada (4). All these septs are in Karnataka. The is a variation in population regarding the families of Devas and septs.

## Kinship

Blood relations among them are very strong. In fact they forbid weddings among the families of same Devas. They marry only the members of differing Devas in the same region. Some times they allow marriages among the members of same of different Devas provided the septs are different. Not all Rajgonds allow this because they strongly believe that members or the same Devas are brothers and sisters and only other different Devas are relatives. Hence they identify themselves with the sept name along with their name. For ex; Shama Raiseedam, Vasant Jamakar, Shama Pusnake etc. Here Raiseedam, Jamakar and Pusnake are the names of their sept or clan.

## Deities and Rituals

The Rajgonds have their own rituals and cultural practices. According to "Gondi Dharma Darshana" Rajgonds worship 12 deities, 750 clans and 2250 totems as their deities. Today there is no worshipping on that large scale of their totems. They believe in animism. Now a days they worship gods like Pherasapen (Mahadev), Baradev (Beerdev), Bheemalpen, Mahakali, Mariyamma etc.

Besides, Rajgonds celebrate the festivals like Shivarathri, Dasera, Holi etc. The Rajgonds of Bidar observe fast for Shivarathri, spending the whole night in singing devotional songs and Gondi dance. And the day they break the fast with a community lunch. They have great reverence for Shiva and worship him as Pherasapen.

Rajgonds of Harihar celebrate Dasera with great pomp. They spend the night in dancing. Both gents and ladies participate in Gondi Dance.

## Economic Organisation

Rajgond nomadic tribes in Karnataka are economically very poor. They are not engaged in agriculture and domesticating animals. So they do not have even an inch of land of their own. They are very innocent and do not know any kind of cheating. Thus they are forced to wander in search of their livelihood.

Unless they bring transformation among their traditional Ayurvedic practice, rules in caste panchayat and their beliefs, it is hard to improve economically.

Ayurvedic medicinal herbs are the support for their life. They call the herbs "Jadi-Booti." It means the leaves, roots and stems of herbs that are used as medicine. They get the herbs (Jadi-Booti) from Vindhya, Satpuda, Narmada, Godavari etc. in the river belts where the forest grows thickly. When they are not available, they buy Jadi-Booti from the local Ayurvedic shops, prepare medicines and sell them. Women and old people sell medicines in the locality in which they camp. Since they sell on roadside they do not get the right price for it.

Now a days Government Ayurvedic hospitals have opened and hence the families depending on Ayurvedic business are dwindling. The new generations among them have taken to cleaning ears on road sides and winding wires to steering wheels of vehicles. The children have taken to collecting of plastic bags that are used and thrown. If this condition continues, in a few years the Ayurvedic knowledge among this tribe will be completely lost. It is necessary to think and make plants to retain their invaluable Ayurvedic knowledge.

**Overview :** After a continuous struggle, a semblance of establishment and identity has been found by the Rajgonds through their bases at Bidar, Bangalore and Harihar in Karnataka. But they are yet to stabilize at these bases, as they are still moving around distant places in search of their brown bread and green pastures. They just cannot afford to be at one place and hence their traditional identity is not fixed and stationary

Dr. Merty has rightly depicted their social-economic life based on his anthropological survey and studies. He is a dedicated scholar who has been working on nomadic communities of south India. I write the 'Foreward' to his book entitled 'Forest Blossoms and the Central Jungle' from which I am reproducing some excerpts to find the similarity in nomadic centre of North and South Indian shepherd communities.

*Chandrakant Khandoji Wagge :* President, Gulbarga District, Gond Sangha, Kori Matha, Dhangar Galli, Brahmpur, Gulbarga gives a historical background of Gonds as under.

The original name of Kuruba is 'Halumata.' There are many evidences to categorise them under scheduled tribes.

The reason for calling them 'Halumata' sect is based in 'Brahamanda Purana'. As recorded there Brahma was born out of Vishnu's 'Nabhi' in the ocean of milk and Beereshwar is the son of Brahma-Saraswati. In Halumata Purana, Brahama is name as Bhramanna and Saraswati as Survatiand their son as Beeranna and thus he is God and they become original Dravida sect of people, as recorded there. Another version is that Shiva (Hara) and Skakti (Hari) both gave birth to Brahma and he is called the Muddanna and Saraswati as Muddavve.

Another folk version is that Parvati, the Shakti, made the clay-dolls out of her breast milk and called them as Muddanna and Muddavve and Beeranna's forefathers are the Gonds, writes Rastapur Bheemakavi in Halumata Purana. In this way Halumata into vogue.

Further definition of Adi Gonds could be : 'Gond' means 'thickest' or a group of huts. Gondaranya means deep thick forest. In such wild forests 'Adivasi Gondas' live. When these people began to rear 'sheep' they were called (sheep people) Kurubas. Their forefathers are from 'Adi Dravidas.' These people are differently called as Adigonda, Amma Gonda, Kadu Gonda, Kari Gonda, Siddha Gonda, Shiva Gonda, Beera Gonda, Padma Gonda, Deva Gonda, Dhool Gonda, Mala Gonda, Honna Gonda, Chinna Gonda, Jeta Gonda, Raya Gonda so on and so forth. These synonyms are recorded in the revenue records of Karnataka.

**Kadu Kurubas**

These people are known as Kadu Kurubas they rear sheep in the forest. Some are 'Jenu Kurubas' as they collect and sell honey. They are also nomads as they ever wander from place to place. Those who become leaders of the forests are called Raja Gondas. Common people are mere Gonds and those who carry messages from place to place are called as Helava Gonda or Kuruba.

**Nomadic Kurubas**

These nomadic Kurubas are spread at all places in Karnataka and those from Belgaum and Bijapur wander in the districts of Gulbarga and Bidar. These people have neither their own villages nor their own homes. Wherever they go that becomes their place and wherever they see water source they camp and that becomes their place. They bring the big fleets of sheep along with their wives and children and the things they require for their life. Those sheep are not their property but they belong to the rich. They get their payment from them. Wherever they land their sheep in the night and day the land owners give them 10-15 kgs of paddy, ragi and jawar because their lands became fertile with the excrets of the sheep. This is the fate of nomadic Kurubas. They are apt to be classified under scheduled tribes.

**Raj Gonds**

The leaders of such groups of huts are referred to as Raja Gonds by the city people and politicians. They are also called as Hire Kurub, Metre, Heggade, Gonde, Dhori, Wodeyas. The elders of these Gonds in the villages, towns and cities became the 'Raja Gonds.' Helvavaru (tellers-messengers) as they are called, on instructions of Kayaka-Kuruba-Gonds, carry the messages from place to place and keep and account of the people residing and leaving the village. As they wander on the oxen, people must have called them Helavas-the Cripple. When they reach the villages, hanging a placard around the neck of the ox and ringing the jingling bells in the morning, they stop each house of 'Kurubara hati' and narrate and praise their respective history and thus collect ration, calves, lamb, worn clothes in the form of charity. These people are also economically weak and they are fit to be included in the scheduled tribes.

**Gods of Kurubas**

Mailarlingeshwara, Beeralingeshwara, Malingeshwara, Amonghasiddha, Revansiddha, Siddha Purusha are their gods as per the Puranas.

**Mailarilingeshwara**

When the demons of Manimallarasa started destroying sheep the sage Kaurambi undertook penance and got the darshan of Shiva and appealed to him regarding their unjust suffering. Then Shiva, moved by the sage, took the avatar of 'Bhairava' on earth and destroyed the demons. Thus, Shiva got the name of

Mailarlingeshwara for safeguarding the sheep and shepherds. These are available in the Malatesh Vijaya or Mailarlingeshwara Purana and in the songs of 40 Voggayyas and Goravayyas.

**Beeralingeshwara**

Beeralingeshwar, a god man, guided and enlightened the sect of Kurbas (Gonds) on this earth.

**Malingeshwara**

Born and bred up in the Gonda family, Mahalingeshwara worshipped his guru intensely with flowers untouched by the insects, with water untouched by the frogs. He wandered far and wide and build the 'gaddugaes' (temple) smearing these walls with Chandra Varuna and drawing figures of Sun, Moon and Adishesha on their back walls for his guru at high places in all the villages he wandered. Even today we find no villages without the temples of Mailarlingdeva. At some places there are temples of Malingaraya. The folk songs relate that temples for him are built by Baragal Siddha Jattingarayas.

**Amukha Siddha himself is Amogha Siddha**

There is an interesting account about among Siddha in the purana and in his biography.

Veerabhadra cut the head of Dakshabrahma and put sheep's head in its place. The original head fell down on the earth. While grazing sheep the Kurubas heard a bodyless-voice. "O master, I have fallen here in the thick forest, take me out to your village near Kallurur and establish me there by building a stone temple and worship and inhabit me amidst you, I make your speeches a prophecy" then that 'wodeya' asked him, "Who are you?, what is your name?" He replied "Call me Amukha Siddha". Then they brought him, installed him in a temple and started worshipping. These people, as per his promise forecast the futures of people—their present, past and future. This is the divine origin of Amoghasiddha, according to puranas and drum-beat folksongs.

Vaggayyas, Wodeyas and Veeragasis are considered to be Swamijis or Jangamas. Vagga means big and ayya means Swami.

They are worshippers of Swami Mailarlinegehswara. 'Kambal' (sheep wool duppatta) cloak, bear-cap are their usual dress. At some place, they wander from place to place narrating 'Mailarlinga Charitra in their yellow clock, crimson coloured turban, 'Bhandar jolige' (bag filled with turmeric powder) round the shoulder, 'damaru and trishul' in their hands and beads of Rudrakshi around their neck. Some of them establish a home at certain place and give 'Shiva diksha' to the kurubas/gondas. The devotees call them to their houses every Sunday, worship them (padapooja), take 'tirtha-prasad' and send them with profuse gifts. Every district has big Mailarling temples. Hundreds of 'goravas' are housed there. The vaggyas in the temple are called 'Karanikas.' They get that name because God appears in their body and then they cut strong iron chains, crack coconuts on the heads, tell prophecies, fall from the top of high pillars, but lifted by the people before their ground-touch. Like this they do so many miracles. Their 'joliges' are their only property and they are their feeders. Such tribes rarely have property status. So these tribes should be classified under scheduled tribes.

**Wodeyars and Muttayyas**

These people are born Kurubas and they are vegetarians. They alone are the worshippers of Amoghasiddha and Revanisiddha. They did miracles in 'Kalyana' Anubhava Mantapa in Bidar district during 12th century. For miraculous rejuvenating of the dead goat, Shantamuttayya was given 'Shivaddksha' and 'linga' was initiated by Rambhapuri Jagadguru, one of the Pancha Mathadeeshas. There is Revanasidddeshawar Gurupeetha in Saroor village Muddebihal taluk in Bijapur district. Shantamuttayya's dynasty people are still there. They live in 'Hattikankana' and in Kudaki village of Aland Taluk in Gulbarga district. Still in Budihal, a village in Bijapur district, there are 'Unnikankana' gurus in Revanasiddha Gurupeetha. They are also 'trikal jnanis' and prophecists. The historical folklores say that they are the 'Rajagondas.'

**Veeragaris/Veerakars**

There is a mythological origin for these people. Beerashwara in his 'veeravesha' used to do miracles under the spell of 'dollu' music, untying his hairknot, wearing the heavy iron balls on the body, piercing needles on the tongue, cracking coconuts on the head, prophesying to the people around. So his devotees, even now do miracles like that in Malingaraya temples. They offer sheep to Beereshwara and celebrate. They not only feed themselves with that meat but it is also served to all their devotees are. Their rites and rituals, hailed from their ancient Dravids, have not changed. Like Kurubas (Gondas) Veerakars lead their life adjusting life, with all. Really they have remained in 'Girijan' culture only.

### Unnikankan Kurubas/Hattikankan Kurubas

Kurubas have the above two divisions. There is a mythological story for that. Padmagonda, an ape man, spread all the sheep, got from the sage Jabal, on the earth. While wandering and rearing sheep, he freed the princess from the clutches of demons and married her binding her with a 'Wool Kankana.' When he returned to his native place as per the wish of his mother, he married another lady. Here he tied her a 'Cotton Kankana.' Thus Kurubas are divided into 'wool kankana kurubas' and 'cotton kankana kurubas.' All these are originally from Dravidas.

### Shakti Worshippers amongst Kurubas/Gondas

These Kurubas install the Devi (Goddess-Shakti) idol on the Deepavali amavasya night and offer pregnant sheep to the deity. They cook that meat and eat and finish off everything before the day break, giving no impression of the past incident. It is told that they do like this because the people should not come to know the pooja of their family deity, Laxmi.

### Another Story

Another Shakti Goddess is Yellamma. For her worship, they take a lady of this tribe and make her naked but covering her body with neem leaves, smearing 'halad-kumkum' to the body, keeping 'arati' on her head and grass in her mouth, amidst the fanfare of music they reach the Yellamma temple. After reaching the temple, that lady is given a new dress and they cut the sheep and offer its meat to the deity. All of them enjoy the 'meat naivedya' accompanied by arrack, wine and dance. This is also a 'Girijana' culture.

### Priests (Pujaris)

The sheep came before 'Time' (Kala) and then came the Kurubas and thus that group became sheep rearing Gonda Kuruba community.

This community people got the title as 'pujaris.' They are called so, because they, starting from a child to a grandparent, worship their Kuladevatas—Mailarlinga as, Malingaraya, Amoghasiddha, Revanasiddha. They consider Mailarlinga their tribe-deity as He was the first, and the present generation of Kurubas and they worship Mailarlinga as family deity also. In other communities, those who worship Gods are called 'Pujaris.' But in Kurubas even newly born child is called a 'pujari.' They mean that 'pujaris' are those who know what worship (pooja) is and whose worship has become their life-style and they live and believe in the superstitious belief that God is different from man. In toto, they are very backward.

### Marriage 'Gondhal' amongst Harijans and Girijans

Vaggayyas of Kurubas initially marries the first male child with the deity Mailarlinga and then conduct the marriage between male and female. Traditionally the other marriages were performed for seven days—first day bringing the deity home; second day the sheep is offered to God and then it is cooked and catch; third day carrying the pot of Yellammadevi; fourth day performing Ababai 'gondhal' for which they go to Tuljaopur and then purify and bedeck the house and keep the 'Divati' and call the 'Gondhali' people to get the Devi story sung in the form of songs and skits; fifth day, binding the newly married couple with 'kankan' after 'surugi' with wool thread; sixth day, children and mother take oil bath and send of the bride; seventh day, sending the deity after offering sheep and concluding the whole function in drinking, singing, dancing and merry-making. Even today this system is prevalent with all Harijans and Girijans. Though they have migrated to towns and cities they have not left these rites and rituals of the marriage.

### The Miracle of 'Dollu'

Dollu in the hands of Shiva is Damaruga which is called 'cremation vadya.' When the dollu was rung the sound was heard around three leagues. This 'dudi' is to be rung only for God's pooja not otherwise—so say the pujaris, voggayyas, veerkas and wodeyars. With the dollu music the pujaris, tell prophecies when they are divinely full. The Gods and Goddesses of paradise come down and enjoy the music of drum specially when they are wearing the drum weighing about 10 kgs round their neck, they jump in dance and sing melodious songs.

In too, Kurubas are the Gonds and Gonds are the Kurubas, as per the mythologies and histories. They are called Kurubas as they generally eat sheep. Such kuruba community should be included in the scheduled tribes.

I agree with the plea given by the scholar in this research writing, Tontapur NB, President, Karnataka State Gond Sangha, has extended Gond Kuruba, claims as under :

This issue is presently about the Gond people in North Karnataka area of Karanataka state. North Karnataka area comprises Hyderabad Karnataka and Bombay Karnataka District i.e., Bidar, Gulbarg. Gond people are called and known generally and popularly as Kuruba, Dhangar and Halmath, which are synonymous to Gond tribe only. The name Gond is in the list of presidential notifications 1950, 1956 and 1977 as scheduled tribes where Kuruba or Dhangar name has been mentioned as synonymous to Gond name in those lists.

G A Grierson, who conducted the Linguistic Survey of India as per 1921 census, has said, "There are 179 languages and 544 local languages in India." Further he expressed with an opinion that it is not possible to mention names of every and each castes/tribes's synonymous names of all these (179) languages and (544) local languages in the presidential notification of SCs and STs list. So the caste certificate issuing authorities are at liberty to find out equivalent names to that particular caste or tribe in those areas or place while conducting local enquiry at applicants place by the Revenue authorities. To this effect, the then Government of Mysore issued a Government Order No. ED 60 SCL 57 B'lore dated 10-09-1958 only limiting to respective integrated areas of the new Mysore State. And also it authorised officers and non-officials to issue caste certificate on the personal knowledge of caste or tribes names popularly known in those places/ areas.

Secondly, in support of the verdict rendered by the Hon'ble Supreme Court held that even if, synonymous names are not declared by the President of India under Article 341 read with article 366 (24) of the Indian constitution with regard to scheduled castes and as per article 342 read with article 366 (25) of Indian constitution with regard to scheduled tribes communities, if the literature and customs are identical and common in its practice supported by public history books as provided under section 57 of Indian Evidence Act, 1872, entitled to be treated on the line of scheduled castes and scheduled tribes.

In the light of the above mentioned Hon'ble Supreme Court verdict and G A Grierson's opinion, Beda and Nayak, Lambada and Lamani and also Bovi and Waddar caste/tribe have been treated synonymous names to the concerned caste in Karnataka State at present. So also on this simple concept only the name 'Kuruba' was treated as synonymous name to Gond. Accordingly the caste certificates were being issued to the candidates belonging to Kuruba community as Gond till 1981 by the authorities concerned. The Government of Karnataka issued a circular stating that the Tahsildars of the Taluk concerned alone should issue the caste certificates to the persons belonging to SCs and STs in the prescribed form, vide letter No. SWL 314 SET 81 dated 17-7-1981. Since then the Tahsildar of Taluk started to reject the applications of Gond caste applied by all Kuruba Community candidates putting forth the legal point that there is no word (name) of the Kuruba in the list of schedule tribes of Karnataka State. Now, the problem of obtaining caste certificates by Kuruba community as Gond ST certificate has arisen in the North Karnatka area.

**Review of Literature**

Enormous literature is available in public history books with regards to Gond as synonymous name of the Kuruba community in North Karnataka Area as under:

(1) Gond means a mountaineer (page No. 469. Practical Sanskrit and English Dictionary, published in 1890 by Sri V S Apte)

(2) The Form of 'KO' or 'KU' refers to mountain in Dravadian languages and Kuruba connotes 'Mountaineer' (Page 15, Tribes of Mysore by A A D Luiz).

(3) Gond: A man of low tribe; Mountaineer especially one resides in Vandhya Range between the Narmada and Krishna rivers (Page 367, Sanskrit, English Dictionary by Sir M Monier Williams).

(4) In fact, the term 'Kuruba' in Kanada, Kurumban in Malayalam or Tulu, Gollawadu or Golladu in Telugu denote shepherd refers only to Kuruba shepherd. (Page 218. The original inhabitants of India by Gustave Oppat.)

(5) KO (KOV) means Kuruba (Page 5000, Kannada English Dictionary by Rev. F. Kittle).

(6) In fact, those (Gond) found in Andhra Pradesh, Madhya Pradesh and Karnataka are wings of Kuruba Society. (Page 65. Shepherds of India by Dr. S S Shashi).

(7) Russel and Hiralal describe the Gond as the principal tribe of Dravidian family. This classification seems to be on the linguistic similarities between the languages of Gondi and the Dravidian language. The name by which they designate their tribe as 'Koitur' or 'KO.' The word Gond is an imposition of the Hindus and Mohmedans (Page No. 31, Tribals Economy in Central India by Ranvir Prakash Sexena).

(8) They (Gond) call themselves 'KO' (in plural form Koitur). The name gond has been given by their neighbours which means in 'Gondi' language 'cow-killer' and 'bear-eater' and so the higher class members of the this tribe object being called as Gond (Page 75. Indian Tribes by M Chakroborthy and Mukharji)

(9) The name Gond is an imposition by Hindu and Muslims. (K L Bowmilk - Tribal India -Page 91, Mukul Chakroborthy and Dipak Mukharji - Indian Tribes. Page-42, Sethu Madava Rao Pagadi - Gonds of the world - Page 1).

It is crystal clear that the name Curuba is a synonymous name to Gond because the literature and customs are identical and common in its practice. Moreover, Gond is mentioned as ST in Presidential Notification in North Karnataka area only.

**Analysis of the Issue**

The Gonds are found to be distributed in the following states of India.

(1) Madhya Pradesh 2) Orissa 3) Maharashtra 4) Andhra Pradesh 5) Bihar 6) Mysore (Now Karnataka) 7) West Bengal 8) Gujarath (Page No. 90, Tribal India by K H Bowmik.)

Dr. S.S. Shashi rightly said, "Social habits, costume, way of living and values also undergo a change with time, climate and tongue. This is not only true of shepherd community but of others too."

People who are aware of synonymous names to the Gond Community and who also supported politically in respective states, are able to enjoy the benefits of Gond i.e. as ST category. After independence of our country, the re-organisation of states on linguistic basis, have been formed all over India. Accordingly, Kannada speaking areas i.e., Districts of Hyderabad State and Bombay province have been merged with new Mysore State in 1956. (The population belonging to Kuruba community in North Karnataka is 42,05,516 and South Karnataka is 14,13,918 as per 1991 census. But literacy as such is only 3% in North Karnataka area and 15% in South Karnataka area. Therefore the exact position of North Karnataka Kurubas is that the population is three time more than south Karnataka but the literacy progress is five times below that of South Karnatak.) More over the Kuruba of South Karnataka are educationally, socially, culturally and financially are more advanced than the Kurubas of North Karnataka. Therefore, all round development of Kuruba community of North Karnataka particularly is only possible is Kurubas of North Karnataka are given scheduled tribe's tag only.

**Origin and Development**

History as the story of the past, is essentially a narration of a change. We see changes occurring constantly around us. Over longer periods, not only ways of life of the human beings but also the pattern of their thought, beliefs, language and customs, have been subjected to change. Kurubas are prominent aboriginal tribes of Karnataka State. These peoples' primary occupation was sheep rearing and wool weaving. Sheep rearing has deteriorated now due to paucity of pasture lands. They are now working as workers and now doing agricultural labour also.

These people are totally illiterate. All are below the poverty line and depend on daily wages. They are socially, educationally and economically backward. These people send their children to labour work instead of sending to school due to poverty. The Government has evolved a number of welfare schemes for the scheduled tribes. But it is doubtful if the benefits extended to these downtrodden communities reach immediately and properly. The implementing agencies in various fields particular officers are not giving attention wholeheartedly towards these unfortunate people. The Constitution of the India has provided ample facilities for the schedule tribes. The officers, unnecessarily in recent days, raise objections or create legal problem starting from issuing caste certificates to providing opportunities to these people. How is it possible to effect the real upliftment of the schedule tribes?

**The State of Art (Analysis for Present Situation-Social Transformation)**

**The Present Situation :** The name 'Gond' has been included as Scheduled Tribes in the Presidential Notifications for Karnataka State. But in the North Karnataka, the name Gond is not popularly called but generally called as Kuruba, Dhangar, Halmath etc., which are actually synonymous words.

The literature and customs of both—Gond and Kuruba people are identical and common in practice. In view of Grierson's opinion and also verdict of Hon'ble Supreme Court, as already mentioned in problem of the issue, the Government may act on the humanitarian grounds with Kuruba community in North Karnataka area as has been doing now in respect of Adijambhav and Kembatti castes people which have not been included in the scheduled caste list of Presidential Notification. The caste certificates as Madiga and Holaya caste are being issued respectively by treating them as synonymous words to Adijambhava and Kembatti castes in Karnataka State.

As said in Marathi Language No orders of any kind will work out before the political power. Mere political force can work now to solve this problem of treating Kuruba, Dhangar or Halmath as synonymous to the Gond in the North Karnataka area. In Karnataka State, Late Sri R.K. Rathod, Minister of Horticulture, Sri G Basavannappa, Minister for Food and Sri L.G. Havanoor, Minister for Social Welfare were in the forefront and fought for the cause of inclusion of their castes in the SCs and STs list i.e., Lambada, Waddar and Beda castes/tribes respectively. There are no leaders in the Kuruba community, unfortunately, to work out fully on this issues and assert with Government that Kuruba, Dhangar, Halmatha names are exactly synonymous to Gond community in the North Karnataka area.

## Social Transformation

There are a few who have availed of the benefits as Gond found tremendous changes in their living conditions. A number of young people have compelled their degree course (in Arts, Science and Commerce), technical courses, medical courses etc., in the field of education. At present, there are doctors, engineers, lecturers, officers and employees in Railway, Banks and in various departments. In North Karnataka area, people of Bidar district only have availed of highest benefits as Gonds so far.

If Kuruba community of North Karnataka area is given an opportunity of schedule tribe's tagged-provision, there will be definitely tremendous developments socially, educationally, economically, financially and culturally in them.

Government of India as well as State Government of Karnataka have envisaged a number of welfare schemes to uplift these tribals. And also the required funds are being floated scheme-wise individually and generally as per their needs.

The transformation means an act of transforming or change. An education to all is the first and foremost factor required in tribals, living conditions. The education and economic benefits in the tribals, lives brought the progress much. For dwelling purpose, the housing scheme is found favourably to them. Regarding health side, still much more attention is required, because this task is itself difficult one, and all these wandering tribals are moving people, changing their residing places in the hills and forests.

## Transformation Targets and Findings

The need of tribals development in all respects is to be tackled:

(1) The implementing authorities have to act liberally and socially with the tribals.

(2) Tribal sect is very sensitive. The offer concerned and working persons in the field need to be sympathetic and tolerable with these tribals.

## Suggestions and Recommendations

The name Gond has been already included as Scheduled Tribes particularly in North Karnataka area in the Presidential Notification of 1950 and 1956 SCs and STs list. Further in the Notification of 1976 SCs and STs list, the area restriction i.e., districts, has been removed in Karnataka State. But the Revenue authorities are merely depending upon the literal meaning of term God without considering the intention of legislature for which it is framed regarding synonymous names–Kuruba, Dhangar, Halmath etc., are in North Karnataka area on the ground of identical and common in practice of customs and literature between Kurubas and Gonds.

In the light of the verdict of Hon'ble Supreme Court and opinion of G A Grierson, the synonymous names of Gond as Kuruba, Dhanagar and Halmath names, are to be treated in North Karnataka area.

## Summation

The assertion of name Gond in North Karnataka as synonymous names as Kuruba, Dhanagar, Halmath is a Must from all points of view i.e., political force and the real demand of people of North Karnataka, with Government of Karnataka as well as Government of India. Due to the lack of knowledge among people of North Karnataka so far, the facilities of Gond as ST were not availed by these unfortunate people, even 56 years after Independence of our country. At least, the future younger generation can avail of facility as ST for their upliftment.

Tontapur's claim and suggestions are worth consideration. We have similar research material by various scholars to evaluate and analyse research material by various scholars. During our research on South Indian Nomads we found some Brahmin gotras among beggar clans who by way of singing devotional song, earn their livelihood. Infact, there are Carpenter and Blacksmith Communities, known as Vishwakarma, who have Brahmin gotras like Angiras, Upadhyay, Vashisth and Bhardwaj. They add Sharma like with their names is North India but the higher Brahmins consider them as lower communities and not as Brahmins .

We have an interesting account of Dhangar Gouli Tribe of South. Bhagu B. Pingale says:–

"Goulis or Dhanagars are economically and educationally backward tribes spread over upper ghat taluks of Uttara Kannada District. Their origin and ancestry is unknown to the public as they are illiterates; of late, some people have tried to know about them. But there is no proper evidence about their origin and development.

It is learnt from the elderly people of the tribe that they were the original inhabitants of Maharashtra and came to settle in the forests of Karnataka, in search of fodder for their cows and buffalos. Their main occupation is rearing of buffalos and cows for milk. Agriculture is secondary occupation. Presently they live in the forests of Mundagod, Yellapur, Haliyal, Joida taluks of Uttara Kannada, and also thinly spread over Belgaum, Dharwad and Shimoga districts.

They construct houses with bamboo and wood with roofs of grass. We find such houses in groups. There groups are called 'Wada', each 'wada' is headed by a 'Pramukha' (leader). Their houses are divided into four parts for their convenience; (i) 'Kona' (Kitchen) - here the God is installed and they call it ("Devara") and (ii) 'Majar' (inside room.) These two are divided by a bamboo curtain. Mud or cow dung is pasted on these curtains to make it as a wall. There is a 'Nan' (Bath room) in the last corner of the house and another corner in a 'Gooni' place for cubs of cows and buffalos which are formed by bamboo curtains.

Their walls are completely made of bamboo pasted with mud or cow dung. On these, during the festival of Dashara and Diwali, the figure of plants, trees and creepers and drawn by gross sticks by the women.

Their cowshed is called "Ghota". This Ghota (Cowshed) and Major (inside room) are divided by 2 1/2 feet wooden bars called 'Gathadi.' This 'gathadi' is removed if a member of the house dies. It is replaced again after the last rites.

Their mother tongue is Marathi. They can not speak any other language; of the late, some people have picked up Kannada and Hindi languages. Dhanagar men folk used to wear 'Langoti' and Buniyan on top. They used to wear a headdress called pagot or paud a type of petha and a type of earring called Bhikbali, Mudi in their ears. They also used to wear metal bangles called 'Kada.' Woman used to wear saree in their own special style up to their knee like the *dhoti* style and blouse called choli on top. Wearing 'Kap' in ear and 'nattu' on the nose was common with bangle in the hands, wearing 2-3 necklaces is also at common fashion. In addition to that they used to erect green tatoos (Hachche) here and there on their faces. Of late, all these style are changing and they have started adopting modern styles.

**Origin:** From the tribes of Dange, Kurub, Mendke, Zende, Dhanagars of Maharashtra, these people are shoot outs from Dhangar who came to Karnataka. Since they sell milk in Karnataka they are called 'Goulis.' Presently Dhanagars are called Goulis in Karnataka.

These people should have been included in the scheduled tribe category, but the Karnataka government has included them in category A. Hence they do not get proper benefits from the government, they do not find places in political parties. They are unable to recognise which party is good or not good for them. During election time they are easily trapped by political parties. They cast vote for cheap gains. They do not cross the community for cheap personal gains. "Vanavasi Kalyana Ashram" is well known to these people. They have got high regards for them. "Vanavasi Kalyana Ashram" has created a stir in them. They have full faith in 'Vanavasi Kalyan Ashrma.'

## Shepherds of North India

I have written a complete research thesis on this subject of which some experts are given below —

The Shepherd community live in forests, in villages and in cities, too. They lead a community life in Uttar Pradesh, Punjab, Haryana, Rajasthan, West Bengal, Bihar, Orissa and Himachal Pradesh. They are found in large numbers in Uttar Pradesh, Karnataka, Madhya Predesh is regarded as the old principality of this community. There had been Dhangar rulers and Maharani Ahilyabai was the most famous of them. Vijayanagar in Karnataka, which was founded by two Kurabas, Hukka-Bukka, is regarded as their stronghold. The royal family of Karoli believed to have links with this community. Sheep, a pet animal of this community can be seen in the royal seal. It is said that the Ghosipura railway station of Gwalior is named after his community.

Dhangars, Oreaon Dhangar (shepherd) also settled in Chota Nagpur, West Bengal, Bihar and Assam. It is said that they belonged to Gujarat and Konkan in the early period. They migrated and settled in other states in due course. Some consider them as tribals of Chota Nagpur. Those who live in remote areas or forests in Madhya Pradesh or Karnataka have been declared as Scheduled Tribes.

The Gaddis are the shepherds of Himachal Pradesh. They are a semi-nomadic tribe and are found in Chamba and Kangra districts.

Some scholars are of the view that the shepherds who migrated from the west and call themselves Marathas have settled down in Gwalior and Anupshahar and later in Bullandshahar. It is said that Dhangars migrated from Maharashtra and settled in these areas.

## ETYMOLOGY

Though this community is known by different names, colloquially it is associated with sheep of cowherds. For instance, the Hindi

---

1. William Crooks : *Tribes and Castes of North West Frontier of India,* Vol. 2 (1806), P. 146 & 361.

word *Gadariya* is a compound on of *Gadar* and *ya*. *Gaddar* is a Prakrit word which means sheep and the suffix *ya* makes it pertaining to the community of shepherds. Some scholars hold that the words *Gadar* and *Arya* formed *Gadararya* or *Gadarya.* Possibly it later became a derivative of *Gadariya.* There is also a view that they were the custodians or defenders of *Garh* (fort) and hence were called *Gadariyas.* Similarly, the Kannada word *Kuri* means sheep from which the term Kurba was derived.

The word Dhangar is derived from cattle wealth. The suffix *Gar* is indicative of cattle-grazers or shepherds. 'Dhangar' is inscribed in a Buddhist cave in Pune district of Maharashtra. This cave, it is believed , has its origin between the first and the third centuries. Dr. Bhagwan Lal Indraji maintains, it is derived from the word 'Dhangar.' Some scholars believe it is associated with the Sanskrit word 'Dhang' which means a hill. This community is called Dhangar because it dwelt in hills. The Sanskrit word *Kandaka* means the dwellers of jungles. The Marathi *Maidapal* is of shepherds. We find *Dan* and *Kuri* in Kannada and hence some feel that the word 'Dhangar' originated from this class in Maharashtra, Madhya Pradesh, Uttar Pradesh, Rajasthan and other States. In this class is reckoned 'Nikhar' a sub group. In fact, when the practice of offering sacrifice increased, Buddhists influence permeated. Many cattle-grazers became Buddhists. Later Shankaracharya gave the call for purification. Meanwhile differences arose between the Hinayana and Hahatana Buddhists. Consequently, those who took to Buddhism rejoined the Hindu faith. And those who want through the purification, began to call themselves 'Nikhar' i.e. purified. Many, however, did not change their names and used the old term *Dhangar.* In fact, the customs, habits and traditions of *Dhangarsa* and *Nikhars* are almost similar and there are inter-marriages. In this context, we hear of different practices in some parts of North Indian which will be discussed later.

The most prevalent word in Uttar Pradesh is Pal or Baghel. Many of this community add the words Pal, Rajpal, Pali or Baghel to their names. *Pal* means one who rears sheep or cattle and Baghel is equivalent to lion. Endowed with the strength of a lion, whether they call themselves Pal or Baghel they take pride in calling themselves Kshatriya, Marhatta, Rajput or Thakur. Their genealogy would reveal that they belong to a branch of Kshatriyas.

The majority of *gotras* are of Kshatriya class. The *gotras* of other classes are also found this community. It looks as if it is a mixture of Brahmin, Kshatriya, Vaishya and other communities. Some *gotras* of this community are also from tribals. In fact *Gadariya* (shepherd) of *Gwala* (cowhered) was no particular community but an occupation which the Brahmins, Kshatriyas and other castes have taken to. Those wol fled to jungles and hills to escape conversion during the Koghal period made cattle grazing their profession and were called Ahir, or Gadariya. Initially, they were economically sound but their condition deteriorated in jungle surroundings. Thus an honourable community came to be looked upon as nomads and were reduced to the plight of *Sudras.*

It is essential to mention here some theories. The word *Dhangar*, historians believe, must have been associated with Dhaval village. V.S. Srivastva has also referred to four princes of this village. These princes were Ajpal, Dhanpal, Gopal and Ranadhval. This proves that Dhangara are part of Maratha Society.

In this context, according to Chintamani Vinayak Vaidya, the Gaikwad, Holkar, Scindia states of Gujarat and North India cannot be different. Pallav, Rashtrakoot, Kadamb, Sendrak and the pure maratha Royal dynasties were connected with Chalukyas. This leaves, no doubt that it is an ancient Maratha sect.

Baghel is a branch of Solanki dynasty whose ancestors are found in large numbers in Bundelkhand. This word is also used for Meshpal society but it is surprising that its use was more in vogue in Mathura, Agra and Gwalior districts and not elsewhere.

Jagdish Singh Gahlot, a historian says that Solanki were in the south of Ayodhya from where they went to Gujarat and there from to Rajputana. Their kingdom was in Sirohi, Marwar, Chitor (Mewar) and Bagad. Charan-Bhato Called this sect Agnivansh but the stone and copper edicts of 600 B.C. to 1600 did not inscribe them as Agnivanshi. They certainly belong to the dynasty of Chandravanshi and Pandavas.

---

1. *Are Rajput Maratha Marriage Morganatic ?* Aitishashik, Gaurav Granth mala Gokhle Building, Poona 1952 P. 198-201.

Emperor Alaudin Khiliji's brother Ulgakhan seized the Solanki ruler's, Kingdom, Anhilwada in 1356 (1299 A.D.). A branch of Solanki's having stayed in Vyaghrapalli (Begheli) village, ten miles from Anhilvada Patan and hence they were well-known as Vyaghrapalliya of Bhagghpels. The ruler of Rewa in Madhya Pradesh belongs to this Baghela branch. The present area of Solanki is Rewa, Loonawada, Bansda and Tharad.

In certain districts of Haryana and Rajasthan, they are referred to as Maratha Rajput. The ruler of this society, Maharani Ahalyabai Holkar had sent them there to settle. Virendara Kumar Vidyananand Srivastava[1] holds that the Maratha village Dhawal in Maharashtra derived its name from the world Dhangar. He says:

The word *pal* is a derivation of *Mashpal.* Alongwith cattle rearing, it carries the sound of welfare of people. Its use is found in many places. It is interesting that Palistan is a place near Chitor and Palestine was the birth place of Jesus Christ. Jesus himself was likened to a shepherd. *Pal* in Nepali and Sikkimese means of good goat from which wool garments are made. *Paleej* means ewe. She was the ancient goddess of shepherds in Europe. Another meaning of *Pal* is group. Among the Moes of Rewari Tehsil of Haryana are Dhangar Pal, Ahir Pal and others of whom some embraced Islam.

The word Pal might well be in use to describe this community since the days of Raja Kushal Pal Singh but there is, doubtless, a lot of history behind it. This word was in evidence ranging from the Pal Dynasty rulers of Bengal to those of Pallavas of South India. Let us have a look at the available names of rulers of this dynasty.

*The Ruler of Pal dynasties of Bengal (543 AD—1947):*

Gopal, Dharampal, Vakyapal, Devpal, Jaipal, Vigrahpal, Rajyapal, Mahipal, Nebhpal, Rajpal, Mahendrapal, Govindpal.

*Rathores of Badaun and Rulers of Pal Dynasty* :

Vigrahapal, Bhuwanpal, Madanpal, Devapal, Bhimpal, Surpal Amritpal, Lakhanpal etc.

---

1. Virendra K. Vidyanand Srivastava : *Are Rajput Marathpa Marriagges Morganatic?* p. 200.

*The Rajas of the ruling dynasty of Indraprastha*—Delhi :

Rajpal, Mohanpal, Samudrapal, Chandrapal, Sahaypal, Devpal, Narsingpal, Sempal, Raghupal, Govindpal, Amritpal, Valipal, Mahipal, Haripal, Seespal, Madanpal, Karmpal, Abhyapal, Dhujhabpal, Udaypal, Yashpal.

*The dynastic genealogy of the Raghuvanshi rulers of Kannauj* (800 A.D.—1021) :

Mahendrapal, Mahipal, Vinayakpal, Mahendrapal, Devpal, Vijaypal, Rajyapal, Trilochanpal, Yashpal etc.

*The Ruling family of Punjab (977—1027)*

Jaipal, Anantpal, Sukhpal, Trilochanpal, Bhimpal, etc.

## THE RULING COMMUNITY

One finds in this community Gahlot, Tomar, Rathore, Pramar, Chauhan, Solanki, Parihar Sengar, Baghpel, Yadav etc. The names of the 36 Kshtriya clans are as follows :

1. Eksevak Ichavakukakusya or Suryavanshi (Sun Race); 2. Indu Somvanshi or Chandravanshi (Moon Race); 3. Gaholt Sisodiya, Raghuvanshi; 4. Yadu (Bhatti, Jareja, Jadoo, Banaphar); 5. Tabar or Tomar; 6. Rathore, Rathod; 7. Kuchwah; 8. Pramar or Panwar; 9. Chauhan (Hada, Bhadoriya); 10. Chalukya or Salanki (Baghel); 11. Parihar or Pratihar; 12 Chobda ; 13. Tak or Takshak (Snake Race) ; 14. Jeet Gate or Jat ; 15. Hun or Hul (Dhangar) ; 16. Kathi or Katti; 17. Balla ; 18. Jhala Makvana; 19. Jaitva or Kamari ; 20 Gohil : 21. Sarviya; 22. Silar or Sular; 23. Devi or Davi; 24. Gar or Goud; 25. Dar, Doda and Dodha ; 26. Dharobal (Garhwal) or Geharvar (Budela) ; 27. Bir Gujar or Badh Gujar; 28. Sengar; 29. Sikarwal; 30. Baees or Bais; 31. Dahima ; 32. Joyiya ; 33. Mohil ; 34. Nikump; 35. Rajpali; and 36 Dohima.

According to a Karnataka saying, there was no community or gotra before the advent of Kurba community's gotra, came into vogue after its birth.

Ahir, Gadariya and Gujar are classified as one in North India. Many proverbs are current :

(1) Ahir, Gadariya, Gujjar

The three are one

(2) Ahir, Gadariya, Gujar, Gwala

All four are one.

Gaderi of Bengal, Ghosi of Bhopla, Gangajali of Bihar, Bharwad and Rabari of Rajasthan and Gujarat denote the meaning of cattle grazers. The Meshpal society is called by various names in different States. Following is the list of the names by which they are called:

| *Name of State or Area* | *Name of Caste or sub-caste* |
|---|---|
| 1. Uttar Pradesh | Pal, Palkshatriya, Baghel, Baghela Dhangar, Nikhar, Gadariya, Gawal, Bhedwar, Gangajali, Bharat. |
| 2. Haryana and Punjab | Pal, Rajpal, Marhatta, Gadariya |
| 3. Bihar | Pal, Rajpal, Gadar, Gadariya Bhedwar, Gangajali, Bhagat. |
| 4. Rajasthan | Pal, Gadariya, Rewadi, Banjara, Bhaghela, Bharwad. |
| 5. Maharashtra | Dhangar, Khutekar, Hatkar, Hatgar, Banjara, Waghle, Gwala, Maratha. |
| 6. Madhya Pradesh | Dhangar, Baghel, Gadariya, Ghosi, Neekhar, Pal, Baghela, Ahir, Yadav, Gval, Gvali, Bharud. |
| 7. Mysore | Kurba, Dhangar |
| 8. Bengal | Gaderi, Pal, Haldhar |
| 9. Himachal Pradesh | Gaddki, Pal. |
| 10. Orissa | Agrayya, Orawan, Oraon, Kurkh, Saile |
| 11. Madras | Kurumba. |
| 12. Gujarat | Rabari, Bharud |

## MIGRATION

Scholars hold different views about their migration, just as some think that Aryans originated from Central Asia while others believe that India is their original home. Gandhar is known as land of Sheep grazers. The Dhangars and Nikhars of Uttar Pradesh, a branch of Maharashtra shepherds, travelled through Madhya Pradesh, Rajasthan and Delhi to far-flung areas with their cattle. Another branch went towards Karnataka and Tamil Nadu and a third towards Bengal and Orissa. Some tribals went from Uttar Pradesh to Bihar while others to Haryana and Punjab.

Some anthropologists are of the view that this society is older than the Aryan residents of India. Risley says they belonged to the Dravidian group. The Gaddi tribe, however, belong to the Aryan race. Similarly the ancestors of North Indians were also Aryans of a mixed blood of Aryan and Dravidian. Being in jungles they became black but in physical features they resemble Aryans. Infact there is no pure race in the world. There has been a mixture of blood by way of inter-caste and inter-tribe marriages.

Bharwars are the residents of Gujarat. A folk-tale classifies Bharwars as belonging to the community of Mahars; Krishna's father Nanda, was of this caste. It is also an accepted fact that they went from Gokul) Brindavan near Mathura and settled there. Some scholars are of the view that these people went from Mewar to Gujarat, Kathiawar and Kutch. It is surprising that while they move with Rabari society they have no matrimonial links.

The Gaddis of Himachal hail from Punjab, Rajasthan, Delhi, Uttar Pradesh or Bengal. As many Rajputs were being deprived of their sacred thread and were being persecuted in Aurangzeb's reign, they took refuge in the hills. There was no other option except rearing cattle, sheep and goats. Hence they took to this profession. In course of time they emerged as a caste.

The Shepherds have progressed in many fields but still a long number is backward and leads a tribal life in hills, forest and villages.

*(On this subject, my books entitled 'Shepherds of India', including Hindi, Tamil and Kannada editions. Hamara Samaj and a large number of research papers / articles are referred Dhangar.)*

# 11

# Roma, the Gypsy World

The Roma of Europe and America do not like to be called as Gypsies now-a-days, but refer to themselves by a generic name 'Rom' and to others as 'Gaje,' word which seems to have been derived from 'Ghazi.' The word 'Roma' seems to have been derived from 'Rama' which means one who pervades and operates all or roams about, a dark coloured person or a husband. The word 'Lava-Kusha' in old Sanskrit means a singer and musician. Since Gypsies are popular musicians also, they may have some association with the Lava and Kusha dynasty.

Roma are known by different names in different countries. They are 'Zigeuner' in Germany, 'Tsyiganes' or 'Manus' in France, 'Tatara' in Sweden, 'Gitano' in Spain, 'Tshingen, in Turkey and Greece, 'Tsigan in USSR, Bulgaria and Rumania, etc. and 'Gipsy' in Britain. Most of the Roma of Europe and America now believe that they are Rajputs, or Jats, from India who had migrated from India, their 'Barothan' (great land). They number more than nine millions, and now lead settled or semi-nomadic life. It is an established fact now that they are mostly Jats from old great Punjab, Haryana, Himachal Pradesh, Delhi and Rajasthan. The community is divided in various groups known as Sinti (Sindhi), Luri or loar (Blacksmith) and Bargujjar, etc.

David Mac Ritchie has collected a number of facts which prove that the Roma were not only the Jat or Rajptus of Punjab but they also belonged to Bharatpur, Lahore and Karachi and other parts of India including Maharashtra and Gujarat. A group of Gypsies called 'Sinti' (Sindhi) was from the land of five rivers and Sind in particular. They were also called *Jate* but now generally known as 'Sinti.' I believe a number of groups of Roma belong to Banjara. Gujjar Sansi, Sikligar, Dhangar etc.

The Roma are engaged in various jobs. They are metal workers, mechanics, horse traders, basket makers. The women folk are known as good fortune tellers. Many Roma are born artists of repute. Mrs. Raya and Mrs. Reshma are renowned Gypsy singers.

According to Shahname of Firdousli, the Persian Monarch, Behram Gour received from an Indian King, 12,000 musicians of both the sexes who were known as Luirs. This fact is again confirmed by Arabian historian, Hamza of Ispahan who wrote half a century before Firdausi, was well versed in the history of the Sassanides. He writes that Behram Gour called 12,000 Indian musicians known as zott for the benefit of his subjects. *Zott* is the name by which the Gypsies were known to the Arabs. In the Arabic Dictionary *al-Kamus* this entry occurs. Zott Arabicized from Jatt, a people of Indian origin. The word might be pronounced as *zatt* with equal correctness. The single individual is called as 'Zotti.' In the lexicon Mohit we read:

> "Zott, a race from India, arabisized from Jatt; Zottish clothes are named after them, a single piece being called Zotti. These are the people who are called Nowar in Syria and sometimes they are styled motribiya i.e. musicians, their avocation being that of players upon stringed instruments and drums. They are like-wise dancers."

Roma arrived in Europe in the 10th to 13th Century AD via Iran, Turkey and Egypt. They had behind them two or three centuries of fateless life in the countries through which they travelled. Those days the feudal system governed in Europe. The human relations and the economic structures were quite different from those of the Gypsies. In the feudal system, the basic principle was the unequality of people. The peasants were made into serfs. In this kind of society, status was based on the cruel economic use of the people. There were the serfs and nobless.

While staying in Helsinki, I had an opportunity to discuss the old history of Gypsies in Finland and other countries with Finish Gypsologist Dr. Kari Huttunen. He said that the feudal class society had thrown Gypsies outside. They lived in their own separate camps, where it was possible for them to follow their own customs and talk their own language. They did not mix with the host population.

The history of Roma is full of torture, sufferings and miseries. Like Jews, they were persecuted through the centuries. In Spain, they were banished by royal edict under threat of terrible penalties as early as 1499. The Spanish Kings made many laws to protect their subjects from the so-called pernicious people. This was a cruel beginning of suppressing the Gypsy race. In Germany, the Nazis tried to impose severe restrictions on Gypsies and thousands of Gypsies were choked to death in gas chambers by Hitler. They were treated in the same fashion as Jews. Dr. Kenrick and Puxon in their book "*The Destiny of Europe's Gypsies*" have given detailed account of this persecution of the Roma. According to them, a quarter of a million Gypsies were killed by Nazis. They were imprisoned in concentration camps and then exterminated.

The suffering and torture continued in Europe for decades and the Government of Poland, Norway, Denmark and Sweden tried to expel them from their territories. In Romania, Bulgaria and Communist countries they were forced to work under inhuman conditions. They had also been enslaved and deprived of the freedom of movement in various countries. In 1782, the Hungarians hanged, beheaded or broke on the wheel forty one Gypsy men and women. Others were driven by soldiers into dangerous swamps to die by drowning.

The Roma arrived in Britain in the middle of the 15th century and scattered all over the country. How they crossed the English Channel, is still a mystery. In the beginning, they had not many problems, but during the reign of Henry VIII, severe measures were taken against them. According to an Act of Parliament passed in 1530, Gypsies were asked to leave England within sixteen days or be imprisoned and forfeit their goods. The Act was not enforced vigorously, but the Gypsies were horrified. When they could not leave the country, they were given severe punishment. Merely being a Gypsy was esteem to crime worthy of death. Even today again most of the British are biased the Gypsies.

In Scotland, during the year 1627, all Gypsies were ordered to be forcibly recruited into the Army, and in 1665, they were banished to the West Indies, Jamaica and other places. They were also transported to Verginia and this is how they were forced to leave Europe and wander in America, Canada and other countries.

When I asked Dr. Rena C. Grooper, a gypsologist in New York about the history of Gypsies in America, she said that Americans, did not torture them like the Europeans, In America, their big group is know as Kaldersa. From the 1880 to 1914, numerous Gypsy bands carried in the America, many from Serbia and from Russian dominated areas. During the age of exploration and colonization, Gypsies arrived there with the European settlers.

The Roma with black hair, black eyes brown wheatish or black complexion look like Indians. The anthropological blood Group Studies have proved them of Indian origin. They have vast kinship relations and the head of the family is the eldest person. The Gypsy chiefs are still called Thakur, and the old lady is known as Phuri dai (old lady). Gypsy marriages are generally arranged by the parents. The bride is supposed to be chaste beautiful girl. They do not allow courtship like Europeans. Adulteries are not common amongst Roma like Hindus. They look down upon marriages between close relations, but surprisingly the bride's price among Roma is up to 10,000 dollars.

The Roma are "decastified" now-a-days and do all sorts of jobs. They recognise three tribal divisions among themselves. (1) The Kaldaras from the Balkans and Central Europe who are the most numerous of Gypsies; (2) the Gitanos, mostly from the Iberian Peninsula, Northern Africa and Southern France and (3) the Manus or Sinti from France and Germany. Members of each tribe of sub-tribe tend to marry among themselves. They are monogamous. Kaldaras or Laledarai (Coppersmiths) and Lovari (horse dealers) are in large number. Sintis are not divided into castes. The Kris of Roma is like old panchayat system of India.

The Roma worship the Hindu Goddess Kali (Durga) which they call Sat Sarah and the rituals are more or less like Hindus. A big Roma international festival is celebrated in France every year where the idol of the Goddess is worshipped and taken in a procession, and later immersed in water in the nearby pond in the same way as is done during Durga Puja in India.

The Roma have, however, now converted to Muslims or Christians. During my second world tour last year, when I conducted door to door sociological survey in Skepjo (Yugoslavia), I was surprised to find a Hindu, a Muslim and a Christian living under the same roof, but following their old traditions. Khuda Baksh, son is Deveshran and daughter Minakshi. His brothers name is George Methew. I came across a number of girls and women named as Ram Kali among Roma. Yugoslavia is the only country where the Roma got nationality for the first time in the world. They are now an integrated part of the Federal Republic where all nations and nationalities as well as ethnic groups are equal.

Sait Balic, the president of Yugoslavia delegation of Roma and President of World organisation of Roma says—'Roma-people in Tito's Yugoslavia are integral part of our Federative Republic. They are equally engaged in all working organisations educational, social and scientific institutions depending on their personal qualifications and educational degrees. I met Prof. Yusuf Saip and Traiko, a research scholar and other Roma people in Skepjo and found them leading a happy life. I was welcomed by Roma youth artists with Indian film songs' *Mere Mitva re o mere*' and '*Jhooth Bole Kauva Kate, kale Kauva se Dario.*' Due to the welfare projects undertaken by many Govt. and NGOs for upliftment of Roma nomads there are tremendous social changes have taken place in some European countries and America. I attended a number of conferences in various countries and also organised some International Conferences in India.

I can never forget the affectionate words of my Roma friends like Dr. Jan Kochanowski, Mr. Aleka, Prof. Saip, poet Rajko Djuric Tarjko Petrovski, Agnes Vranckyand others who frequently uttered '*tu mera Ratt*' (you are my blood relation) and *Bharat mera Barothan* (India is my great country).

*"ROMA WORLD"*

Here are some excerpts from the 'Roma World' journal edited by me about 2002 Roma Conference held in Roma Research Centre of New Delhi by Research Foundation —

Research Foundation had earlier organised an international Conference on Art, Culture, Literature and Human rights in 1995.

The conference was attended by over 500 scholars, Faculty members of various universities in India and abroad, Research Associates, Authors and Social Activists. Some Roma Scholars also participated in conference. In the year 2001, the Roma Research Centre of Research Foundation helped Hindu Heritage Pratisthan and Modi Foundation, in organising the International Seminar on Roma Heritage and Culture with the cooperation of Ministry of tourism and Culture, Govt. of India.

We have a large number of Banjara and other nomadic people in India who want to have their association with Roma, the Indian Gypsies abroad. This journal will be a media of communication among the International community of scholars.

"Roma world" is the only journal on Roma people being published from Delhi to interact with Roma, the Indian origin people abroad. We published in our introductory issue a brief report of Roma conference held in 2001 in New Delhi.

Mr. W.R. Rishi, Founder Romani Institute Chandigarh had served the noble cause of Roma Welfare by holding Roma festivals in India and bringing out another 'Roma' Journal from Chandigarh.

According to my Anthropoligical research, Roma are ancient Indian emigrants. We have a large number of Indian emigrants who migrated from India from time to time. We can classify them in three phases in general. The first pertains to Roma Gypsies who left India between 1000 and 800 years ago. The second number is that of emigrant Indians living in Mauritius, Surinam, Fiji, Trinidad etc. and the third one left India is recent period, to get jobs. Brain drain is a common term used for Indian engineers, doctors and experts who are going every year to other countries in search of jobs.

As regards the Roma Gypsies, there are many theories prevalent among the scholars on the migration of Aryans. One theory holds that the Arctic region was the original home of a people who, in the course of centuries, migrated south populating Central Asia, Afghanistan and finally India. Beginning with the greater Punjab which included the modern Haryana, Himachal Pradesh and parts of Delhi State as well.

This theory has, however, been under increasing challenge and contemporary scientists and scholars believe, on the basis of the depiction in cave and rock paintings that the migration was actually in reverse and that it was from Indian that people moved out to Central Asia and thence to Europe.

These ancient migrants were known as 'Aryans,' which means the noble and honourable people. There is irrefutable evidence sufficient to disprove the theory of Aryan invasion to India. It is proven fact that Roma Gypsies are of Indian origin and they migrated from India to western countries in different periods. Their forefathers lived as Hindus in various parts of India particularly in western India, which included old Sind, Punjab, Rajasthan, Maharashtra, Gujrat etc. The number of Roma today may be between 15 and 20 millions in Europe and 10 millions in Americas.

*(Refer my books entitled "Roma-The Gypsy World" and "Roma culture and Heritage" for detailed studies).*

## International Conference on Roma (Gypsy) Culture and Heritage (A Brief Report)

"The two-day conference on Roma culture and heritage was organised by H.H.P. in collaboration with Ministry of Tourism and Culture, Govt. of India. Modi Foundation and active support from Roma Research Centre, Research Foundation International Delhi, India Inter-continental Cultural Centre, Chandigarh and other organisations. The venue was National Museum on 8-9th April , 2001 in New Delhi. The eminent Hindu Cultural leader Mr. Ashok Singhal inaugurated the conference on 8th April which is the Roma Flag Day and celebrated all over the world. He was of the opinion that Roma Gypsies should be treated as ancient Indian emigrant. He shared his opinion with the Roma leaders that they should be recognised as a Nation and given proper representation in U.N.O. The Secretary General of I.R.U. Dr. Hristo Kyuchukov, Mr. Nikile Gherorghe, Dr. Vaia Kochanawaski, Mrs. Anisa Agnes and others participated in the discussions. Dr. Lokesh Chandra presented his paper on Roma Culture and heritage, Prof. Som Dixit spoke on Hinduism and Roma Culture. Mr. J.S. Pathania and Lilyana interpreted the speeches into Romani language. Dr. B.K. Modi, the President of H.H.P. was of the opinion that there are many tribals and Dalit communities which were forced to leave their home and hearth during British rule in India as they fought against the rulers. There are many Banjara and nomadic people who like Roma Gypsies had to wander here and there and many settled in forests and hills. Roma had to struggle hard for their livelihood and existence in European and other countries. Earlier Dr. Shyam Singh Shashi, Romanologist; Chairman, Research Foundation Research Centre, well known Arya Samajist leader Mr. Anil Vadhawan, Vice President Sarvadeshk Arya Pratinidhi Sabha and Ved Vrat Sharma, Sect. Gen. Arya Sabha also spoke on this occasion. Secretary General. H.H.P., Dr. Shashi presented his key note address explaining the theme of the conference and other details based on his Gypso-anthropological research in the field. Mr. Ranjit Naik, President, All India Banjara Sangh and Mr. B.K. Naik also addressed the conference.

There were four sessions besides Inaugural and valedictory functions of the conference- (1) Roma Culture and Heritage (2) Roma people and human rights (3) Romani language and literature (4) Journey to roots and Roma religion. Thirty three delegates from 11 countries viz. France, Belgium, Bulgaria, Czech Republic, Yugoslavia, Poland, Romania, Albania, Slovakia participated in the conference.

**Journey to roots :** Roma *caravan* left from Delhi on 9th afternoon on a heritage tour and had its first halt at Modipuram where Dr. Bhupendra Kumar Modi addressed the delegation at a function organised by the Dayawati Modi Academy. Mrs. Parbha Thakur, a politician-poetess recited her poem, Padma Shri Prof. Satyavrat Shastri, are renowned scholar and Dr. B. Singh also participated in the deliberations.

**At Haridwar :** The Roma *Cravan* left for Haridwar afternoon and reached Har Ki Pauri. They had achaman and offered flowers to mother Ganga Chanting "Jai Ganga" words for the first time in the past one thousand years of Roma history. They also lightened the earthern lamps which were flown in the sacred river and remembering their forefathers' roots. After visiting temples, they left for Rishikesh next day; they attended the discourses of Swami Nirlepanandji and Swami Dayanandji.

**At Chandigarh :** The *Caravan* left for Chandigarh next day carrying Gangajal with them. No doubt, the inconvenience was faced by the delegates due to change in food habits and culture as many have given up their Gypsy way of life and now are almost westernised. Though they have adopted Christianity and Islam but they don't follow the same rigidly.

The Roma delegates stayed at Chandigarh on 11th and 12th. Mr. Dev Bhardwaj, Director, IICC organised cultural evenings and one-day conference. Mrs. Nanda, the Advisor to the Administrator inaugurated the function and the Secretary General of the International Romani Union and others participated in the deliberations. Dr. Shyam Singh Shashi paid his grateful thanks to the organisers for the hospitality they extended to the Roma guests. The Roma also visited Romano Kher (Roma Museum) of late Dr. W.R. Rishi, the founder of Indian Institute of Romani studies. The Roma enjoyed Punjabi culture and their way of life. (Scholars Rishi and Bhangwatji died recently).

**At Kurukshetra :** On 13th morning the Roma *Carvan* left for Kurukshetra, the place of Mahabharata war where they learnt about the history of Mahabharata and the message of *Bhagvad Gita.* They took keen interest in Gita and the Secretary General Dr. Hristo Kyuchukov requested the Indian scholars to help him in translating *Gita* into Romani language.

**Book released :** The president, international Roma Union released a book entitled, Roma Culture and Heritage authored by Dr. Shyam Singh Shashi and the inaugural session of the conference. There were other publications entitled *Indian Gypsies abroad, Videsh men Rahnewale Roma Gypsy and Heritage Souvenir* edited by Mr. Shardendu Sharma released on this occasion.

**Dr. Murli Manohar Joshi addresses :** After the cultural programme and kathak dance by the twin eminent dancers Ms. Nalini, Kamalini, the Minister of Human Resource and Development, Govt. of India, Dr. Murli Manohar Joshi addressed the delegates and assured them to give all support in cultural and literary exchange programmes. He also advised Dr. S.S. Shashi and Mr. B.K. Naik to chalk out the programme in this connection for which a task force of scholars was also to be formed with the help of

Roma Scholars. (The programme was chalked out and sent to the Minister but no results).

**Other functions :** On 9th morning in his valedictory address. Mr. K.S. Sudarshan said that the Roma should not depend on the Govt. Assistance as there are some devote non-Govt. organisations also, which will be more useful than the Govt. organisation. He assured the delegates to help them in socio-cultural areas. There were felicitation programmes at Sankat Mochan Ashram where Acharya Giriraj Kishore, Mr. Vishnu Hari Dalmia, Late Mr. Caman Lal, Mr.Baleshwar Agrawal, Dr. B.R. Grover, Dr. Ramrang, Mr.Champat Rai etc. were also present.

**Research Foundation Fellowships :** On the concluding day of the journey to roots, the Roma delegates visited Roma Research Centre of Research Foundation International at Rohini, Sector-9, Delhi where two eminent scholars namely Dr. Hristo Kyuchukov and Mr. Nikole Ghereghe were honoured with Hon. fellowships for their extra ordinary contribution in the field of Romani studies.

**Roma met Prime Minister Vajpayee :** Roma delegates met the Prime Minister Mr. Atal Bihari Vajpayee at his residence on 14th April. at 12.00 noon. The Prime Minister welcomed the delegation and said that the Govt. of India will help them in their fight for social justice. The President of IRU Dr. Emil Scuka spoke about the painful history of Roma migration from India. Mr. Gheorghe, Advisor on Roma and Sinti issues, Dr. S.S. Shashi, Dr, Kyuchukov and others also spoke on this occasion. ***(No follow up action from the Govt.)***

I had bitter experience in holding this conference and wrote a poem on this occasion as below —

**Glory Be Yours My Roma Friends!**

*My dreams were torn*
*When I was reborn*
*I thought I would say*
*Good-bye to all*

*But the surgeons and doctors*
*Gave me a divine call:*
*We will not allow you to die*
*Till your dreams are alive*
*Trust me my friends*
*My Roma brothers and sisters*
*I wanted you to take*
*The ganga water of your forefather's sacred river*
*Which I preserved for ages*
*Since Ganga flows in my veins*
*Hardwar the land of my birth*
*I survived and lived for you only*
*Never wishing anything from you*
*Except the brotherly love.*
*The pure love from you.*
*We may or may not meet again*
*My pen will share your pain*
*And my soul will always say-*
*Glory this copious world!*

**Resolutions**—The resolution were drafted by Nikole Gheroghe in consultation with the International President and Secretary General of International Roma Union.

1. Roma preserved Indian ancient culture. They had Hindu roots and strong affiliation with India. They contributed precious Indian elements to the world but suffered a lot in various countries. They should be recognised by Govt. of India as ancient Indian emigrants like Indian Emigrant of Mauritius, Surinam and Fiji, etc.

2. Roma should be allowed to associate with GOPIO and considered as PIO to participate in the Indian funded projects addressed to the Indian Diaspora.

3. Govt. of India should help in translation, teaching and propagating Romani language, viz Hindi, Punjabi, Rajasthani,

Gujarati and Marathi. Knowledge about Roma roots in India and the rich Roma cultural heritage should be included in the text books of India and the countries in which Roma reside. Ministry of Education may like to use distance education system in this regard and other techniques of education through correspondence method.

4. There should be books and literature of Indian culture in Romani language also. Ministry of Human Resources Development may take up this issue with the Govts. of those countries where Roma reside in big number.
5. India Houses may be set up in the respective countries well equipped with documentation and cultural facilities to get people conversant with Indian culture. Later, these India Houses can be set up in each district.
6. To implement the resolution passed, a Task Force should be constituted immediately for which devoted scholars should be nominated by IRU. In his connection, Minister of Human Resources Development Dr. Murali Manohar Joshi has asked the Indian scholars and Romanologist Dr. Shyam Singh Shashi and Shri B. U. Naik to prepare the draft proposal and line of action to prepare the draft proposal and line of action of HHP in consultation with Ministry of Tourism and Culture. PM Office may be convened during OSCE
7. International Conference on Roma to be organised by the Ministry of Foreign Affairs of Romani on 10-13 September 2001.
8. International NGOs and Roma representative in cooperation with Indian delegates (Govt. and NGOs) should coordinate, to fight against racism and discrimination in the UN world conference to be held in Durban, South Africa on 28th August 2001.
9. An International public fund is to be established for development and promotion of the Universal Human Rights of Roma people of the world. The fund should be used by Roma people themselves.
10. Indian Govt. should help to protect the interest of the Roma people in UNO.

**Roma Conferences 1983 —** The Roma visited India in 1983 to attend 2nd world Roma Festival, to be held at Chandigarh from 29th to 31st October. They last came in 1976. Here are glimpses of their migration, history and culture by Roma Scholars and Gypsologist in their own language and style.

Roma scholars and delegates from various countries were felicitated by Research Foundation from time to time. On October 23 1983, three Roma scholars viz. Jean Michel, Gilles Eynard (France) and Agnes Varuna Vranck (Brussels) were felicitated by the Foundation.

Dr. Sait Balic (Yugoslavia) President of Yugoslavia Delegation of Roma and President of World Organisation of Roma spoke—

During recent years all over the world are being done considerable efforts for human rights, especially those who were oppressed and without any rights.

Roma people in Tito's Yugoslavia are integral part of our Federative Republic, where all nations and nationalities as well as ethnic groups are equal, nowhere in the world as here. They are equally engaged in socio-political structure beginning from local community, commune assembly, regions, republics and even Federation depending on their personal qualifications and educational degree. Roma people are equally engaged in all working organisations educational, social and scientific institutions. In the field of "written world," Roma people in our country have in recent time considerable success. There have been many collections of printed poems in Roma—language whose author is our well-known and very active member Rajko Djuric.

The Rom poet Rajko Djuric from the then Yugoslavia, whom I met in Belgrad in 1982, presented his poetic collection to me. Here is a poem in Romani composed by him—

*Indaras e slike merimase*
*Ande jakha*
*Duj rote galbene*
*Galbene an kalo*
*Sar chonut an rat*
*Duj galbene rote*
*Amaro dikohipe chinen*

*Po muj e devlesko perel to korhipe*

W.R. Rishi, Chandigarh writes —

With the support of the Indian member, United Nations Sub-Commission on Prevention of Discrimination and Protection of Minorities passed a resolution in August 1977 appealing to those countries which had a Gypsy population to accord to it all the rights to which they are entitled under the United Nations Character, set forth in the Universal Declaration of Human Rights without distinctions, such as those of race, colour, sex, language, religion.

In March 1979, again with the active support of India's Permanent Representative at the UN, the Romani Union representing more than 71 Romani organisations in various countries of the world have been granted consultive status with the Economic and Social Council of the United Nations. The Romani Union will now be able to participate as a non-governmental organisation in the work of UNESCO, the UN Commission on Human Rights and other agencies of the United Nations.

**Dr. Vania from Paris says —** The Universal Declaration of Human Rights is the exaltation of freedom and expresses the profound desire of freedom and expresses the profound desire of implantation of this freedom in all human beings. We shall briefly examine to what degree the conception of liberty of the Universal Declaration of Human Rights.

"Romane Chave does not have special treaties on liberty. However, not only their tales and legends but all behaviour from the cradle to the grave is living illustration of their conception of freedom.

"If one thinks of the history of Indo-European civilization, one is tempted to make the following synthesis the Indo-European barbarians were civilized by contact with Mediterranean culture and formed their own cultural nucleus between the Danube and Aegean Sea; this is the first "Europeanized" and definitely gave the biggest cultural centres in Athens, the in Roma. Due to conquest, with the decadence of the peoples of the Near East, the Greco-Roman civilization followed the same fall. New invasions renewed the vigour, but barbarianized the conquered peoples. The Judeo-Christian religion softened, at first, the customs and reviewed agonizing values, but soon the representatives of this religion got entangled in wealth and became instrumental in smoothing every new thought.

Here is one report about tortures given to the Roma even today in various countries of Europe by Simon Wiesenthal —

"In my functions as President of the Union of Jewish Victims of the Nazi Regime and as a human being who personally suffered from persecution. I have always been ready to do my best and to help get rid, the world of oppression and injustice. This I owe to the people who suffered with me and did not live to see the day of liberation. It is a debt which can only be repaid by standing up for all innocent victims of persecution anywhere.

Eynard Gilles France writes about Roma Marriage as today —

"Although still traditional as far it is the parents who decide even some times before the birth or in infancy to be effective at a quite tender age (16) this use is vanishing and young lady some times refuses to marry in the family. Mostly, I pretend this actual cross-cousin marriage is the fact of the poverty rather than of an existing snobbism. Who would indeed accept to marry such a misery? Who would be unable to insult this belonging if not the one who is of the same family? Inversely, in rich families is the exogamy is the use with some taste for the same tribe. Would they have to cross the ocean up to USA.

Roma Social Activist Mrs. Agnes Vrancky, Belgium says —

'In Western Europe where the industrial development was conditioning whole populations, we feel very often the unbalanced personality of them. For us, the ROM-HOM (perfect human being) is three : intellect, sentiment and body and it is our duty to observe and to develop the harmony of this. Very often we have the impression that in this modern world only BRAINS are developed and estimated, the nobleness of feelings is far under-developed so as the beauty and resistance of the body is quite ignored.

In order to act better, to be less invulnerable too, I don't like the cult of own personality. An old "warriors"—attitude of Indians' Maya was : don't have any history, nor own ambitions, be always vigilant and never underestimate people. It is also a good defensive attitude.

Sam Beck, Brown University & Nocolae Gheorthe, Bucuresti write about Gypsies in Romania—

Some administrators and some segments of Romanian society consider that the Gypsy problem is based in their nonconformist behaviour to "accept" modes of conduct, that they are deviant, criminal, and parasitic elements in society. Others believes that no Gypsy problem exists and assume that education and the raising of their standard of live will bring about spontaneous cultural convergence and socio-economic homogeneity. This is an ethnocentric perspective which sees Romanian values and world view as superior to that evolved by Gypsies. Yet others see the Gypsies as an increasing demographic presence in Romanian society. One that is viewed as a drain on local and national educational, health, and legal services and facilities and thus reduces the resources available to other people. To some, the Gypsies are an embarrassment, an anachronism of Romania's underdeveloped and "primitive" past. The impact of the sedentarization of previously nomadic Gypsies has made them not only more visible within the communities of which they have become a part, but their entrance into the formal structures of such communities has necessitated new and special response which communities have been unable or have found difficult to provide...

*(I collected hundreds of books and journals on Roma life and culture from foreign countries, which are available in Roma Research Centre of Research Foundation Library situated in Shiksha Bhavan, Rohini, Delhi. My D. Litt. thesis on Roma entitled 'Roma-The Gypsy World' and 'Roma Cultura and Heritage' and a large number of articles are referred for advanced studies in this field.)*

# 12

# Among the Indian Americans

During my research on Roma and other nomads of the World, I came across some literature reflecting Hindu influence on primitive American culture. I was deeply inclined to know the 'Patal Lok' the land of mistry the place of 'Shesh Nag' and the country of Kerala King Bali as narrated in our mythological scripture. In my childhood, I met Swami Satya Dev Privrajak, an elderly scholar who travelled from India to America carrying with him only twelve annas (less than one rupee) in his pocket. He wrote some books about his journey and founded an Institution namely 'Satya Gyan Niketan' and library in Jwalapur, Haridwar near my village in Uttaranchal. This was all prevalent in my sub-conscious mind. Swami Vivekanand's lectures in Chicago and Bhikku Chaman Lal's book *Hindu America* interested me most.

In 1981, after my tour in European countries, I went to New York and travelled in the Eastern part of U.S.A. and Canada. I spent some time in Niagra Falls where I wrote poems on this great wonder of the natural world. I met Dr. Rina Gropper, Professor of Anthropology in Pace University and author of several books on Roma Gypsies of America. Now when I peep into the past, it looks like a dream. I do not know how I succeeded in establishing rapport and making many friends in my journey by train and buses and stayed there for about twenty days with a meagre money. Those days, Indians were not in a big number like today in U.S.A. and Canada. Of course, I had an advantage of having specialisation on nomadic studies and Indian culture which helped me in contacting Professors of the Universities and researchers who arranged my lectures in sociology and anthropology departments. There is a long story of my maiden journey to the unknown fairy land where I had no friends, no relatives and no financial resources to help in my sociological surveys. I, however, could collect a lot of literature and first hand knowledge about Roma, Red Indians and a little bit about the socio-economic conditions of NRIs (Non-resident Indians) also.

In 1992, I was invited by a writer's organisation of South America to participate and present my paper in the International Conference held in Mexico. It was amazing to observe that a number of scholars asked me about *Gita* and mystic sciences of India. Many of them were studying philosophy including Indian culture, may be due to the influence of Octo Panz's poetry who had been to India as diplomat and he wrote on Indian culture and religion. Since, he was out of station, I had detailed consultation with his wife only. I also had interaction with Mexican families but could not meet there any NRI (Non Resident Indian). I had to seek the help of an interpreter being Spanish as a common language of the country. I visited Sun temple, and studied the sun worship in the ancient age and the heritage of Maya culture. A family took me to various places and showed me traditional cities of Mexico. The land lady provided me lot of literature about Aztec and Maya culture and their history. I visited anthropological museums and found their cultural heritage similar to that of Indian culture in many respects. The idols of Vishnu lying in Ksheer Sagar depicts Hindu mythology whereas the incarnated snakes on stone shows serpent culture (Nag Sanskriti) once prevalent in the entire South America.

Before I quote from authentic studies on this subject, I would like to mention about my recent visits to U.S.A. and U.K. in 2004, where I stayed for about two months. I was invited as a Hindi poet and writer by an NRI organisation to address the various conferences and poetic symposia as chief guest. I never knew that within a short span of time twenty lakh Indians could reach U.S.A. and earn a handsome money, name and fame as well. We may call it a brain drain but we should be proud of their rich contribution in American life and achievements in various fields. I also met the people of Indian origin migrated from Guyana, Fizi, Surinam to America and Europe. While travelling from New York to San Francisco with my host, an eminent cardiologist and Hindi poet Dr. B.K. Mehta, visited silken valley where Dr. Shyam Narain Shukla organised a big function of Hindi lovers in my honour. He wrote a travelogue covering his journey from Ganga to Missisippi river. Here I met my old friend Mr. Jagdish Seth, who after his retirement, settled with his son in U.S.A.. Dr. Indira Mehta, daughter of Dr. B.K. Mehta working as lecturer in California University, took us to her house and hold us that new generation of Indian settlers does not believe in Indian way of arranged marriages. I noticed this fact when I was in Carry, a city of intellects in the northern parts of U.S.A. I stayed with an ideal family of Dr. Sudha Dhingra. She is a well known Hindi poet and her husband is a software Engineer. No doubt there are families who observe Indian culture even today but most of them are becoming Americanised. Thank God, that some Ashrams founded by Hindu scholars like Swami Prakashanand in Austine and other Indian Missionaries, are working to preserve Indian culture in America and other parts of the world.

This was my literary journey and hence a number of Hindi organisations invited me to participate in their get-together and functions. I was interviewed by American press and a number of time by Asia and India T.V. in which communicated my message of peace and brotherhood to the world. Some printed interviews and write ups about me appeared in American news papers which are given in the appendices of this book. I also contributed a number of articles on this journey after I returned to India via London where I stayed for about a week. I was received by Dr. Dauji Gupta a scholar, politician of repute and the International President of the World Hindi Council. His son, Dr. Padmesh Gupta, a learned scholar and Hindi writer organised a big function in the University of London which was presided over by me. A number of Hindi and Urdu writers attended the conference. After this programme, another scholar and Hindi writer, Dr. Krishna Kumar organised a grand function in my honour held in Birminghm. Well, this time in my journey in America and U.K., I felt very homely as there was no problem of language or money as this was a special visit on which I am writing a separate travelogue. I however had again a language problem in Budapest in the year 2004, the capital of Hungary where I was invited by World Hungarian Congress to participate in an International Conference and to present my paper on my new subject of research, i.e., Shakas and Hoons, the primitive nomadic clans who ruled in India in 5th century and founded Hungary in Eastern Europe. After the programme, I travelled from Hungary to Germany where, I stayed with a Roma family and also visited Indian German families in Berlin.

To avoid more narration about my personal data of travelling, I am confined here to my advanced studies and further research on Indian Americas only.

**Red Indians**

Once upon a time, in all the length and breadth of the Western Hemisphere, there was not a single human being. Mankind was unknown. The wild beasts had all this magnificent land to themselves.

Then, on one historic day, most anthropologists, agree, a band of Asiatic hunters came from Siberia to Alaska. They had probably been chasing polar bears, walruses, or seals. In any case, they kept going south, making their camp each night when darkness fell in a shallow cave, if possible, or under a protective outcropping of rock. They were garments made of fur, and carried stone hatchets and stone-tipped spears. They had shaggy hunting dogs that resembled wolves. They made their cooking fires by rubbing dry sticks together. As the centuries, passed on in that long-age, other groups of nomadic hunters followed them. In time, the trickle developed into a slow but steady flow of people migrating down through the ridges of the Canadian Rockies into what is now the northwestern United States. Wherever these wanderers, went, some settled down and remained. But the more adventurous ones kept moving.

Among the earliest traces of man in North America are some square-toed, sandals of shreded bush. Found in a cave in Oregon, they are believed to be 9000 years old. Found in the early 1930's in a cave in the Grand Canyon in Arizona, a twig deer is about 3000 years old. Scientists believe that it was used as a fetish for a successful hunt. Primitive Stone Age spear points are among the many relics we have found to date of the early inhabitants of North America.

And now we describe where, the Americans of great Vedic, serpent and sun culture like modern way of life.

As the seeds of herbs and trees are carried to distant place by wind and birds, so in ancient times mankind and culture spread over the world through the tides of great Indian and Pacific oceans. The Hindus were mighty navigators and pioneers of culture centuries before Columbus was born. They established their cultural empires in Java, Bali, Sumatra, Borneo, Philippines, Cambodia, Champa, Annam and Siam and ruled there until after the 14th century. Even today Cambodia's King bear the title of the great Varman rulers of India, and Bali has Hindu Raja. Hindu migration to America was vigorous from the first to the twelfth century A.D.

According to Bhikku chaman Lal, Cambodia, the ancient Kamboja, was one of the earliest to receive the culture of India. The name of its river Mekong was derived from Ma Ganga (mother Ganges). In the first century A.D. a Brahman called Kaundiya came to Kamboja from Kanchi, the capital of Pallava kings in South India, married the Kamboja Princess Soma and was elected king of the country. Champa, at present *Vietnam,* figures prominently in the story of India's cultural expansion. *Vietnam* was the footboard for the pilgrims to America. A Prince of Kalinga (Orissa) founded the Hindu State of Java in the first century A.D. Java is the ancient Yava Dveepa mentioned in the Ramayana and other Sanskrit texts. Bali Dveep is still a stronghold of Hinduism. Borneo is the ancient Suvarna Dveepa or Sri Vijaya. On the Indonesian national flag still flutters our Garuda. From Angkor Vat to American Hinduism and its gods and temples have left their imprint. Siam was the centre of Hindu culture for centuries and boasts of rulers with names such as Rama, Praja Deepak and Dharmaraja. The same pioneers of culture who ruled such large areas in the Pacific for fourteen centuries also went to far off Mexico and Peru and established cultural empires.

*Ship-building* : Indian ship-building had developed at least 2,000 years ago and according to Dr. Ekholm, Director of the Museum of Natural History in New York, and Dr. Rovert Heine Geldern, there appears to be little doubt that ship-building and navigation were sufficiently advanced in southern and eastern Asia at the period in question to have made trans-Pacific voyages possible. As early as the time of Ptolemy in the second century. A.D., Indian ships sailed to the Malayan Peninsula and Indonesia not east-wise but across the Bay of Bengal. In the third century horses were exported from India to the Malayan Peninsula and Indo-China, an indication that there must have been ships of considerable size. When the Chinese Buddhist scholar FaHein returned from India around A.D. 400 he embarked on a ship which carried more than 200 sailors and merchants and which therefore must have been larger than the ships of Columbus and early Spanish explorers. "Ships of that size able to cross the Indian Ocean and the China Sea with their dangerous cyclones could certainly cross the Pacific as well." According to French and British historians the Hindus excelled in the art of constructing ships and for centuries the British and the French borrowed from the Hindus many improvements in the naval architecture.

Bhikku quotes two authorities in his 17 years long research writings—

"In ancient times the Indians excelled in the art constructing vessels, and the present Hindus, can in this respect, still offer models to Europe, so much that the English, attentive to everything which relates to naval architecture, have borrowed from the Hindus many improvements which they have adopted with success to their own shipping. The Indian vessels unite elegance and utility, and are models of patience and fine workmanship." *(Lees Hindus*—P. 181). Astec *Calendar*

"Those who first arrived on the continent later to be known as America were groups of men driven by that mighty current that set out from India towards the east."

The U.S. Ambassador Miles Poindexter states in his book *The Ayr-Incas* that primitive Aryan words and people came to America especially from Indo-Arya by the island chains of Polynesia. The very name of the boat in Mexico is a South Indian (Tamil) word: Catamaran.)

Let us begin with the Astec calendar known as the Astec Chakra to the Hindu astronomers. It is the foundation stone of Hindu culture in America. The ancient Americans live in the four Hindu ages (Yugas or cycles). This Astec calendar (of Hindu origin) depicts the Hindu ages of the world. Mackenzie, author of *Myths of Pre-Columbian America*, says "The doctrine of the word's ages (Hindu Yugas) was imported into pre-Columbian America. The Mexican sequence is identical with the Hindu. It would be ridiculous to assert that such a strange doctrine was of spontaneous origin in different parts of old and new worlds." The very sculpture of the Sun in this calendar bears the imprint of India.

Witness the complicated game of Pachisi as it is played in India and Mexico. Seventy years ago Edward Tylor pointed out that the ancient Mexican game of Patollit was similar in its details to the game of Pachisi is played in India and the whole region of Southern Asia. "It seems clear," he wrote, "that the Mexican game must have come from Asia." Subsequently Stewart Culin showed that even the cosmic meaning of the Mexican game, its relation to the four quarters of the world and to the calendars ascribed to them was essentially the same as in Pachisi. Dr. Kroeber, leading anthropologist of California, observes that "the mathematical probability of two games invented separately, agreeing by chance in so many specific features, is very low. The close correspondence between the rules of the two game indicates a real connection." Dr. Kroeber however could not find more evidence to link India with America and decided to leave the issue unsolved, expressing the hope that fuller and more accurate knowledge would some day solve the dilemma. Dr. Robert Heine Geldern, the famous anthropologist of Vienna, and Dr. Gordon. F. Ekholmhave now presented enough evidence to support the thesis that Americans had definite cultural links with the people of South-East Asia at least 200 years ago.

*The lotus motif* : Their research in the last three years support the thesis, I presented 26 years ago in my book *Hindu America.* They begin with the lotus in India and Mexico. (Lotus is one of the most sacred symbols of India. Hinduism is essentially embodied in the lotus. One of the most frequent motifs of early Indian art is the lotus plant). The same kind of lotus motif occurs in America at Chichen Itza (Mexico) as a border in the reliefs of the lower room of the Temple of the Tigers. "It is certainly remarkable that in India as well as in Middle America, the rhizome, a part of the plant not normally visible because it is submerged and deeply buried in mud should have been the basic element of a whole motif and, moreover, be stylized in the same unrealistic manner as an undulating creeper." The two learned anthropologists are definitely of the view that "such a combination of highly specific details cannot be accidental. It suggests the existence of some kind of relationship between Maya art and not only Buddhist art in general but the school of Amravati of the second century A.D. in particular."

The most obtrusive factor in the customs and beliefs of the Maya civilization according to experts is unquestionably Indian. Maya architecture bears unmistakable seal of Hindu architecture as you can see from the picture of Maya palaces and temples.

Atlantean figures appear in India in the second century B.C. They played an important role in Indian art and are found even on very recent Siamese temples. In America they can be seen at Thula in Central Mexico and Chichen Itza. Gods and ceremonial figures standing on crouched human figures are found in India from the second century B.C. onward. In Central America they occurred in many Maya sculptures, especially at Palenque. From Sanchi to Central America the pattern is similar.

Those anthropologists who until yesterday completely denied any contact between ancient America and Asia are much perturbed today to find that their so-called 'cross' of Palanque (Mexico) is no longer a cross but an exact copy of the Hindu Tree of Life on Mount Mere (Sumeru), the mythological centre of the world. A representation of the Hindu Tree of Life is presented in a shadow play from Java. This depicts the Hindu celestial tree on Mount Meru. This Javanese specimen and the so-called Mexican cross have the same demonic figure in the centre and branches of the tree are clearly visible even to a layman. Javanese specimens are of course recent but the fact that the motif appears in an already highly conventionalised form among the reliefs of Angkor Vat in Cambodia about the middle of the 12th century indicates that it must be of considerable antiquity. We find stairways flanked by serpent-balustrades in South-East Asia and Middle America. The use of half columns characteristics of Cambodian architecture. Highly similar combinations appear in certain Maya buildings.

*Common Ceremonial* : Most of you in India are familiar with the Charak Puja ceremonial observed in Bengal and several States in South India. This Hindu ceremonial was also observed in Mexico and Peru. The Spanish historians call it the Mexican Valador ritual. A relief of Byaon central temple of Angkor Thom in Cambodia represents a rite similar to the Mexican Valador. The use of parasol

*(Chhatra)* is an age-old sign of royalty and rank in India, Burma, China and Japan. The Maya Astec and the Incas also used it as a sign of royalty. Frescoes of Chak Multum in Yucatan show two types of parasols both of which correspond to types still in use in South-East Asia.

In reading descriptions of the palace and court of the Astec emperors of Mexico, any one familiar with South-East Asia cannot fail to be reminded of the courts of Burma, Siam and Cambodia. The same applied to the form of government. Thus the institution of four chief officials in Mexico and Peru corresponds to the found ministers of state and Governors of the four quarters of the Kingdom in Hindu Buddhist empires of South-East Asia. In both cases this institution is based on cosmological principles. This indicates similar pictorial story of the Hindu Buddhist origins in the field of art, religious architecture, government, kingship, cosmology and mythology prove close cultural contacts between ancient India and countries of South-East Asia with the countries of Central and South America. Dr. Robert Heine Geldern and Dr. Ekholm have come to the following conclusion:

"The large number of highly specific correspondence in so many fields precludes any responsibility of mere accidental coincidence nor would it help us to take refuge in any kind of explanation based on some alleged psychological laws. There is no psychological law which could have caused the peoples on both sides of the Pacific to stylize the lotus plants in the same manner and to make it surge from the mouth of a jawless demon's head, to invent the parasol and use it as a sign of rank and to invent the same complicated game (Pachisi). There is no explanation other than the assumption of cultural relationship. We must bow to the evidence of facts even though this may mean a completely new start in our appraisal of the origin and development of the American Indian higher civilizations."

*The ayar rulers* : The use of throne, the litre and of fans mounted standard like on long poles as insignia of rank and royalty on the countries of Central and South America bears the strong imprint of India. It may be observed here that the last Ayar ruler of Peru was carried in his palanquin on the day the Spinards invaded Peru. His turban with the plume and his Mudra of the hand are unmistakable proofs of his Hindu origin. His four Ranis performed Sati after he was murdered by the Spaniards. A hundred Ayar rulers ruled Peru.

The Mexican national throne preserved in the National Museum of Mexico bears the typical Hindu Buddhist disc of the Sun. The Mexicans also had the Hindu Simhasan (Lion throne) and the Padmasan (Lotus throne). A scene of Buddha-Sangh as preserved in a relief temple in Java has its parallel in the famous pyramid temple in Piedras Negras, Guatemala.

Bhikku Chaman Lal has published two photographs of two women to compare their costumes. One is a Maya woman from Mexico and another is a Gaddi from Himachal Pradesh. Both are similar in costume and feature also.

Though the Aztec people of Mexico are no more travellers like their forefathers in the past, I have included them in this book to have an idea of travelling people of India since time immemorable. Similarly, I am including the socio-economic structure of Indian Americans today. This material is based on a recent survey when I visited U.S.A. in 2003. They are neither nomads nor travellers as such but according to the philosophy of nomads sociology, we have studied those Indians also who migrated from India to various countries in search of jobs or business and settled there as NRI or PIO. Here is a survey report of Indian Americans based on little India Business Directory Vol. 9 No. 12 which I collected from New York during my visit in 2003.

**The Indian Americans (N.R.Is.)**

The most comprehensive nationwide survey ever conducted of Indian Americans yields a complex picture of a financially thriving and rapidly growing ethnic community, which has simultaneously embraced American economic and public life, but erected a guarded fortress around its social and personal space.

Indian Americans are intensely religious, prefer to speak Indian languages at home and fret over the moral values of the second generation. An overwhelming majority value economic security, but almost half are ambivalent about whether they are better off in the United States than in India. The exclusive survey conducted by Little India also found that Indian Americans confine to have an affinity for Indian traditions and food and almost a third mix predominantly with Indian friends.

The public and private dichotomy in Indian American life is reflected even in their language preferences. English is overwhelmingly the preferred language of public discourse among Indian Americans, even though 95 percent also speak a language other than English. Inside the home, almost two-thirds speak Indian languages Hindi 43 percent, Gujarati 27 percent, Bengali 3 percent, Punjabi 6 percent, and South Indian languages 15 percent.

Even though the vast majority of the Indian population is first generation, and for that reason still tied to its language of origin, Yashodhara Pawar, a scientist, says she sees the commitment also in the second generation. "I have second generation Indian friends, in their twenties and thirties, who are taking a keen interest in their Indian culture and background. They are making an effort to learn the language on their own. Had they been force-fed they say, They would have been less inclined to learn the language or understand it."

Sujata Chinchankar, of Edison, NJ, says retaining the mother tongue is exceedingly important in her family "I send my 8-year old son twice a month to Marathi classes so that he can learn to read and write the language and polish up his grammar. The idea is that he should be comfortable whenever we visit family and relatives back home."

Chinchankar says she wants her son to understand the significance of festivals, Shlokas, Strotas, as well as to be able to read public sings and boards in India. "He should be able to read and write letters to his grandparents in Marathi. Recently, when we performed his thread ceremony in Pune, the priest was very impressed by his understanding and the fact he didn't need to translate instructions in English for him. Since we already speak the language at home his teachers have been saying that his command over the language is very good. "

According to Chinchankar, nearly 50 students attend Marathi language classes in her area and she regrets starting her son late with the language. "With my daughter who is three years old, I'll be starting sooner."

However, Mikta Daga, of Woodbridge, NJ, says while she recognizes the importance of language instruction, "Kids should be taught the mother tongue and since one is abroad the effort will have to be that much more. I have known friends who get basic language textbooks to teach kids the language at home. However, if my kid shows resistance towards it, like many do, it will not bother me. I grew up in Bombay and a kid insisted in speaking in English and not my mother tongue, Hindi. So I can understand that feeling."

The language is getting rusty in this new environment, Pawar says, in any event. "Since my mother tongue is Marathi I am fluent in it. However I have met people, both parents and their kids who spoke to me in a strange archaic Marathi that made regular easy-going realize that back in Pune, the Boston of Marathi culture, the young don't speak in such a stilled, bookish manner any more. Listening to them speak is like as if you are at a Marathi book reading session instead of chatting across the dinner table."

Among the most striking funding of the survey is the Mr. Portance of religion in the lives of Indian Americans. Almost 85 percent rate religion as being very or fairly important in their *life*. Almost half visit a temple, mosque or church at least once a month and nearly two in three pray daily.

Chitra Khorana, an occupational therapist, is typical of many Indian Americans. "I am very religious. I go to the temple frequently and fast every Thursday and observe festivals. I was equally religious in India also, except that over here sometimes I lose track of some of the smaller festivals."

Ram Mallappa, computer consultant with Sofsys, Inc, Atlanta, Ga, who identifies his family as "slightly religious," however is dismissive of religious rituals. "I believe God exists and we do visit the temple once in 15 days. But we don't observe any fasts, do pujas or chant any mantras. God understands all languages, I think, I also don't believe in rituals and how people have simplified these things. They have no meaning really. The idea should be to do the right action, then the right results follow."

The ambivalence many Indians have towards their new life is at its starkest in the unease so many of them experience over the upbringing of their children. Nearly four in 10 Indians identify moral values of the second generation as their single most important concern. Such moral issues are traditionally the bastions of the right fringe in American polity.

Pawar says, "Now that their kids have grown up and ready to enter college and live away from home there is this tremendous fear among Indians that they will lose their culture. There is major conflict between the generations over this issue and both the parents as well as the kids are equally confused. The gap here is wider because unlike parents in India, who have the advantage of seeing change in society, these people have isolated themselves and remained in the sixties. They have continued to live the way they did in those days in India."

Education also primarily a second generations issue, ranked second among Indian American concerns with 22 percent. Traditional mainstream issues did not have quite as much resonance among Indians; health care came in third at 10 percent and care for the elderly fourth at 7 percent.

Indians appear to be politically apathetic, with four in 10 indicating that they have no sympathies with U.S. political parties at all and almost as many refusing to label themselves as liberal, conservative of middle of the road. Democrats have a 2-1 advantage over Republicans among Indians who do have a political preference. Surprisingly, the political apathy among Indian Americans spill over into political opinions in India as well, with a majority of Indians saying that they don't care which political party leads the government at the centre in India. Among those with a preference, the BJP was the runaway favourite with 32 percent, followed by Congress with only 9 percent.

Financial security is central to the Indian community; almost 95 percent said that it is important to them. Almost four in five Indians feel they better off financially now than they were five years ago and almost as many expect to improve their finances in the next five years. However, only about half could bring themselves to claim that they were better off in the United States than in India.

Nearly one in six thought they would have been better off in India and 31 percent could not make a judgement.

Subbu Iyer a Chicago-based consultant with Oracle Financials, is among the slim majority of Indians who are convinced that they are better off in the United States. "I came here to study and that's an experience I cherish, because as a student one is able to participate in the American way of life. Those who come directly on the job miss all that aspect of getting to know and understanding the culture of a country."

The social life may be unsatisfactory for some Indian Americans because in India they are surrounded by relatives and friends, which is not possible here. "If you have only Indian friends here," he says, "You are bound to feel isolated. In that sense, college experience here allows you to make many friends in the mainstream community. However, in the professional sphere, Iyer insists, "Nobody can honestly say that back in India, if one were to work hard they will certainly reach their goals. Here to a great extent it is true. There are that many fewer variables. One has a degree of control over those variables."

But even that is changing. Pawar has elected to return to India early next year to work with a multinational company with offices in Bombay, "Professional it's getting to be good in India so much that I am planning to move my base to Bombay and now I can combine being close to family and a good career. Things were not so clear even four years ago and I was unable to decide with so much confidence."

Nonetheless, even as she prepares for her move, Pawar bridges the ambivalence of many Indians by keeping her feet planted in both worlds.

"Even now, the deal have would have me visiting the U.S. on work at least twice a year, which makes it that much easier for me to decide. If this was not there, and I had no option of returning to the U.S. I would think twice. I like this concept of being set across both countries."

Iyer acknowledges the discomfort some Indians experience towards their life in the United States. "There's been a flood of people on H1 visas who directly come on the job. Most of them are in companies that already have a large number of Indians working in those specific departments. As a result, they have very few or no friends in the mainstream community. They are also less inclined to know more about the country where they live." These people, Iyer says, are bound to feel they are better off in India, "because money can be a motivation for only the first few years."

Pawar adds, "I Have been looking closely at the kind of people who have returned to India for good and I notice that most are very religious Hindu conservatives who have made up their mind that this culture is harmful for their kids. They don't realize that things in India have changed vastly in the past few years. America has so much to offer if you only take the trouble to look, so to simply dismiss this country and say that one is better off in India, would be drastic."

Cooking for pleasure, eating out and visiting friends emerged as the most popular social pastimes of Indian Americans. Almost six in 10 attend an Indian social or cultural event weekly and about as many attend a party or read an Indian newspaper. Almost half shop at an Indian store or play a sport or jogging, running or biking every week.

Mallapppaa is representative of the Indian social set. He says, "Indians don't know how to entertain—they will not rent a movie or arrange some games or even discuss some topics with their guests. So everything tends to centre around cooking. They are usually good at it and so talk revolves around recipes, etc."

"The biggest past time is food. Social get-togethers are centred around food. Even if one were planning a trip to Niagara Falls, Indians will begin thinking first of what foods to carry with them. Americans tend to take a break from routine by playing some sports, going dancing or socializing, but for Indians who cook daily at home, eating out is considered a big break for both husband and wife," Mallappa says.

"The survey also paints a picture of the consumer habits of Indian Americans. More than nine in 10 Indians have credit cards and over one -third purchased a car in the past two years. Only 44 percent of Indians say that brand names are very important in their purchasing decision, whereas 51 percent rate price as being very important. Almost 82 percent purchase most of the spices at Indian grocery stores. An overwhelming majority turn to mainstream stores for their purchase of meats, general grocery, electronics and general merchandise.

The survey also found that physical ties to India in the past two years. The popular image of Indians lugging major electronic appliances on their trips home is undergoing a revision, perhaps with the wide availability of Western consumer goods in India. Clothes, followed by perfumes, were the most popular gifts Indian Americans took to friends and relatives in India. Cameras were a distinct third popular gift, followed by telephones, cigarettes and other electronics. TVs, VCRs and other popular electronics which no returning middle-class Indian could once be seen without, barely registered in the survey.

Mallapppa says he sees the changes in gift patterns in his own experience. " I came to this country four-and-a-half years ago. I have been to India each year and already see the change in the type of gift I carry home. Nowadays, electronics goods are available easily in India. There are big showrooms with several models to choose from. They also offer genuine warranties, etc. so people to buy them there. Also cost wise it adds up to the same amount."

He recalls taking an Olympus camera as gift last year to a relative. "Then, on MG Road in Bangalore I happened to see the same model for the same price." Computer companies, such as IBM and Compaq, have their own showrooms so Indians don't hanker after them either. Brand name consumer goods, like Nike, Levi's, Allen Solly, Van Heusen, are all widely available. "My shopping has turned more complicated now" says Mallappa. "I have to think hard about what my family back home can't get in the local shopping centre."

Whatever their level of assimilation into American society, Indians seem to hang tight to their culinary habits. A majority eat exclusively or mostly Indian food. By contrast, fewer than one in six normally consume non-Indian food. Understandably so, says Mallappa. "Indians like to eat only Indian food at home. We do too. When I go out I don't want surprises and I am unwilling to try a completely new dish so we usually settle for the tried and tested. A large number of Indians are vegetarians, so I can understand their reluctance to try different cuisine for fear that they may eat meat unwittingly."

Horror stories, such as one involving a lawsuit filed by an Indian graduate student against Taco Bell after being served a beef burrito instead of a been one, feed their apprehensions. Says Daga : "We are vegetarian so are less inclined to try different cuisine and prefer to eat Indian food. Whatever other cuisine we have tried like. That or Mexican has been those other family members have tried and recommended. On our own I don't think we would be willing try a new cuisine."

One third of Indians also say that they socially mix primarily with Indian friends. Almost half share friendship equally with Indians and non-Indians. Iyer says he understands the trend among recent Indians immigrants to socialize only among other Indians. Although New Jersey boasts of being a "racially diverse" state, he says, "I think its the most segregated state in the sense that there are pockets of Spanish, Indian, Polish communities, etc., which tend to live in an insulated world."

Iyer asserts that there is a difference between the early Indian immigrants and those who arrived move recently. "Back in the sixties and seventies there were no cheap calling rates to India, no emails to stay in touch with family back home. So many Indian stores to cater to their grocery needs didn't exist so they adapted their food habits accordingly. They had no choice but to assimilate quickly with the mainstream community."

However, Pawar rejects the proposition that all early Indian immigrants assimilated. "There are those who still live in a time warp. You meet people who live in posh neighbourhoods in tiny American homes. But when you enter, you'll find huge posters of their favourite Gods and Goddesses and the ambience is that of a Mylapore (Madras) suburban home complete with rangoli, fresh flower garlands, and the aroma of rice and sambar cooking in the kitchen."

Census bureau studies reveal that Indians are economically most successful ethnic community in the United States, with the highest median household income and the strongest educational background. The survey bore out that image. Nearly 45 percent of Indians traded in stocks, bonds or mutual funds in the past year. Almost nine in 10 have health insurance and three-quarters have life insurance. Indian Americans had a home ownership rate higher than the national average.

The latest date of American Indians' migration is available in American Census reports. There are a large number of Indian origin people from British Guyana, Fizi, Surinam, Trinidad etc. They have their own Sanatan and Arya Samaj temples. A sociological study of people of Indian origin and Non Resident Indian is required to be conducted on university level. This author tried to collect some material on the subject but the red tapism and dirty politics in every sphere in India does not encourage the committed scholars to undertake such uneconomic matters. Better not to say anything in this regard as this author has already faced a lot of problems and could not complete his studies on these subjects due to lack of financial support from private or public sector—whatever was possible, I am offering to my readers.

*(My Travelogue on my literary journey to USA and UK in 2003 will throw more light on this subject. Advanced sociological studies on NRIs and PIOs are required to be conducted by Indian scholars of social sciences).*

# 13

# Mexico, the Land of Sun Temples

"...........We only came to sleep, we only came to dream; It's not true, no, It's not true that we came to live on the earth, We're changed into the grass of springtime: Our hearts'll grow green again, and they'll open their petals, but our body's like a rose tree: It puts forth 'nd then withers........." Translated, so runs a song of the great Aztecs, the Indian people who ruled the central and South America for age, even before the discovery of the New World by Christopher Columbus in 1492. Next year is the 5th centenary of Santa Maria's famous voyage.

I was fortunate to have attended an International conference of philosophers and social scientists hosted by Mexico in the last week of April. It turned out to be a memorable visit as I studied the glorious primitive culture of various ethnic Indian groups viz. Mayan, Hopi and the latest migrated Gitano, known to be the real Indian Gypsies. A glance at Gitano, would reveal their resemblance to our own Punjabis, Rajasthanis and other Indians. Dark hair, black eyes, sharp features, mixed blood and other customary life styles depict their closeness to our Indian races.

It is believed that these pioneers to settle in America over 1000 years ago were primitive Asians who traversed from Siberia to Alaska along what is presently the Bering Strait. A few other scientists are of view that a land bridge existed between Siberia and Alaska over the frozen Bering Strait as a passage for Asian migrants and other nomads from India. Some Soviet scientists contend the usage of big-Diomede (Russian) and small Diomede (American) as transit islands that "abridged" the total distance from 60 nautical miles to just 25 miles. However, now all historians are convinced that the original immigrants and their descendant American Indians were long established prior to Columbus, Vespusi and other Europeans could set their foot on the sands of America.

My visit to Mexico offered me a golden chance to trace the great historic pre-Hispanic Mexican cultures, the Meso-American in particular. This trail took me to the Maya temples, the Sun Temples, the Pyramid and the court of the Moon to Tula reminiscences and the Aztec architecture. I was astonished to learn that the Red Indians do not digest referring them as Red Indians. Inspite of their glorious cultural heritage, a good number of them are backward and a family may have around 10 children on an average. I met the Gypsies of Indian origin known as Gitano in Mexico who still lead semi-nomadic life. Although Gitano have intermingled with Red Indian and Mexicans, they are proud of their Indian forefathers and regard our Indian as 'Barothan', to mean great land.

My studies convinced me of the fact that there existed direct land route from India to Mexico through Africa which in course of time submerged under the sea. A remarkable aspect of my studies pertained to the Mexican temples which resemble South Indian architecture. Similar to our Puranic concept of 33 crore deities, they too had a large number of Gods. The Red Indians and Gitano believe in 4 'yugas's the pious bird eagle (Garuda), God of Fire (Agni), God of Rain (Varuna), God of Wind (Vayu), God of Jaguar etc.

The International Conference I attended, was a profitable venue to meet and interact with numerous like minded philosophers and scholars. Among them were Ms. Lic Alicia Rodrigues, a film artiste deeply interested in cultural topics, Mr. Jose Onderon Alvardo an academician at whose Institute young scholars like Jaun Funny and Javier impressed me very much. I am indebted to the generous and pious family of Mrs. Teresa Gomez Lopez who made my stay truly a memorable visit. Her daughter Laura Mercado, son Oliver and a scholarly couple Mr. and Mrs. Lic Sergio J. Quero Oritiz and host of others deserve a whole hearted special mention of gratitude. At the Conference I was delighted to meet eminent scholar Dr. Veleril Geidt, his duo Soviet friends Dr. Svetlana Vasilieva and Inna

Chevaleva. Apart from the Conference theme, Mr. Valeril shared most of my habits and tastes, being a teetotaller and vegetarian. Friends from the land of cigars, Rolando and Gerurde were one of the best go-getters. My hunt for information about Sun temples and worshippers was aided by many of the delegates that included Mrs. Marla Jose, incidentally the wife of world renowned poet Pat Octavic and precious advice from the American scholar Mr. James. Even the managers of Hotel Fleming where I stayed were very helpful and of course our own ambassador Mr. U. C. Soni and his staff Om Dutta and Kapoor who endeavoured to make my visit fruitful. A detailed treatise in book form is in the offing.

Bhikku Cham Lal has studied the Indian culture abroad and wrote a monumental work Hindu America. I am given some descriptions from his book on Maya Culture. *"The Mayas were the most advanced people of ancient America"–Frans Blom.*

*"He who raped a virgin or took a woman by force was put to death and the some lot befell him who attacked a married woman, or who broke up a home. It is said that one of the rulers of Mayapan had his brother put to death in the most brutal way because he had raped a virgin"–Father Landa.*

The fall of the Maya Empire which took place between 580 and 680 A.D, resulting in the emigration of the last survivors of this population constituted until quite recently one of the enigmas of history. The American geologist, with Wythe Cooke, after a prolonged study of the country, thought that the mysterious disappearance of the civilization of the Mayas could be attributed to great epidemics, of malaria.

All that we know of Maya customs, beliefs, religion and philosophy has been conveyed to us by the Spanish missionary, Landa, who lived in the land of the Mayas at the time of the invasion and played his full share in burning Maya literatures destroying Maya religious customs and converting the people to Christianity. Most of the later writers on the Mayas depend on his information and interpret it in their own way. I rely on the story of the Mayas by Frans Blom, who bases it on the writings of Landa, which are in Spanish. Landa gives a graphic account of the Maya life in the 16th century. The Mayas always built their cities and towns around temples. The place of the ruler or the chief of the province, the houses of traders and the nobility were built around the temple (as is even now the case of India). These people had fine buildings of stone and mortar. Around them were built thousand of houses of farmers, soldiers and artisans. These were mostly thatched houses, but very clean and well white-washed.

*Daily Life.*–The mayas did not roam in the forests like the English and the Gauls in Europe, but they had a settled and civilised life like the Hindus. Their present day life is much the same as it was centuries ago. Both men and women were early risers (and still are). The women's first task (like our village women of two decades ago) is to attend to the grinding of maize into a fine dough of which they make fresh round cakes like our Hindu bread, exactly in the same manner and same size. They call it tortilla. Their main diet is tortilla and beans, with plenty of chillies and herbs. They have plenty of vegetables, practically all Indian vegetables. They also eat fowl, eggs and meat, but only few can afford meat. The peasants, while leaving for the field, carry a ball of maize dough, which dissolved in water makes a drink, called Posole; this is their noon meal, like our *sattu* of Barley.

*Taste for Beauty.* – The maya women are generally beautiful and they have fine aesthetic tastes. They are lovers of beauty and want to look beautiful. Their dresses are always colourful, blue, red and yellow being the favourite colours.

They have long shiny black hair, which they sometimes arrange in two beautiful braids hanging in front and sometimes twist around their heads. Like our womenfolk in many provinces and especially like those in Kullu valley, the Maya women adorn themselves with beautiful flower ribbons. They have a wonderful carriage and the way they carry big water jars on their heads, is characteristically Hindu.

*Hindu Features.*—Their skin is of a delicate brown colour and the few Mayas I met during my short stay in Mexico, liked more like Hindus than any other race. Among them I met a former judge of the Federal Court of the Republic of Mexico, who evinced much interest in India and was proud to say that his people, though now in their decline, were yet very proud or their origins, their high culture and the glories of their ancestors, the Hindus.

*Hindu Dress.*— The Maya women's dress is similar to the dress of our women. They dress in a hand woven cotton skirt, like the ones mostly used in the villages of Central and Southern Punjab, United Provinces and Rajputana. The upper part of their bodies they cover with a light cotton blouse, often embroidered with gaily coloured designs around the arm and neck openings. It is similar to the blouses we give in dozens in dowry in Punjab villages and are also used in Marwar and Gujrat.

The men's dress to-day bears traces of European influence, but in the past they used to be dressed in loin cloth. According to Landa it was "a piece of cloth one had wide, which served them as trousers and they wound it several times around their waists so that one end hung down in front and the other behind (Like our langot) and the end of this cloth were richly embroidered by the women with threads in colours and with feathers. They also wore cloaks; large and square, and tied them on their shoulders (Like our Hindu Kurta which is buttoned on the shoulders). On their feet they wore sandals made out of rope or dried deer skin and this was all they wore."

Mexican sandals, it may be noted, are exactly similar to our centuries-old sandals made in Peshawar and several other parts of India. I had some Peshawar sandals with me and Mexican people were surprised to find that they were so similar to theirs, but they were always polite to add–"But Hindu sandals are superior to ours. Look you have gold work even on your footwear! How rich must the Hindus be!"

*Hardworking Women.*— The Maya women are quite hardworking; while men go to the fields or mines, the women take care of the children, weave, make household goods of clay, embroider clothes or do other household work.

In ancient times most of the industries were in the hands of specialists and different villages were reputed for different articles and the professions were handed down by father to son for generations.

*More Hindu Customs* — The Mayas are a very clean race and they bathe and wash quite often, like the Hindus.

The men always eat in the company of males only and are served by women; such was the custom in the past and such it is to-day.

Among the highland tribes, the young women serve the meals. They serve a bowl of lukewarm water to each guest to rinse his mouth with and another bowl of water to wash hands before touching the food. (This is a Hindu custom).

*Panchayati Co-operation.*—The Mayas Preserve the ancient Panchayati co-operation system of the Hindus even to-day. Field and harvest work is done in teams, peasants helping each other in each other's fields.

*Maya Prayers.*– No task can commence without a prayer. The Mayas, as well as other Indian tribes off America, are rich in prayers meant for different gods at different times.

J. Eric Thompson translated some of these prayers with the help of Maya friends and I quote two samples:

"Here before you I stand........Three times I stand before you to worship you. Behold, my Lord, how I stand in your presence now to venerate. I stand in the presence of your holy name, lord God and in the presence, too, of the lords of the forests, who are mighty men. Forgive me my sins because I am here to worship these gods. That you may not forget me without cause, I offer these five gourds of *posole* in order that the mighty men, the lords of the forest, who live on the mountain tops and who are the true lords, and are those who pass before to clear the roads, in order that they be pleased I repeat my drink.

"Behold my lord, my good intentions in the presence of the gods. I am preparing the drink offering for my field. Forgive me. O great masters. Accept then but one cool drink of *posole* (similar to Hindu drink of barley flour called *Sattu*) that the anger that lies in your hearts toward me may be cooled."

*Prayer to Mother Earth.*–"O Goddess, my mother, be patient with me, for I am about to do as my fathers have ever done. Now I make my offering (of Copal Incense) to you that you may know that I am about to trouble your soul, but suffer it. I pray. I am about to dirty you, to destroy your beauty. I am going to work that I may obtain food. I pray you suffer no animal to attack me nor snakes to bite me. Permit not the scorpions or wasps to sting me. Bid the trees that they do not fall upon me, and suffer not the axe or knife to cut me, for with all my heart I am about to work you. "(Prayer offered before ploughing).

How beautifully innocent and childlike prayers they are!

*Love for progeny.*—Both among the Mayas and the Astecs the love for progeny was exactly Hindu-like. The birth of a child was regarded as a great gift from the gods. *It was regarded as most shameful for woman to be barren.* Father Ximenez writes that the women of Quiche people (a Maya tribe) went to the springs with their prayers for a son. At the time of childbirth a medicine women was sent for and she used to place under the mother's bed an idol of the goddess lxchel, which they said was the goddess of childbirth. The notorious missionary, Landa, who destroyed all written records and literature of the Mayas and destroyed hundreds of temples, describes this goddess as a 'devil' forgetting that his acts were nothing but devilish.

*Flattening the Head.*— Among the Mayas it was customary to flatten the heads of the children by placing them in boards and bandage, so that their heads would have odd shapes when they grew up. The Mayas painted their bodies red (sacred hindu colour) wore large ear and nose ornaments. They filed their incisor teeth, and sometimes they had them inlaid with small disks of jade or pyrites.

Landa says, "when a child was born, they immediately bathed it and when they had finished torturing(?) it by flattening its forehead and head, they brought it to the priest, so that he could tell them what future it would have and give it a name to carry during childhood, because they had the custom to re-name it in a different way before it was baptised."

This means that they were re-named after some years, just as we Hindus re-name the children after the sacred thread ceremony.

**HINDU AMERICA**

(This ceremony entitles children to be classed as "Twice born" (dwija people).

Landa adds, "The sciences which they taught were the count of the days, months and years, the feast days and the ceremonies, the administration of their sacraments, the science of evil days and times, astrology, and the remedies for evil things, their ancient history and to read and write."

*An Interesting Custom*— The Mayas had a rather interesting custom, which would be good to introduce in India in these days of economic hardship to newly married young men. The young man after his marriage stayed with his father-in law and served him for one year, when in the meanwhile he became the father of a child. Then he was given a plot of land, considered large enough to feed a family, and was allowed to build his own home and move into it.

*Great Moralists* — The Mayas were a highly moral people. They practised monogamy as a rule; few chiefs and nobles infringed this rule and married more than one wife. Moral crimes were punished very severely according to Landa.

"He who raped a virgin or took a woman by force was put to death and the same lot befell him who attacked a married woman, or a girl while she was still under her father's care, or who broke up a home. It is said that one of the rulers of Mayapan had his brother put to death in the most brutal way because he had raped a virgin."

Doesn't it sound like following Manu's Code of Laws?

What a highly civilised and just people they must be, whose ruler executed his own brother for a crime which is being repeated thousand times a day in, for instance, London alone, which boasts of being the metropolis of English civilization.

The Mayas, according to Landa, had a great fear of death, and when death did come, "they cried silently during the day and at night with loud and wailing cries, which were pitiful to hear. For many days they went most marvellously sad, and observed fast for the dead one, especially the husband for his wife."

*Rations for Next World*– Like the Hindus, the Mayas gave the dead some rations for the next world. "When dead they shrouded the corpse and filled its mouth with ground maize, together with their native money, so that, in the next life he would not lack food."

*Cremation of Bodies*–Landa says, "Rulers and people of great importance were generally cremated (the Hindu ceremony) and they placed their ashes in urns, and built a temple (Hindu Samadhi) over them, as we found that they had done at Ixmal. Now in our days we have found they gathered the ashes in the hollow statues of clay when the dead were great rulers." Landa adds that the bodies of ordinary people were buried and cremation was reserved for the high class only. (In Malabar in India this is still the custom).

But Frans Blom has discovered the ashes of thousands of people in one buried city alone, which shows that most of the dead must have been cremated; it is possible the custom of burial cropped up at later stage.

*Cremation-an Old Custom*–That cremation was the original and old Maya custom is proved by the following facts

Frans Blom who was in charge of the John Geddings Gray Memorial Expedition conducted by the Tulane University in 1928, found fragments of cremated human bones in pottery urns and pieces of white cotton cloth, clean and strong-the only well preserved cloth ever found ever found in the Maya area upto the present date.

In the cavity were set hundreds of years ago, before the conquest, great clay urns containing the cremated bones of mankind. The urns were closed their lids of clay, and sealed with resin and gums.

The explorer found cremated remains of hundreds of people in different places within an area of fifty miles. He also discovered thousands of broken pieces of pottery along with the human ashes in urns or in the graves.

He accounts for broken pottery pieces in the following manner:-

"Among many peoples, in the most separated parts of the World, there was the belief that any object made by the industry of man contains life as it is manufactured by a living being. When man dies, it is obvious that a living thing cannot follow him into the unknown, and therefore every object, which is placed in his grave, for his use in the other world, must also be dead. Hence we find that beautifully carved jade pendants have been broken, exquisite gold ornaments have been crumpled and clay vases and urns have been 'killed' by punching a small hole into their sides."

It is interesting to note that the Hindus also break earthern pots before the dead body is cremated. In my village, I still remember after twenty years' absence, there used to be a mound on the way to the cremation grounds, and this mound was called the 'place of the broken pots.'

How similar were the life and death philosophies of Hindus, the Mayas and the Astecs!

*A Refined people*– In this age of rouge, lipstick and cheap perfumes (especially the ones that a visitor is compelled to smell in London), the reader will be surprised to know that the so-called nomad Indians of ancient America and especially the Mayas had very refined tastes in the use of cosmetics. The finer arts of making up and the use of perfume, face powder and other toilet materials were well developed among them, but instead of seeking beauty in man-made beauty salons, they went to Nature's beauty parlour and used natural cosmetics as beautifying agents. By combining ingenuity with nature's bounty, the Indians were able to obtain paints and powders, perfumes and soaps, just as the Hindu women of ancient India were expert in the use of cosmetics and no modernised woman dare deny that ancient cosmetics were genuine beautifying agents and caused no injury to the face, unlike modern cosmetics. The Indians of America like the Hindus loved perfumes and incense burning since that was a part of their religious life. An American writer has said:-

"The Indian is ever a lover of the beautiful. His choice of colour harmony, his imaginative designs, his appreciation of music of oration and of the exquisite in Nature's perfumes, all indicate his aesthetic soul. He is a lover of subtle odours and has used them frequently. Being a child of Nature, he chose the delicate perfumes suggestive of the wholesomeness and freedom of the out-doors."

The Indians had many varieties of powders and perfumes made from corn (maize), flowers and different grasses and herbs.

*Mayas-Talented Artists.* — Their women, like our women in Assam and Burma, were talented weavers (and still are) and their artistic products are admired all over modern America. Among the ancient Hindus, too, it was the women's duty to weave fine textiles, since it was thought a feminine type of work: the same was the feeling in ancient America.

The Potteries of ancient Mayas are still the wonder of the world. They were lovers of music. They used several Hindu musical instruments, such as flutes and small and large wooden drums covered with deer skin on the sides.

The Mayas, the Astecs and other races of ancient America had master-builders and great architects, whose works, though in ruin, are still marvels of the present day. American modern engineers are still unable to solve the mystery as to how these palaces and temples were built without any mechanical aid. This is what an American writer has said about them in "Mexican Life".

"The pre-Columbian architects were fortunate, no doubt, in the religions they served. Astronomical observation was a sacred rite in ancient America, and immense importance was attached to the four cardinal points. This necessitated on unimpeded view of the sky and a clearly defined lay-out. A pious Astec would have found it impossible to worship in the holy slums of ancient Greece. He needed space for the practice of his religion, and geometrical order. At Delos or Delphi he would have had overcrowding and confusion."

What a refined and cultural people they must be!

The Rigveda describes *Surya* or *Savita* as the God of Gods. Hindus pray to sun God chanting various *mantras* and *slokas* from sacred books. *Gayatri mantra* is also *Savila* or *Surya mantra. Sun* worship had been very popular in Bharat and abroad through the ages. Man made temples in the name of Sun God. There are number of Sun temples in India and other countries. The Konarka, Sun Temple is known for its typical *Bhartiya* culture.

Hindus worship sun in many ways viz *Surya Pranam* (salute to Sun God), offering, *Arghya* (water) to sun and performing *Yajna* (fire worship), with the following *Mantral*:

*"Om Suryo jyotir Jyotih Suryah Swaha*
ओम सूर्यो ज्योतिर्ज्योतिः सूर्य स्वाहा
*Sun is light, light is sun, hail*
*Om Jyotih Suryah Surya Jyatih Swaha*
ओम ज्योतिः सूर्यः सूर्यो ज्यातिः स्वाहा

*Light is sun, sun is light, hail*
*Om sajur deven Savitra sarurushendrawatya*
*Suryo Vetu Swaha"*
ओम् सजुर्देवेन सवित्रा सजूरूपेन्द्रवत्या जुषाणः
सूर्यो वेतु स्वाहा।

In conjunction with God, the actuator and all powerful dawn, let the sun be auspicious to us, Hail.

The *Rigveda* glorified Sun as the source and substance of life and creator of light shining through all ethereal space. The sacred book says–

*Emerging up above the bark,*
*Towards the higher light we turn*
*We have attained the God of Gods,*
*The Sun itself, the highest light*
(Rigveda . 1 50. 10)

The concept of *Surya* as *Narayana* is an obvious corollary of a lose knit concept, source of light, upholder of Dharma and sustainer of life. Surya holds the lotus in both his hands. He is not the embodiment of the three Vedas but, is also of the very nature of the three *gunas*, *satva*, for creation of beings, *rajas* for creation of the universe and *tamas* for the deluge of in all.

When we look at the pages of Indian history , we find Sun dynasty (*Surya Vansh*) and Moon dynasty (*Chandra Vansh*) of *Bharatiya* Kings. The same type for empires of the Sun was in Mesopotamia, Egypt, and Peru, Mexico and Japan etc. The Nile cults once upon a time like Greek philosophy were very popular. From the early times, the Sun was worshipped in Egypt, but when about five thousand years ago, the whole land became united under the pharaohs, the Sun god assumed to glorious a Sovereignty that it is doubtful whether man's relationship with the Star was ever more exalted than there in the Nile valley. Finally the Sun God was pharaoh and through all, Egyptian history the Sun God made the great journey by boat. The Egyptians gave many titles and meanings to Sun God. Earlier Ramezess the emperor of Egypt had the title of Rama, the son of Darsharatha like Thailand kings. They were all Sun worshippers

People of Iran and Iraq worshipped the Sun God and fire God in their own way. Germans and Russians had number of deities and nature-Gods and they used to worship during the period of paganism and Vedic philosophy, which were prevalent throughout the world.

If we look at the world map, we find many Sun Temples in the tropic of cancer right from Konarka to Mexico. The idol of Sun God having chariot of horses or in other human form can be seen in Indian Sun Temples. The mythology of China depicts that there were ten Suns in the time of Emperor Yao (2357-2255 BC), which burnt up grass and trees causing confusion and death on earth. The Lord Archer shot to death nine crows and thus nine suns vanished and the present remains. Japanese were also sun worshippers before the Buddhism entered in their country. The highest temple in the world is in Mexico, perhaps rebuilt in 500-600 A.D. The place is known as Teotihuacan, which seems to have been derived from a Sanskrit word *Jyoti-wahan or Jyoti-sthan (*The carrier or the land of light. The height of this temple is 210 feet but is no idol of sun like many other temples. It has a large *Vedi* (Altar) where *Yajna* used to be performed and the people from various parts of South America would come there and sacrifice their *Ahutis*. In *Ramayana* and *Mahabharata*, there are references of *Patal Lok* and its rich culture, which was carried by Aryan and Pagan communities to various countries of the world.

Unfortunately, the sun worship in Mexico turned to the sacrifice of man in the name of Sun God. Infact, sacrifice of animals to please God and deities had become very common in India and abroad for many decades. Priest used to play an important role and in many places he used to be an emperor or a king. The temples were cultural centres where various modes of Art developed. Sun God in the Aztec manuscripts, the Codex Borgia had Claws that reached hungrily for human hearts. In the name of, these hungry Gods, human sacrifices started as dictated by priests. The official history of Mexico proves that the Aryans (Hindus) were the first to reach this continent. They imported their Gods to South America. Peru is another imported place known for sun temples. The meaning of Peru in old Sanskrit is the "land of Sun ". According to Bhikkhu Chaman Lal and other Indologists, it appears that Vamana Vishnu drove the *Mayas* (Danavas) under the leadership of Bali with their counterparts

Daityas and Nagas, out of India. Bali, Daitya Monarch reached *Patala* (*Atala*) or America about twelve thousand years before Christ. With the progeny of Maya, Asuras, and Nagas reached there and colonized Atala and built their beautiful cities having magnificent places, gardens, temples and roads. The *Puranas* also say the same story. Many cities were known by the names of chief *Asuras* or *Mayas*, the descendants *Maya Danava* the Monarch of Atala continent. Thus the name *Maya*, Mexico, Meshika or Mayarastra became famous and the history of *Mayas* (*Danavas*) can be seen in the light of *Ramayana, Mahabharata* and *Puranas*. It is evident from the *Mahabharata* and *Puranas*, that *Mayas* were the great builders and architects whose wonderful palaces and temples tell still, their glory in Mexico, Being the great architects, they were also mighty navigators and ship builders.

Eminent Anthropologist-poet Mrs. Jacquetta Hawkeyus in her book "*Man and the Sun*" describes the importance of sun worship all over the world through the ages. She says that Sun is the father of mankind, something more than analogy, for it is the energy in its rays that has made possible the generation and development of sun worship in Zoroastrianism and Mithraism, and shows how solar symbolism has permeated both religions and secular imagery during the Christian era. Today, in a new but perhaps no less ardent form, sun-worship is to be seen on the summer beaches of the western world. Mitra or Mihir in Iran God is also Sun God and Sunday seems to have been named after sun worship

In this paper, we are not going into the details of Sun temples of the world and the Sun worship which has been performed all over the world, what we mean just to put glimpses if the same as studied by various social scientists and scholars. Our study starts from India and leads to Mexico through Royal dynasty of Egypt, Iran, Iraq, Germany, Great Britain and other European countries where Sun worship was prevalent in the form of paganism or polytheism before any other religion emerged in the world.

The oldest scripture in the world, the Rig-Veda is full of hymen to God in nature form like *Agni Devata (fire God), Vayu Devata (Wind God) Varun Devata (Water God)* etc. Similarly in India almost many tribes worship nature and thousands of deities which are very close to ancient Hinduism and Paganism.

Many historians have proved the theory of Aryan's invasion to Bharat or Aryavarta null and void now. In fact, there was migration carried Indian to Mauritius, Surinam, Fiji, Trinidad and other countries where the old Indian culture is still alive. Their customs remain almost the same and they speak Hindi, Marathi, Tamil and other Indian languages besides the languages of their respective countries. Their forefathers carried with them *Hanuman Chalisa, Gita and Ramayana.* This is how they survived their culture and traditions. Another ancient group of travellers known as Roma, the Indian Gypsies in Europe and America follow the Bhartiya traditions in many respects even today.

Now some facts about the relevance of *Ramayana* in the context of sun worship and Sun dynasty as Rama was also *Suryavanshi* (from Sun dynasty). The *Ramayana* is relevant not only in India but it has its impact all over the world. The Ramayana has become the lyric of the men of Asia from Sideria to Bali of Indonesia....In Bali, 80% people follow Hinduism and have the tradition of narrating *Ramayana* through performing art of classical ballet. They also worship sun in their own way. During the period of A.D 251, Ramayana was translated into Chinese in the form of jatak tales by K' ang-Seng-hui. In 16th Century, a classic Chinese Novel entitled "*His-yu-chi* (Monkey Hanuman) Appeared and became very popular. In the 6th Century, the Sinhalese poet, King Kumaradasa composed the Janaki Harana in Sanskrit and later on, C. Don Bastean translated *Ramayana* in Sinhalese. A thorough research is required to find Sun dynasty and sun worship prevalent in these countries through various versions of Ramayana.

To end with a word about the Bhartiya culture which is composite in nature and is based on non-violence, universal brotherhood (Vasudhaiva Kutumbakam), peaceful co-existence and Manava Dharma i.e,. the religion of humanity and way of life for mankind.

**References**

*(For more details read the Rigveda and other Vedic scriptures, Man and the Sun: Jacquetta Hawkes, London, The Chesset Press, 1962, Surya Mandiron ki khoj Mein: Dr. Shyam Singh Shashi,*

*Pustakayan Delhi 1993, Roma-The Gypsy World: Dr. S.S. Shashi, Sandeep Publications, Delhi 1990, and other books available in Mexico Anthropoligical libraries.)*

# 14

# The Nomads of the World

The growing interest in research among nomadic peoples during the last few years at an international level is derived mainly from practical demands and as a consequence of the integration of nomadic peoples into the contemporary economic, political and social development of many Asian and African countries, especially those in arid zones. During the past, mainly historians, ethnologists, geographers and philologists were engaged in research into different aspects of the life of nomads, but of recent years they have been joined increasingly by economists, sociologists, psychologists, medical specialists and representatives of various other natural and technical sciences. These experts are searching by means of complex investigations for ways of integrating the nomads into the modern society of their respective countries. These activities frequently take place under the guidance and with the financial support of international organisations such as UNESCO, WHO FAO, ILO and other specialised institutes for research into nomadism have been founded in a number of countries.

As a result of this development the literature on nomadism and associated problems has increased considerably. Not only are there many monographs based on fieldwork but there are also many papers dealing with theoretical aspects of nomadism.

I am quoting here in composite manner from researches conducted on nomads of various countries by eminent scholars viz., Lother Stein, Martha Brill Olcot, Benjamin, Sebastian Orlove, Daniel A. Bradburd and Brian Spooner.

*Social Differentiation*: The nomads occupy a special position in the development of society in so far as social differentiation began to develop very early—earlier than this was possible with tillers of the soil. There are two reasons for this: first livestock very early became private property and secondly, extensive livestock breeding permitted a rapid accumulation of wealth much more rapid then in the case of extensive tillage.

The great Chinese wall, for instance, is a reminder of the constant threat posed by the inner Asiatic nomadic peoples. Such tremendous efforts in the making of the wall were justified only if they were to preserve even greater values. On the other hand however, it was the Mongols who, after their conquest of China, were to set up such an imposing system of communications and to achieve such wonders in organisation, both in a symbiosis of their own and the Chinese economy and in creating an efficient military and state apparatus.

The pastoral nomad's economy represents a new form of specialisation of production which contrasts with what might be called "Occupational forms" such as those of gatherers and hunters, fishermen and -to a certain extent—extensive tillers of the soil. The cultural and historical importance of nomadism lies in the fact that it enabled new regions in deserts, steppes and mountain areas to be opened up for occupation. It also promoted facilities for far-reaching communication and thereby exchange of goods. One of the most characteristic features of nomadism is the ability of its socioeconomic conditions.

The number of Bedouins who lead a nomadic life has been gradually diminishing for many years. They are changing more and more to occupation other than animal husbandry and are finding new ways of subsistence in the fast developing oil industry where they preferably work as truck drivers, watchmen, unskilled workers, etc. Moreover, they engage in the retail, entrepot trade and in border areas—in smuggling goods. In tourist centres they act as guides and service employees. But seen proportionally, the majority find employment in agriculture or horticulture and in the armed forces of certain Arab countries, for instance in the "Bedouin Legion" of the Hashemite Kingdom of Jordan and in the "white Legion" of the kingdom of Saudi-Arabia, it is well known that these armies strongly support their respective regimes. For widening professional opportunities for former nomads, the improvement and extension of the schooling system and vocational training are of great importance, a special role in this respect is played by adult education.

Kazakhstan, the Kazakh S. S. R., is the northernmost part of Central Asia. Until the late eighteenth and early nineteenth centuries it was an area populated nearly exclusively by the Kazakhs, a group of Turkic pastoral nomads. For analytic purposes it is useful to conceive of Kazashstan as composed of distinct regions: the north-steppe land with arable soil and some forest lands, suitable for livestock breeding and grain production, the centre-semi-desert and desert, marginal pasture lands during periods of adequate rainfall, and the south-desert lands and a small mountainous region which, because of the presence of the Amu Darya and Syr Darya rivers and their tributaries, was capable in many places of supporting irrigated agriculture or free grazing of livestock. The northern region was composed of the northern half of the Uralsk, Turgai, Akmolinsk and Semipalatinsk Oblasts, the central region comprised the southern portion of the aforementioned Oblasts, and the Southern region encompassed the Oblasts of Syr Darya and Semirechye. The type of nomadic economy varied by region, with cattle and horses being more abundant in the north, and sheep, goats and camels found in larger numbers in the south.

During the first thirty years of colonial rule the sedentarization of the Kazakh nomads was seen as desirable but was not a priority of the Russian government. Although the nomadic economy was considered to be wasteful, there was really no additional demand for the steppe land. There were some Russian settlements, particularly in the North near the forts on the Orenburg line, but they were numerically rather insignificant, and the increase in settlement was a gradual one because the restrictive Russian policy on internal migration combined with the harsh conditions of travel made it difficult for peasants to move from European Russia to the steppe.

The Kazakhs were mixed livestock breeders. They drove herds composed mainly of sheep and goats, but which included small numbers of horses, camels, and horned cattle. Even in the 18th century, livestock breeding was never the exclusive occupation of the Kazakhs. The distinctive feature of the nomadic economy was that agriculture and animal husbandry were undifferentiated, i.e., the sowing of grain was considered subsidiary to livestock breeding, done only to provide feed for the livestock, engaged in only part of the year and usually only by part of the population. The Kazakhs continued to migrate even at the same time that they were seeding their fields, and resumed a grand migration after the harvest. Agriculture was most strongly in evidence in the southern regions of Kazakhstan, along the banks of the Syr Sarya. In some of these areas agricultural oases communities had existed since antiquity.

The Kazakh lifestyle was a relatively simple one. Most customs revolved around the preservation of the family and the family's herds. Every nomadic community was largely self-sufficient and self-governing. Although constantly on the move, they had little contact with the world beyond the steppe and were even relatively isolated from other Kazakhs except at occasional gatherings for feast days or weddings. The universe of the eighteenth century Kazakh was a closely defined one. Pastoral livestock breeding promoted economic self-regulating and to enable the Kazakhs to maintain the continuing sense of history and common purpose.

According to Rustam Pourzal during the past 2-3 decades or so, anthropologists have paid increasing attention to the nomadic forms of adaptation in the middle East. In particular, a certain amount of ethnographic work has appeared in Iranian pastoral nomads in the southern Zagros range, including the tribes of the powerful Khamseh and Qashofai confederacies.

The precursor of these studies, Barth's account of the Basseri, while inspiring other research, has dominated anthropological thinking on pastoralism in the Iranian area. The Basseri tribe of the Khamseh confederacy has come to be regarded to some extent as the prototype Iranian and even other southwest Asian mountain nomads. Partly due to the lack of comparably detailed knowledge of other groups, the Basseri form of political organization in particular has emerged in the literature as a theme of which others, are variants. Consequently, tribes defined by allegiance to a hierarchy of chiefs and sub-chiefs who dare challenge the state have been vaguely thought to Characterize at least all nomads of Fars, the home province of the Basseri. This notion is incorrect, for while the Khamseh and Qashqai tribes are certainly dominant among

Fars' half-million pastoral nomads, there are other nomads in the area without chiefs.

Several new studies have been published in the last few years on Andean populations which live at elevations about 4200m above sea level of alpacas and Ilamas.

The Instituto de Estudios Peruanos has been publishing several series of monographs and edited works in the social sciences, and the Institutito de Pastoral Andina works with the Catholic church in the southern highlands to develop social action programs among peasant populations. Some authors, such as Nachtigall, only present day practices and indicate continuities with pre-columbian traditions. Others, such as Gow and Gow, present the coherence of the world view and cosmogony of the herders, while still others, such as Flores and Aranguren Paz, stress more strongly the correspondences which exist between ceremonial objects and rituals on the one hand and the puna ecology and the annual cycles of the herders on the other, Flores and Palacios Rios also present a correspondence between ritual aspects of culture and native systems of classification, showing that the herders are very competent and perceptive as taxonomists.

The ritual and symbolic aspects of culture might have two functions. Either they are simply another element in the structure and coherent way of life of the herders or they ideologically reinforce the materia adaptation. This relation among the four elements is demonstrated not only by their functional integration but also by their chronological persistence: the authors share a tendency to find historical continuities. Some of these continuities are indeed notable. The high puna, for instance is the ecological zone where the native languages and certain techniques (weaving for instance) have maintained themselves with the greatest vigour. The Andean herding pattern also can be located well within the pattern of verticality described by Murra. One can also notice the continuity of other elements, as miller shows in an excellent discussion of the practices of camelid sacrifice in the southern Peruvian highlands. Other authors nonetheless go beyond the concrete details of these cases to suggest that continuities always have priority over changes. The continuities in ritual, for instance, can be shown in many cases, but there are other ceremonies which have not continued. More work like that of wing is needed to establish the clear relations between early and contemporary herding, although hear work in Allpanchis 8 suggests certain lines of continuity. It is worth remembering that it is very difficult to establish continuities in aspects of social organization (we do not know, for instance, whether the distribution of herds among households was at one time more egalitarian than it is currently) * while one can—and indeed must examine the settlement of nomads as a problem of settlement and culture change, one must do this with the understanding that settlement (under capitalist conditions) is but a piece of a much larger historical process. In sum, accurate analysis of the settlement problem ultimately requires adequate theoretical reformations of the context in which it occurs.

Reviewing the book '*The Kirghiz and Wakhi of Afghanistan*' authored by M. Nazif Mohib Shahrani, Brain Spooner says —

"The Great Pamir and the Little Pamir are the flat valleys of the Pamir and Sarhad rivers, tributaries of the oxus, which together form the narrow Wakhan corridor and its eastern extension of Afghan territory, stretching across to China, sandwiched between soviet Tajikistan and Pakistan. The valleys average 4,000 metres in altitude and are enclosed by mountains rising at their highest to almost 7,000 metres. Passage into Soviet and Chinese territory, though difficult, is easier than into Pakistan. The route sown into the centre of Badakshan, the northeastern province of Afghanistan, is also difficult and winter travel is preferred whin it is possible to march along the frozen river. Despite the difficulty of the routes trade links through this territory have been important throughout the historical period.

The Kirghiz had only used the Pamirs for summer grazing, or for temporary refuges at other seasons, until after 1949 the combination of the internal policies and closed frontiers of soviet Russia and Communist China led some of them to choose Afghanistan and to develop an annual grazing cycle and pattern of resource use by which they could maintain the year.

It is interesting that despite the general difficulty of the environment and the great extremes of temperature, this niche appears to be less vulnerable to drought than other arid and semi-arid pastoral areas, since the Kirghiz did not suffer from drought in the early 1970's they are, however, highly vulnerable to unusually heavy shows and spells of extreme cold.

Like most other nomadic pastoralists the Kirghiz are organised in a standard segmentary tribal system. Descent rather than residence is the basis for political unity, but there is the usual compromise between descent group and other factors in meeting the labour and logistical needs of the pastoral technology and in the formation of herding groups. The Kirghiz camps are mostly cooperative herding groups. Where they differ from most other nomads is in being some times also local corporate pasture-owning groups.

According to the old studies, they developed private ownership of winter pasture, and have become widely differentiated in wealth and authority. Summer is the time of plenty and summer grazing is public or is owned corporately by kinship groups, the camps are larger and people work together in milking, shearing, felt-making and collecting fodder for the winter. In winter the camps are smaller and more widely distributed. However, while total animal holdings have not changed significantly many households no longer own animals (less than one third of the household units now own sheep and goats and only just over two thirds own yaks). Meanwhile a paramount Khan has emerged, who is the wealthiest man in the community (with 16,000 sheep and goats and 700 yaks). Families without animals either work for the wealthy (who also hire some Wakhi) or enter into arrangements whereby they shepherd and use the products of some of their animals. A great deal of time is also taken up in trading trips down the river corridor to the nearest market centre, khandud. The author makes no association between this factor and the concentration of animal ownership. The point of interest here is that unlike comparable situations where loss of animals has led to impoverishment and sedentarisation the Kirthiz have maintained their internal organisation has ensured that loss of animals has not led to impoverishment. Despite individualisation of rights to grazing, which might suggest the opposite trend, the tribe has become the unit of production in a way that is rare in the middle East though it may be familiar to Africanists.

This description is fascination for anyone interested in Central Asia, nomads or adaptation to extreme environments. It is unfortunate, however, that the explanatory aspects of the writing are not so successful. There are competent sections on the political aspects of Kirghiz adaptation and on the inadequacy of the familiar nomad-farmer analytical dichotomy which is implied in other discussions of middle East pastoralism. But the data are largely behavioural and the reader gains little insight into the most interesting aspects of the process whereby pasture became individualised and part if the population lost their animals without apparently changing their identity. Similarly, there is sufficient reference to the literature on other nomadic populations but little is made of the significance of the Kirghiz situation in that context. If recent reports are true that they have moved across the border into Pakistan, these Kirghiz are encapsulated historically between the Chinese revolution and the Russian invasion of Afghanistan and such an adaptation may never recur in the Pamirs.

As narrated earlier, besides pastoral, trader, warrior and other kinds of nomads there are begging clans who have talents of singing, dancing, acting acrobatics and fortune telling. Here are some facts about Indian nomads : Prof. Ram Krishna Kaushik has studied the nomad beggars and has collected a very interesting account of them. According to him, the beggars are found all over the world. The orbit of their beat is limited to a few square miles. They roam about begging and then come back to their homes. A beggar does not require nomadism to facilitate begging. As all nomads are not beggars, similarly all beggars are not nomads. It will be more correct to assume that when some of the traditional nomads found their food-gathering sources dried up, due to some reason or the other, they took to begging as an alternative means of sustenance. It may also be possible that certain types or groups of nomads, on getting tired of their wander lust, wanted to stay and settle down and till they or their children learnt an avocation, would have taken to begging as a stop-gap.

Begging is the easiest of all professions, if a profession it can be called. In countries like India, Burma and Thailand begging had attained a semi-religious and dignified status, practised by astelus and *sanyasis in orange rodes. Sanyasis or* monks are those who have renounced the world to lead a life of self-abnegation. A housewife would think twice before sending back a monk or a *sanyasi* disappointed, particularly when he turns up at meal time

Music is a powerful aid to beggary. The musician draws up a few melodious notes either upon his stringed instrument or with his own voice and attracts listeners' sympathies, if not admiration. For this purpose, he chooses religious themes and mythological subjects, for swaying the sentiments of the women folk.

Beggars in India keep wandering not only from district to district but even from State to State. Two sects of religious mendicants, known as Ramaswami and Rangaswami and who are reputed to have migrated from South India to spread the cult of Shri Ramanuja in various parts of the country, have stayed back in Rajasthan, Punjab, Madhya Pradesh and small pores of miles with the aid of singing devotional songs. They keep an account of the genealogies of respectable citizens, mostly the farmers and businessmen and collect fixed doles from the so-called disciples from year to year. They wear the religious symbols of Patron saint on their fore-heads and use small stringed instruments for heightening the effect of their melodious vocal tunes. They are regarded by those whom they visit as vererable persons, possessing spiritual attainments.

## The Karwals

The Karwals are nomadic beggars of Bihar and Uttar Pradesh. Their beat covers extensive areas, embracing hundreds of miles. They go about in small bands pursuing a systematic and organised begging. They carry their portable tents on pack bullock and ponies and stay at convenient lengths of distances to avoid fatigue and at the same time to make the best of their occupation. They fix their tents in shady mango-groves or the place suited to them.

The karwals have rigid system of control. The head of a gang is invariably a middle aged energetic and assertive woman. Neither her husband nor son has any control over the gang. She is called a *mukhiya. Mukhiya-ship* descends not to sons and daughters but to the eldest daughter-in law of the ex-mukhiya.

A *mukhiya* controls the movements of the gang, plans the next camps, punishes indiscipline and settles all social disputes of the gang. They are treated by the Bihar State Government as a criminal tribe. Their movements are closely watched.

*Gulgulias* are also nomadic beggars mostly found in the State of Bihar, though they do not keep an organised gang like the Karwals.

The Singiwalas are beggar nomads who move in small groups. They use a conical tube made of horn, the tappered end of which is pierced by a hole. They also carry a small, long iron instrument with a sharp cutting edge. When called upon to cure a patient they select the place of ailment where they incise small cuts with the instrument . Placing the horn on the spot they suck through the hole with their mouth so hard that impure blood woozing from the cuts collects in their mouth which they spit out. They carry out this sucking operation to a number of times. After this they remove the horn, rub some turmeric powder on the spot. This is done for curing muscular pains. They also live by snake-charming and curing snake-bites. They move in smaller groups of less than ten.

*Dheas sell* glass bottles and tumblers. Their chief profession is to make good windows for the use of the farmers. They are found in North Western India, in Punjab, Rajasthan and even Jammu and Kashmir States. They carry their belongings on donkeys, keep pet dogs, are too lazy to exert and prefer to starve, when begging fails to earn any earnings.

*Singhikats* are nomadic beggars of North Western India, totally devoid of ambition, scantily clothed and poorly fed. They collect rags, pieces of cast off paper and profess to be quack-doctors, possessing charms, talismans and drugs.

*Jogis* are inter-State vagabonds, like beggars. Some of them are also called Bengalies, though they do not have traditions of ever having come from Bengal. They always are found wandering and do not like to be settled.

*Mundunttas* and *Kelas* belong to the tribes of acrobats, earning their livelihood by giving performances of rope-dances in villages. They are few in numbers and can be found in Ganjam District, around Cuttack in Orissa State.

Other beggar tribes like Adi Pandavas of Madras State and Helvas and Bacchiwalis lead nomadic life. They exercise rights to secure alms from certain specified communities as a relic of a lost grant or remuneration for services in days of yore, now fallen in disuse. Thus, a right once exercised with pride has now degenerated into begging and is disgracefully continued. Madaris (Andhra Pradesh) Darashas, Hareas, Bhopas, Durga Murgis (Andhra Pradesh) claim divine blessings, sanctions and commissions for pursuing the usual discredited beggar's profession.

In Karnatka and Andhra Pradesh, Budgajangam is a begger community who earn their livelihood by singing devotional songs. Similarly there are similar groups of artists known as Chennadas, Dombidasara Dombara, Handi Jogi, Dombaru, Gondhali (fortune teller) and Helava. Now they have formed their association and want reservation in education and employment to get rid of begging tradition.

## The Welfare Programmes

During the Five Year Plans, measures, taken up for the welfare of nomadic and semi-nomadic groups, largely aimed at their rehabilitation and to integrate them with the rest of the society. These groups, being poor and unable to educate their children, Ashram schools have been set-up for them and these have proved to be quite useful. Scholarships, stipends and other educational aids are provided to help and encourage their children to attend the school and pursue their studies. Boarding grants and hostels facilities are also provided. Peripatetic schools have been started for the children of nomads. This scheme has met with little success, though correct assessment has yet to be made.

*(Read my papers on Sociology of nomads and Encyclopedia of Social Sciences and Humanities (50 Vol), Encycledia of Indian Tribes (10 Vol) Encyclopedia Indica (150 Vol) edited by me and published by Anmol publishers, Delhi for further study).*

# 15

# Nehru—The Lover of Nomads

When we remember the dynamic personality of Jawaharlal Nehru and his varied interests in different subjects, we recall his own words because we cannot put them better. He said: "If any people chose to think of me then I should like them to say this was the man who with all his mind and heart loved India and the Indian people. And they in turn were indulgent to him and gave him their love most abundantly and extravagantly." These words depict how Nehru loved his people and how he got abundant love from them.

His humanitarian thinking, indomitable courage, wisdom administrative ability, statesmanship and, above all, the charm of his magnetic personality have had a deep impact on our social, political and economic structures which he shaped in its formative years. He had unparalleled sincerity towards the people in general and weaker sections in particular. Though he had reached the Himalayan heights in every sphere of life, Panditji was the commonest among the commons and was always approachable to the common man.

Nehru was a great friend of tribals, and an ardent lover of their art and culture. His interest in the tribal people transcended the political, cultural and economic affinities of the tribals with the rest of the community. He regarded them as the repositories of original human culture of India. Their way of life to a great extent was still not adulterated to tribal people. Every year, he would spare some time from busy schedule to be with tribal folks coming from the distant tribal belts for the Republic Day celebrations in Delhi. Hew would sing and dance with them and forget for a moment the cares of a prime Minister. Panditji was very critical about the vices that were replacing the virtues of the tribal social life in the name of civilization. He found the folk songs and dances more inspiring than the cinema and theatre. To him the open hostility of the tribal society seemed much better than the evil practices prevailing in the urban society.

He once said: "They are a virile people. I approach this simple folk in a spirit of comradeship and not like someone aloof who had come to look at them, examine them, weigh them or try and make them conform to another way of life".

He opposed the idea of keeping tribals as a separate class or group. Nehru had great admiration for tribal way of life. He liked their innocent behaviour, clean heart and straight forwardness. He once remarked: "they are an extremely disciplined people, often much more democratic than most others in India, without a constitution and the rest, they function democratically and carry out the decisions made by their elders or their own representatives almost without exception. Above all, they are a people who sing and dance and try to enjoy life; not people who sit in stock exchanges and shout at each other and call that civilization. I would prefer any day to be a nomad in the hills to being a member of stock exchanges or being made to sit there and listen to those frightfully ugly noises. Is that the civilization we want the tribal people to have? I hope not. I am quite sure that ultimately the civilization of the tribal folk, of song and dance, will last when stock exchanges have ceased to exist in this country and other countries".

Nehru had a poetic heart and was ardent lover of nature. He liked hills, rivers, trees and natural environment for which he desired to be a nomad and live among nomadic communities. It was Nehru, who helped the nomadic people, particularly Gadia Lohar of Rajasthan and Gujjars of Kashmir and Himachal Pradesh, in rehabilitation. But this adjustment was not based on damaging the tribal or nomadic culture. His approach was different from theoretical anthropologies.

As earlier stated I had the opportunity to work among nomads of the Himalayas, particularly Gaddis and Gujjars of Himachal Pradesh. Both the communities are nomadic and semi-nomadic. I have interviewed a large number of Gaddis, Gujjars and other nomads of the Himalayas from time to time while working in Ashok Ashram, Kalsi, Dehra Dun, with Pt. Dharm Dev Shastri. I had privilege of attending the Gujjar nomadic tribal conference addressed by Pt. Jawaharlal Nehru held at Choharpur in Dehra Dun district.

Nehru was also interested in Banjaras and Indian Roma Gypsies who left India over 1, 000 years ago and still wandered from place to place in Europe and America. I had the opportunity to study these people in depth and found the educated Roma were aware that both Jawaharlal Nehru and Indira Gandhi had been very sympathetic to them. The groups of Roma Gypsies met Nehruji and Indira Gandhi whenever they came to India.

Nehru as Prime Minister was directly concerned with the tribal policy and decision-making about the tribal problems. In his speeches and writings he always laid stress that the approach to the tribal people should be one of learning from them and, having learnt, of trying to help and co-operate with them.

In his foreword to the second edition of Verrier Elwin's *Philosophy for NEFA*, Nehru said: It between these two extreme positions that we have to function. Development in various ways there has to be, such as communications, medical facilities, education and better agriculture. These avenues of development should, however, be pursued within the broad framework of the following five fundamental principles:

1. People should develop along the lines of their own genius and we should avoid imposing anything on them. We should try to encourage in every way their own traditional arts and culture.
2. Tribal rights in land and forests should be respected.
3. We should try to train and build up a team of their own people to do the work of administration and development. Some technical personnel from outside will, no doubt, be needed, especially in the beginning. But we should avoid introducing to many outsiders into tribal territory.

*(For further details my book entitled 'Nehru and the Tribals' is referred).*

# 16

# Hoons and Shakas in India and Hungary

Of late, I added two more nomadic clans—Hoons or Hoonas and Shakas in my research projects. In 2004, I was invited by World Hungarian Congress to present my paper on them. I am still working on them. Here is a Summary reproduced with courtesy from a Hungarian Research Journal 'TVRAN' of June 2004, Budapest, XXIIV. VI Edition about my paper—

"The author is Chairman, Research Foundation International and Visiting University Professor (Sociology), India's National Awardee-PADMA SHREE in Social Sciences and Literature.

His most important publications to this subject;

1. "Dr. S.S. Shashi"/=*The Shepherds of India*, ( including Hoons) Sandeep Prakashan, Delhi, 1978, 134, Old/in English.

2. "Dr. S.S. Shashi" *Nehru and the Tribals*, Concept Publications Pvt. Ltd., Delhi, 1989, 1998 Old/in English.

3. "Dr. S.S. Shashi"/=Himachal-Nature's Peaceful Paradise, Delhi Publishers, 1971,310 Old/in English.

4. "Dr. S.S. Shashi"/=*Roma The Gipsy World*, Sandeep Prakashan, Delhi, 1990,230 in English.

5. Dr. S.S. Shashi/ = *Encyclopaedia of Indian Tribes*, Vol. 6 Himachal pradesh and Northern Highland, Anmol Publications, Delhi, 1994,231 in English.

**Short abstract of the paper**

India is a land of multi-racial, multi-religious and multi-linguistic country. People from various parts of the world had been migrating to India from time to time and settled here.

Since there is a strong caste and gotra (lineage) system in the country, they adopted local traditions and customs in course of time. Hinduism is not a religion as such but a way of life and hence, many hoons and shakas are known as *Gotras* among Gujjars, Jats, Yadavas, shepherds and other Kshatriya communities including Shakadwip Brahmins. Similarly, Indians also migrated from their motherland to various parts of the world from time to time and settled there, Roma, NRIs, PIOs are the living example of the history of migration.

This author has written about these communities in his socio anthropological works, viz., *Shepherds of India, Nomads of the Himalayas* and a monumental encyclopaedic work on Indian Tribes etc.

Last year, the author stayed in USA and UK for about two months and studied the socio-cultural change in Indian communities living in various cities of America and England and found many similarities in Hungarian and Indian communities. It is an established fact that the Hoons are Hungarians who had been good horse riders and the marshal people.

Excerpts from my paper presented in the World Hungarian Conference held in Budapest in 3rd June, 2004 are as under :—

To begin with the subject in detail, we find references in Sanskrit literature. Here is a Sloka from the great poet Kalidasa's epic "*Raghuvansa*".

तत्र हूणावरोधानां भर्तृषु व्यक्तविक्रम।<br>
कपोलपाटलदेशि बभूव रघुचेष्टितम्।।68।।

Tatra Hunavarodhanam bhartrsu vyaktavikram.<br>
Kapolapataladesi badhuva Raghuchestitam ||68 ||

Kalidasa says that the Hoons reside in Oxus Valley. They were made to feel the effect of power and cheeks of their wives turned red at Raghu's exploits. Atreyi Biswas has analysed Raghu's victory in his book "*The political History of Hunas in India*".

*Resources: Agni Purana, Raghuvansha, Mahadharata, James Tod, Rose H.A, Metcalf Smith, Vincent, Russel, S.C. Roychowdhry. Viswas Atrey, Romila Thapar, R.S. Kushwaga, D.C. Circar, EvaAradi. A. S. O. I. P. A. Dr. Shashi.*

The Hara Hunas of the "*Mahabharata*" and *Brahat Samhita* and the Hunas of Kalidasa refer to the Huns in the Oxus Valley and not to the Hunas of Bharat or India proper. The Huns who invaded India were the white Huns who also ought with the kings of Persia. In Course of time, Sveta or white adjective of the Hun tribe was dropped and they were known as Huna only.

**The Shakas**—According to many Indian Historians, Shakas were the ex-communicated Kshatriyas from India. Though Greek writers have written about them but hardly anything about their roman culture. The Hindu scriptures describes that Bharat was land of rivers and mountains. Shaka in Sanskrit means teak trees. Matsya Purana says that there was a Shaka mountain in the Shakadwipa, and hence name of this land. In Sanskrit dictionary 'Shaka' means a tree, an island, a kshatriya, a country and a king/ satya Sharva, Shakas in India" p. 3.

In Mahabharata, the Kshiroda Sagar or the Caspian sea was encircled in parts by the Shakavipa.

शाकद्वीपं च वक्ष्यामि यथावदिह पार्थिव।
क्षीरोदो भरश्रेष्ठं येन संपोरे वारितः॥

Bhishma Parva, 12 : 8-9.

There were different kingdoms of Shakas in Shakadwipa. A small band of the shakas inhabited a portion of the Indus region at the time of Duryodhana. The Shaka hordes came to these regions from time to time and the whole region was known as Indo-Scythia or the region of Sindhu Shakas.

Shaka is a *gotra* like Hun among nomadic communities, and Kshatriya castes in India. There had been migration from East to West and vice versa. Kushan dynasty claimed to be the descendants of Kusha, the son of Rama. They were from Sun dynasty and became Buddhist over a period of time.

It has been established that in ancient times, the effect of an union between the different castes was ordinarily the formation of a new caste. For instance the Brahmana Hraishchandra, surnamed Rohilladhi, had two wives, a Brahman and a kshatriya. His children by both were called Pratihara, but the sons of the former were

Brahmana Pratiharas and those of the latter Kshatriya Pratiharas. And the Pratiharas, inspite of their Gurjar origin, became a rajput clan, one of the four Agnikulas.

Prof. Bhandarkar's research again throws light on complex caste system in the context of Huns and Shakas in India. He illustrates the first-named process by some very interesting historical facts, called from all parts of India. He cites the recently discovered inscription at Besnagar in Gwalior for an instance of a Greek Ambassador, a Yavana-duta, with the Greek name of Heliodorus, erecting a Garuda column to Vasudeva, god of gods, not as mere compliment but because he was a Bhagavata of the god and therefore, fairly to be described as a Vaishnava and a Hindu. The Yavana men however, were oftner Buddhist the Hindus.

Sometimes, western scholars don't distinguish between race and castes system in India. In fact, it is difficult to find difference among two or more similar communities who follow the same profession but belong to different *gotras*. For example, the Banjara, a nomadic community is included in the list of scheduled tribe in Andhra pradesh, Scheduled or Dalits in U.P. Backward class in Delhi whereas some of their *gotras* are Chauhan and Rathor of Rajput or Kshatriya clans. The Gaddi nomads of Himachal pradesh are tribals in Chamba district, but are considered higher caste in Kangra district from sociological angle. There are several instances which prove the *gotra* system as the origin of Huns, Shakas and many other unknown people of India.

## Similarities between Indian and Hungarian Culture

There are many similarities between Indian and Hungarian Culture which should be studied in depth. Scholars should have more interaction strengthening our ancestral relations and Kinship or **Magyar** with **Bharat**

## Life–The Endless Journey

*(An emotional letter to all the friends whom Prof. (Dr.) Shashi. S.S. met in Budapest and Berlin in the month of may-June 2004).*

**Greetings** to the president of World Hungarian federation, Mr. Patrubany Miklos, Mrs., Dr. Eva Aradi and other participants of the conference held in Budapest in the 1st week of June 2004 and best wishes to all old and new friends who met and honoured me during my visit to Hungary and Germany and my journey from Budapest to Berlin via Slovakia and Czech Republic in May-June 2004.

**Friends,** Life is like a train journey. We come across many fellow passengers who talk friendly, eat together, enjoy company and part away at the arrival of their destination.

Sometimes, we may be in the crowd of relatives and friends but we may still feel alone. Why? Perhaps we don't get the person, we like or the environment may not be of our choice.

In my recent visit to Hungary, Slovakia, Chezck Republic and United Germany, it was not so of course, I travelled by air from Delhi to Budapest via Moscow and after participating in World Hungarian Conference, I left for Berlin by train. I met people of different nature, different culture and various nations. Some of us exchanged visiting cards which would never be utilised except one or two, that too perhaps far a short period.

Now back home to my country, I remember my new friends whom I may or may not meet in future, nobody knows.

I congratulate Mr. Patrubany Miklos for a very successful conference held in Bubapest under his presidentship. He has a magnetic personality and possesses all the qualities to become a great leader. He is lucky to have an intelligent consort and a dedicated team of scholars of repute and faithful friends. I am thankful to Aradi family (Mr. Martin and Dr. Eva Aradi of Budapest who were kind enough to introduce me to the new galaxy of eminent scholars and writers. I also met H.E. Manbir Singh, Indian Ambassador and Mr. R.C. Nair the 1st Secy. of Indian Embassy in Budapest who were very courteous and friendly to Hungarian scholars and writers.

In the conference, I remember the new friends from various countries, namely, Dr. Sagynbek Tursunov, Ambassador, Prof. Kasim, Prof. Alibek, Mrs. Tildas, Mrs. Boski all from Kazakhstan,

Prof. Dovdoi Bayar from Mangolia, Prof. Marico Alinei from Itly, Bela Tanito from Finland, Sandor Vamosi from Canada, Prof. Istvan Erdelyi, Dr. Maria Negyesi (Budapest University), Ms. Dobos Tunde, Mr. Karpati Gabor, Prof. A. Laszlo, Prof. Csanad Sajgo, Prof. Zsigmond Emese, Ms. Jldiko Fabian, Prof.. Mandoky Ongajsa, Dr. H. Szabolcs, Mr. Olah Janos, Mr. Benyhe Jamos, Prof. Andrew, E. Czeizel Vargaceza, M.S. Clari mostly from Hungary and some from other countries.

In Berlin, my German friends, Mr. Warner Vorner Voight and his charming wife Mrs. Katarzyna Pollok provided me descent and affectionate hospitality. Mr. Werner is an artist and journalist who has been to India number of times and exhibited her paintings in various art galleries. She has also displayed her art work emphasizing holocaust in particular and other subjects in general. We wish her a bright future in her creative work and urge Indian art lovers to organise her exhibitions in various towns as she is from Indian Sinti Roma origin. Though her mother was from a noble Russian family but her father a scientist from Poland belongs to a Sinti Roma family.

Among the Indian community in Germany, I was invited by Mr. Sudhanshu Pandey at dinner along with Mrs. Susila Sharma, Mrs. and Prof. Wani and other NRI German friends. Their sweet behaviour and family culture impressed me a lot. Mr. Pandey's scholarship, sweet behaviours and family culture is superb. My compliments.

I am thankful to Mrs. Sharma, a well known writer for holding a literary function in my honour on behalf of **Bharat Majlis.** This association has the privilege of having Netaji Subhash Chandra Bose one of its Hon'ble Member, Pt. Jawaharlal Nehru, Mrs. Indira Gandhi, Pt. Ravi Shankar, Bismillah Khan etc. Were also honoured by the organization in the past. Mrs. Sharma teaches Hindi to the German students.

I have no words to express my gratitude to a poet-laureate Mr. Rajvinder Singh who is not only an eminent poet but he also entertains his poet-friends with tasty food cooked by himself. I found one of my book "Roma–the Gypsy World" in his personal library. He has written about eight books of poetry in German and some in punjabi. Perhaps, he is the only Indian poet in Germany who has been honoured by German Govt. for his eight collections of poetry in German language.

Among other friends, I met a religious family of Dr. Avianish Kumar Lugani and his Arya Samajist wife Smt. Shashi Kanta who perform Yajna every Sunday. Their daughter-in law is a German girl who also observes Hindu customs and traditions like other family members.

Among other NRI German friends, whom, I met, are namely-Mr. Devendra Paliwal, Mrs. & Mr. Gurdeep Singh, Mr. Hari Singh Kumar, Mr. Avinder Singh, Mrs. Manju Taneja, Mrs. Nirsa B. Beumer, Mr. Forster Ramester and his son Huberdus Ramester, Ms. Claudia Kramatschek, all from Berlin. I also visited Indian embassy with Sinti Roma Artist Mrs. Pollok and met Mr. Amit Das Gupta, Dy. Chief of the Mission, Mr. Sudhanshu Pandey, Counsellor, Culture. I remember Mr. Dhiraj Roy, Dr. N.D. Sharma etc. Forgive me whose name slip from my memory, but they are sure in my heart.

At the end, I would like to pay my regards to all the friends of Hungary, Germany and other countries for their love and affection, they have shown to me during my visit to Europe in the months of May-June 2004. The Gypsy carvans are hardly visible now-a-days as they are assimilated in the society of their respective countries. Will the life goes on like a wheel of time i.e. kaal chakra for endless journey.

*(For higher learning my book 'Shepherds of India' TURAN Journal (Hungary) and Hoons and Shakas in India and Hungary jointly being written by me and Dr. (Mrs.) Eva Aradi of Hungary. Her research papers and books on this subject are referred for further research).*

# 17

# The Journey Goes On

Coming back to the Indian nomads, I recollected my old journeys. I have recently visited Gaddi and Roma families in various cities of India and Germany and found tremendous social and cultural changes. They neither wear old clothes nor typical ornaments which their forefathers used to wear. The Gaddi girls and boys of Bharmor wear now modern dress. I was amazed to see a large number of such families in Delhi also. I revisited Himalayas from time to time. I met recently the educated Gaddis in Delhi. Here are some glimpses of my latest studies.

In 2004, I met Roma families in Hungary and Germany. Many of them have changed their life and many are in transitional phase. During my new research, I interacted with many scholars belonging to various Shaka, Hoona, Kazak and primitive nomadic-clans in Budapest. This may be perhaps my last journey to Europe as I am satisfied with my achievements.

Obviously the journey of life never ends. It goes on even after the researcher is no more.

I am again in Pahalgam, the village of Pohals, *i.e.,* Shepherds. It is situated at the head of the Liddar Valley in Jammu and Kashmir. It is known for its exquisite scenery, springs and streams and possesses healthy forests of pines. It is also the base for treks to higher points like Amarnath and Sheshnag.

I have just reached here after covering the journey of 96 km. from Srinagar. I find a number of tourists and also my favourite nomads—the Gujjars and Bakarwals with their cattle, sheep and goats.

"Salam Sahib, I am Abdul of Himachal Pradesh. Do you remember, we met in Chamba long ago ? a Gujjar asked me.

"O yes, I am recollecting. But what brought you to this place"? I questioned.

"I have my relation in Jammu and Kashmir and also in Azad Kashmir." The Gujjar replied.

The Gujjars have also changed in tune with the time but the percentage in this direction is poor. They are businessmen, traders, teachers and politicians too.

I reach their *Dera* and witness their daily routine. I see a few of them possessing now transistors, watches and wearing trousers.

Walter R. Lawrence has presented a very dark picture of the nature and character of Kashmiris, but he praised Gujjars and compared them with the Kashmiris. He writes :

They are an ignorant, inoffensive and simple people, and in their relations with the State are infinitely more honest than the Kashmiris. Their good faith is proverbial, and they are a generous people, giving all the milk of Friday away in charity. Their women keep the accounts of the butter made over to the middleman by tying knots on a string. The favourite name of the Gujjar is Muhammad, and a man of position among the herdsmen is always addressed as *Bhai* (brother). From the point of view of forestry their existence is to be regretted, but they serve a useful purpose as pioneer of cultivation, and the wise policy of the Kashmir State has been to encourage the Gujjars.

It is also interesting to note that the women of Gujjars and other Kashmiri communities are extremely beautiful. Bernier in his book "Journey to Kashmere, the Paradise of the Indies" says :

'The women are very handsome, and it is from this country that nearly every individual, when first admitted to the Court of the Great Mogol, selects wives or concubines, that his children may be whiter than the Indians, and pass for genuine Mogols'. One ingenious writer suggests that the decadence of beauty in Kashmir is due to the fact that the fairest of Kashmir's women were taken away to India, and that the stock whence beauty might be bred has disappeared. Marco Polo, speaking of the women says, 'Taking them as brunettes they are very beautiful.'

The Gujjars rear not only Buffaloes but also the sheep and goats. They use horses and ponies for carrying the load of their household. The ponies are small but wiry and of great endurance. Nearly every Gujjar family has poney mares.

I see a number of Bakarwals, the goat rearers in migration. Their goats are very fine animals and a valuable property. They supply milk, *ghee*, meat and skins to others. The milk of the goat is considered to be very strengthening. The hair of the goat is used for skin grain bags, but it is not employed in the manufacture of finer fabrics.

"How many goats do you possess"? I asked the Bakarwal.

"Nearly one Thousand, Sab". This was a straight-forward reply and he was of the opinion that education does not help in their profession. Hence, for him education was immaterial.

However, in my last, when, I visited Himachal Pradesh, I found equally interesting results. There were mobile schools for Gujjar children like Roma mobile schools in European countries.

The Gaddi nomad is, no doubt, aware of many new things today, but has changed his migratory habits slowly. He wears a long woollen string around his waste only when carries all his household goods on his back and climbs the high hills with his new born lambs. I remembered I wrote to the then Chief Minister of Himachal Pradesh, Dr. Y.S. Parmer, to help these tribals in making them self-sufficient with fodder and cereals for winter too. Now, I observed the same problem but in a diferent way. Much water has flown in the Ganga but many nomads are still ignorant of railway journey or A.B.C. in a book. They are yet to lead a hard life in the midst of unfriendly natural surroundings and privation born out of unrewarding yields from small, terraced fields.

Here, I may say that the picture is now not, however, so gloomy when we visit the Gaddi villages. They have marched ahead, changed their age-old costume and other traditions to some extent. One can find a young Gaddi pair in bell-bottom with long hippi-type hair carrying a radio transistor and listening to English songs. Many feel jealous of safeguarding their cultural identity and the social set-up which went a long with it. They are eager to take the advantage of modern technology and dislike being treated as museum pieces. Many have joined the national maintream but this does not mean that they want to give up their culture and religion. The tribals are more concerned with the new breeds of their sheep and goats than with their new folk songs and dances.

According to my recent findings, they were never a tribe as such, but descendants of Rajputs, Thakurs and Kshatriyas and Brahmins; they were forced to live as farmers and shepherds in a highly rugged terrain where soil erosion continues to pose a constant threat. In fact, time took away their zest for arms and they took to farming. Surprisingly, once a professional warrior community, today's Gaddi shuns violence. He would rather yield than resort to force. The Changes are no doubt taking place slowly but steadily and in a few decades, the plainsmen may have to make some efforts to meet the plain, sincere and faithful *mitra* as in the past.

Whenever is a call from the Himalayas, I visit them and find the change in nomadic life, but this change is very slow. Hence, they including other shepherds of India need reservation as S.T. till they all are in mainstream.

During my recent survey of Gaddi tribes in Himachal Pradesh, I noticed a considerable change among my most favourite people. I met my *mitras* who come down from the high hills every winter with their flocks of goats and sheep. Many still travel for six months preserving their migratory habits. The young faces of those days had grown older. The children were young men and women and I was again a stranger to them.

I tried to start a conversation but did not get much response.

Soon an old man came forward and said : 'I recognise you Sab ! Are you not the same person who went upto Brahmaur with my flock ? I cannot remember the year but I know you had spent some time in our *caravan*. You also ate *en-ra-sag* with *maki-ki-roti* and slept under the open sky.'

'Oh, you Baisakhu,' where is your fiery dog, who saved my life from a panther.' I asked him eagerly.

'He is no more, Sab. He died of some unknown disease but won a prize at the All-India dog-show at Simla before his death,' the *mitra* spoke in melancholy.

In winter, some Gaddis even today migrate with their flocks of sheep and goats to the lower hills of Kangra, Chamba, Mandi and Gurdaspur in search of grazing lands. This seasonal exodus is of ancient origin, and the people speak of going to 'Jandar' as they call the country to the south of the Dhaula Dhar. Some members of the village community stay back to tend the cattle and look after property. Many Gaddis have acquired permanent grazing rights in some places and some have their agricultural land in Kangra district. Rabari, Bharwad, Raika, Gond Kuruba, Gadariya, Gwala, Ahir, Gujjar and all other shepherds should be given similar rights by all the states of the country.

The forest department as usual discourages the multiplication of sheep and goats to check over-grazing and does not issue grazing permits for more than a fixed number of goats and sheep. This has created some dissatisfaction among the shepherds in some states.

Recently, I was invited by Mr. Rattan Pahl, Secy General, Gaddi Vikas Samiti to preside over their cultural function held on 19th Oct 2004 in New Delhi. I was amazed to observe more than one thousand young Gaddi men and women working in different departments of the Govt. of India, and Delhi State Govt. I met one IAS officer Mr. Suresh Kumar working as Director in the Ministry of Human Resource Development. Mr. Rattan Pahl himself is a Gazetted Officer working in the Govt. of India. His wife is also a Central Govt. employee.

'Had there been no reservation for them, no body could have got employment in Govt. Service from such a remote area of Brahmor and Kangra'—This was the impression, they gave to me while asking them about their progress in various fields.

Now-a-days, there is a great awareness among the Gaddis and many sheep and cow-rearing communities but perhaps among the educated class and not the lower strata of society. I am sure that they will also come up and will contribute in the development of their community and the country as well.

I saluate to my nomadic world both at home and abroad, and wish them a very happy future, I may or may not be in this world, but the carvan will move on with a mission of '*Charaiveti*' (go on) and '*Vasudhaiv Kutumbakam*' (the world is one family).

# 18

# Appendices

(1) Roma Paganism and Hinduism.

(2) Globalization : Thoughts of Dr. Shashi.

(3) Shashi Busts Myth of Aryan Invasion.

(4) A Review of Dr. Shashi's Nomadic Epic 'Agnisagar'.

(5) The Ex-Criminal Tribes : A False Notion.

(6) Dr. Shashi's Interview in '*Caribbean New Yorker*'.

(7) Dr. Shashi in Germany

(8) Anthropologist-Poet.

(9) Anthropologist Felicitated.

(10) Book on Shyam Singh Shashi

(11) Dr. Shashi in Hungary

(12) Dr. Shyam Singh Shashi-A Profile and list of books.

(13) A Brief History of Research Foundation.

(14) PM 'Baro Rani' of Roma Gypsies.

(15) Bibliography.

(16) Photo–section.

## 1. Roma Paganism and Hinduism

There are many similarities between Paganism and Hinduism. According to Hindu Mythology and divine history, the chief deities of the Aryans were : *Indra,* (the God of Thunder), *Varuna* (the Lord of the Waters), *Mitra (*the friend, the personification of the Sun's dynasty), *Agni* (the fire), etc. Their enemies, or demons are *Dasyus, Ahi, Susna, Vritra* etc. over whom victory is sought.

The important feature of the Vedic religion is the tendency towards monotheism and monism, the Vedic Hymns foreshadow the idea of universality and express the belief that God is one although he bears many names:

"They call him Indra, Varuna,
and Agni, he is the heavenly bird Garutmat;
To what is one the poets give many names,
They call it *Agni, Yama, Matrisva*"

*(Rigveda 1 16446)*

God Brahma is the creator, Vishnu is the sustainer, Shiva is the killer of the wicked and evil ones. According to M.I. Kaunavine a Russian research scholar, the Roma in Russia have preserved legends of Brahama, Indra, Visnu, Agni, Lakshmi, Prithvi. The last mentioned goddess they call *Mata* (mother). Roma in Skopje (former Macedonian Republic) call it "Mautia." When the Indian Ambassador in Yugoslavia, late Mr. P.N. Menon, visited Roma of Skopje on 23 October 1974, the Roma Theatre put on a special performance of the drama "Mautia." The drama tells of the departure of Roma from their homeland, suffering on the road and eventual rescue by Goddess Mautia, the sacred Earth, representing Mother India.

A physician by profession, Mikhail Ivanovich Kaunavine was an indefatigable worker in the domain of philological science. He was born in 1820. He devoted 36 years of his life to conduct research into the origins and life of Roma, visiting India twice.

Dr. Lokesh Chandra describes Paganism in the context of universal faith in general and Lithuanian beliefs in particular.

He says "Paganism is the flow of spiritual culture and material civilization in the rhythms of the universe, evolving into the wholeness of an inner unity. The Pagan quest is eternal, even beyond our within. We wonder through all the outer worlds to reach the innermost shrine at the end. We are Cosmic Religions, pilgrims to the yonder shore, we live to have something to outlive. Man and nature are one: banish the delusion of being different.

*Menu sauluze vede (Candra-Mah Suryam udvaha)*
*Pirma Pavasareli Prathamam Pravatsaram)*

What a moving dainos of Lithuania giving a persona to nature, wherein humans harmonise with the universe. The winds of primaeval spring caressing the hearts of men. The light of the sun and moon expelling all dimness and darkness.

*Dainos* is akin to the Rigvedic word *dhena* in the sense of 'speech reflecting the inner thoughts of man.' The *dainos* or *dhena* are the human ascent to the Divine, and not a Divine condescension through a prophet via a book. They are *sadhana* or visualisation, contemplation, luminosity growing from within. *Sadhana* is a epiphany of the divine in human consciousness. In the words of the rigveda it is to find the bonds of being in Non-being *(sato bandhum asati niravindan).* In the ancient Indo-European world, realisation was central to human transcension, as distinct from revelation in the three Judeocentric traditions. Revelation is the body of truth which is made known by a prophetic tradition. It is a communication to a lesser mind and demands unquestioning acceptance. Realisation or sadhana, on the other hand, is a visualisation of truth, a cultivation by meditation, a transfiguration of the individual into the majesty of the Divine. Epic moments of human life are fragment of divine splendour. As the *bhagavad Gita* says:

yad-yad vibhutimat sattavam, srimad urijitam eva va/
tad-tad evavagaccha tvam, mama tejo msa-sambhavam//

The universe is animated by an all-pervading divine radiation: wherever this current attains a particular intensity, a higher voltage, revealing itself as beauty, power, wonder, where the Supreme becomes apparent, there is the Divine."

Dr. W.R. Rishi says- "In the ancient legends, the mythological elements assert themselves most strongly, and the characteristic features of the Hindu mythology are so evident that even the names to be met within these tales recall the analogous divinities of the Hindu theology. Some of these are : Barmy (Brahma), Yag (Agni), Jandra (Indra), Laki (Kali from metathesis), Mata (mother Earth). It may be mentioned here that Sanskrit word Brahma has become

Barma in Hindi and Punjabi languages. Similarly Indra has also been mentioned by the name of Jandra in Panjabi. In the Punjabi language i changes to 'j', e.g. Sanskrit word *Surya (Sun)* becomes suraj Punjabi. Guru Nanak has similarly used *mat for mother earth "dharat mat."* Even the secondary names of the primitive mythology of the Gypsies remind us of the analogous names of the divination of the religion of the Hindu and of Zoroaster. The Gypsy names of Devenni (Sanskrit Devyani, good spirits) and *Mor* (Asur or evil spirits) are likewise etymologically akin to the Sanskrit *"deva* and to the common Aryan root *'mara'* which denotes every being that is wicked and hostile to man. Mura is the evil spirit killed by Lord Krishna and is mentioned in the Hindu Epic, Mahabhrata.

'According to a tale Jandra (Vedic Thunder God-Indra) is the son of "Sun's mother," having brothers and sisters owning analogy in the forms of other Aryan gods, changing of clothes by thunder god, his washing himself with clean water and by his turning himself into night, sun-negative, wintry-Farre of Gypsies and Varuna of Hindus.

The chief terrestrial Vedic deity is *Agni* (Fire), being naturally of primary importance as the personification of sacrificial fire which is the centre of the ritual poetry of the Vedas. Next to Indira he is the most prominent of the Vedic deities. He is celebrated in at least 200 hymns of the Rigveda and in several others he is invoked conjointly with other deities. Agni also is identified with Sun. Agni is a great benefactor of his worshippers.

'Fire is said partake of both the Sun and the Moon and pertains only to earth. It is fire which relates us to Sun and Moon and makes earth livable for us. People are either of sun-descent, or moon descent, or fire-descent, Letters of the alphabet belong to Moon (the 16 vovels), to Sun (some consonants) and to Fire (other consonants). As to breath, the right nostril breath is sun, the left is moon and the Susumna or middle is fire. There are five fires known as live lights- 1. Jyotis 2. Yoga fire; 3. Yajna fire; 4. Jnana fire; 6. Love fire. The Vedic Urvasi is the universal creative fire in all its aspects. The first Rigvedic hymn is dedicated to fire in its forms on earth. The fire god is easily the first, the best, the link between earth and heaven. Its very name Agni (the first goer, up-goer) etymologically means all that.'

The most interesting and relevant story is about the birth of Rajputs as a class distinguished from Ahirs, Gujjars, some back work kshatriya communities and Khatris from fire. They call themselves *Agnikula,* fire-born, Ahirs, Pals and Gujjars on the other. The mixed population eugenically became Jat and Rajput according to their occupation and status as farmer or as fighter ruler. A study of Hindu *gotras* and *Alhs* of pastoral, shepherds, tribal and backward communities prove that they were kshatriyas.

The concept of Roma for fire is, another proof of their Indian origin. Aryanism thrived in Afghanistan and North West and behind Aryanism is Zoroastrianism, which is also a fire-cult in its physical and metaphysical aspects. The influence of Rama as the Sun incarnation and the Devi on the Kshartiyas and the influence of the fire-cult on the Rajputs has been stressed by indologists. Some Shaiva influence on the Rajputs and Jats is also worth study.

Kaunavine has collected the following hymans on this subject "*Brahma,* hidden in Omoni *(OM)* : Thou reflected by you." "In Omoni (OM) is thy body and thy mighty word. Say, O Father of the Universe, who it is that has become guilty before thee that the Sun is hidden in the abysses of the waters and no more illuminates and darkened earth."

"It is in thee, the Omnipotent Omni, who has created the Universe by the mighty word-it is thee. "Omni, that Brahma reposes. In thee reposes Pesawin (Pashupati Sive) the golden eye of the father (Sun), in thee the shining stars, in thee, through all ages beams the pale faced moon, lighting the world of sorrows and gloom."

*From Dr. Shashi's book "Roma Culture and Heritage".*

## (2) GLOBALIZATION : THOUGHTS OF DR. SHASHI

"I believe in globalization of love, peace, equality, non-violence and brotherhood through literature, media and socio-cultural interaction in the context of Indian philosophy. *Vasudhaiv Kutumbakam (The World is one family)*"

*From : Dr. Shashi's speeches, delivered during his visits to Japan (1995). Thailand (1995) and Bangladesh (1996).*

## (3) SHASHI BUSTS MYTH OF ARYAN INVASION

**Irrefutable evidence to prove there migration from India to various countries'**

Social Scientist of repute and noted scholar Padmashree Dr. Shyam Singh Shashi claimed that ample archeological and historical evidence is available to prove beyond doubt that Indian migrants enriched the culture of various countries all over the world.

The irrefutable evidence is sufficient to disprove the theory of Aryan invasion to India. In fact, there were migration from India to various countries, he said.

Dr. Shashi was delivering a lecture on 'Indian culture abroad in Dr. S.W. Bakhle Memorial Lecture Series organised by International Centre for Cultural Studies (ICCS) at Mundle Hall of Dharampeth Girls School today.'

In support of his claim that Indians migrated to various parts of the world since ages and dominated the cultural scene there, the archeologist-poet cited several cases and referred to research findings. Signs of rich Indian cultural heritage are still available in all parts of the world. He said.

He had an opportunity to attend international conference of philosophers and social scientists, held in 1992 in Mexico. The visit prompted him to study the rich culture of various ethnic Indian groups like gypsies in Mexico and elsewhere.

Gypsies in Mexico, known as Gitano, are proud of their Indian origin and regard India as a 'Barothan,' meaning great land, he said. After an extensive study of the ethnic culture, he is convinced that there existed a direct land route from India to Mexico via Africa, which in course of time, was submerged under the sea.

He also studied in greater detail the system of Sun worshipping in various parts of the word. He said, "If we look at the world map we find many Sun temples in the tropic of cancer right from Konarka to Mexico."

The highest temple, in fact, is in Mexico. The temple, 210 ft in height, has a large altar where *yajnas* used to be performed. Another south American country, Peru also provides ample evidence of Indian cultural Heritage, he added.

The epic *Ramayana* is relevant not only in India but it has its impact all over the world, he said adding that *Ramayana* has become the lyric of Asia, from Siberia to Bali. (The Indian Express, Nagpur 3-1.2000).

**(4) *A Review of Dr. Shashi's Nomadic Anthropological Epic*** *entitled Agnisagar by Mr. Manohar Bandopadhyay an eminent English-Hindi poet and Secy. General, Poetry club of India, published in "Indian Literature" (Sahitya Academi, 150)*

Dr. Shyam singh Shashi's Hindi epic '*Agnisagar*' is based on the legendary manu, the first man on earth, his wife, Sraddha; his mistress Ira: his son Manav and the scattered survivals after the great Flood. But then this is the skeleton plot of the epic. The main strength of the work is the reinterpretation of *Manusmriti* and demolition of numerous misnotions popularly held about the class-structure in Indian society. It is, therefore, a poetic attempt to restore the authentic message of *Manusmriti* and to weed out the chunk of social rules added by the interpolators attributing to the sage Manu.

As the history tells us, sometime in the first two centuries A.D., many authored the famous *Manava Dharmashastra* or the Law Code, popularly known as *Manusmriti*. But there were several Manus beginning with Svayambhu Manu (The self-born Manu) who was said to be a hermaphrodite. The tenth Manu was the most famous during whose reign occurred the great Flood. Dr. Shashi considers that Manusmriti is the composition of not one but several Manus at different periods of time. Dr. Shashi is however not very specific about the exact date; his sole objection is the corrupted version of Manusmriti handed down to us which thoroughly misleads the original tenets propounded by Manu. The corruption occurred, Dr. Shashi intimates us, sometime in the second century B.C. It is true Manu regarded status of man not by birth but by action; a Brahmin could be Shudra and vice-versa dependent upon his deeds.

Thus in the epic when Manu confronts the cries of allegations from all quarters he cannot contain himself any longer and bursts forth;

> "No. Never. This is all lies
> These were never my edicts.
> This is someone else's doing
> I never made such odious divisions."

Manu further explains how he made moral tenets of his religion and warned that those who did not follow them in life were all *Shudras*.

The Manu episode, however, appears in the latter half of the epic. Integrally the plot of the epic is similar to that of Prasad's *Kamayani*. The basic departure is that Dr. Shashi embodied all Manus in one defying the limit of time. If this is taken to be of allegorical significance, it would be difficult to answer the Manu of *Manusmiriti*. There are certain with Sraddha, in *Agnisagar*, Manu is shown as an eternal gypsy who sets out on his mission leaving even Sraddha behind; "with faith and resolve in his heart/ Manu walked alone like a gypsy."

'Agnisagar' is then the ocean of fire in which burns the Manu of *Manusmriti*. The epic, therefore, clearly points, to the fact that Dr. Shashi has made the author of the famous classic the hero of this epic and not the Manu who survived the great Flood. It is for his convenience that he has used the available plot with a liberal facility.

'Agnisagar' is divided into cantos; each numbered with a 'direction' such as "Disha One," "Disha Two" and so on. There are thus ten directions, each representing one of the ten doors or ethical paths prescribed in Manusmriti. This is elaborately explained in seventh canto wherein Manu begets his son, Manav, by Sraddha. In that canto Manu exhorts his son about the virtues like restrain, patience, control of senses, forgiveness etc. These principles numbering ten are explained as the righteous way of living, a philosophy of life and not as tenets of any dogmatic religion. Each canto is again sub-entitled as "Brahmratri," "Manwantar," "Uplabdhi" etc. The main gravity again falls on the canto, "Manu Ka Pashchatap" wherein he repents over the lopsided distortions of his social laws. He says: "I never said the men of foul deeds/ are ever high-born." He wonders how the priests-made classification of society on the basis of birth has miserably disintegrated the society. It is this flame that singes Manu of 'Manusmriti' and it is this episode that suggests the title of the epic.

As a form, *Agnisagar* qualifies the traditional traits even as it is far less in detailed treatment than the old epics. It has a lofty theme, grant style, lofty purpose, variety of versification, a mission and description of nature and society. It has more than seven cantos required in an epic. Despite these features the epic may be a bit controversial for its spatial limitation. The epic contains a commentary of our time. This is not an age of epic and the epics attempted by the ambitious poets are merely of academic interest and even there the fate is uncertain. But then, certainly this is a model which will be advantageously seized by the coming generations.

'*Agnisagar*' deserves therefore to be seen as a poetic re-instatement of *Manusmriti* and in the context of modern ethos of society, its tastes, mood and temper and not as a fallout of prasad's *Kamayani*.

— Manohar Bandopadhya

### (5) THE EX-CRIMINAL TRIBES, A FALSE NOTION.

History has been the repetition of events and the incidents are narrated with certain pre-conceived biases. This is the general impression among some social scientists and perhaps the reason behind the caste-based development form this notion. In British period, there were certain castes particularly Nomads who fought against the Britishers either in direct face-to-face warfare or Guerilla warfare. They were declared by them as criminal tribes. In fact, most of these communities belong to tough martial races as they did not bow to foreign rulers and thus branded victims of their bravery. These communities were being tortured by the Britishers. They had to leave their home and hearths in search of their livelihood. At times, circumstances forced them to commit petty crimes like theft, robbery, etc. and occasionally murder also.

According to Dr. Verier Elwin, for centuries natural environment has been the ruler of the tribals. It is in this state of human development and behaviour that the tribals adopted nomadism as the more normal way of life. The pattern was adopted by them according to the needs and their own peculiar modes of trades. It must not be difficult to recall to our mind, even at this colossal span of time, the picture of snowy, hardy, unshaven, half-naked, hairy men striding silently across the shady jungles. Their belongings must have been quite few consisting of sharp edged digging sticks, a dead deer or a stag for the night meal, one or two dogs as pets, for serving as mattresses or warning apparels, hollowed bamboos or wooden receptacles for eating and drinking. They were wandering from place to place as vagabonds. The men and women could not have been sullen; the journey could not have been wearisome; the time would not have been heavy. These so-called Ex-criminal tribes include mostly Sansis, Bhantus, Doms, Bhils, Nats, Ghosis, Gujjars, Banjaras etc.

The modern sociologists' opinion is that the criminals are made and not born. A number of studies have been made on the subject and it is now a proven fact that there is nothing like criminal by birth, but the society is responsible for making them criminals.

During my visit to a Muria village of Madhya Pradesh. There was some quarrel between two tribals on social issues. A Muria became very angry with the other tribal. He could not control himself and killed him with a sickle. When the victim died this man repented and straightaway went to the nearby Police Station and admitted the crime. It was just accidental and not intentional. Can any criminal in a civilised society admit in this manner? The reply is 'no'. Then why should we blame these people.

Forbes Waston and John William Kaye wrote in an old anthropological work entitled "People of India" among the wandering tribes, Sansees occupy a place of pre-eminent notoriety. They are neither Hindus nor Mohammadans in reality, but profess to be Hindus and do not practice circumcision by which alone they could become Mohammadans. They are basically outcastes, admitted to no other caste fellowship ministered to by no priests, without any ostensible calling or profession, totally ignorant of everything. Then they are engaged in the acts of crimes, they are beggars, and live under most abject poverty. Their women and children have the true whine of the professional mendicant as they frequent thronged bazars. He further says the Sansees are not only thugs and dacoits, but kidnappers of children and in particular of females children, who are readily sold, even at very tender ages, to be brought up as household slaves, or to be educated by vicious professional classes for the purpose of prostitution. This applies to many other ex-criminal tribes also.

*(The author has given the reasons of crimes and details about so called ex-criminal communities in his book A Socio-History of Ex-criminal communities OBCs. Infact those who fought against the British rulers, were declared a criminal caste. (This article also appeared in Indian Police Journal — 1986 Sr. No. 1-4 p. 29).*

**(6) Dr. Shashi's Interview by "*Caribean NewYorker*" (May 30, 2003), New York, U.S.A.**

Padma Shri Dr. Shyam Singh Shashi, prolific Indian poet, author and socio-political commentator, is on a literary lecture tour of New York and other cities in the United States. He visits as Guest of Honour of the World Hindi Council (WHC) an organization which pioneers the literary endeavors of people of Indian origin across the world.

Speaking to me from the home of Queens cardiologist Dr. Vijay Mehta, president of the NY chapter of WHC, he says that he is very concerned with world affairs, especially of the recent past. Responding to me, he says that he believes in globalization: "---but for me, globalization is en-nobling of the human spirit: it embodies the reciprocal love of nations: it's clothed in peace, equality, non-violence and brotherhood achieved by way of literature, media and socio-cultural interaction. Globalization, achieved by military exploits, is counter productive to man's destiny." It's dehumanizing, *Vasudhaiv kutumbakam - the world is one family.*

A compelling, yet poignant image of globalization is captured in this verse taken from this anthology, *White Darkness:*

***With claws of ideals***
***Your mechanical hands***
***Have soared beyond the skies***
***But the legacy of Your***
***Ancestors, Your mind and the body***
***Yet remain dwarfed even today!***

For his outstanding contribution to the arts. Dr. Shashi was conferred the Padmashri, India's highest non-military award. In the spirit of the times Dr. Shashi, who has travelled to some fifty-odd countries, has communicated his widely acquired experience to the President of the United States, *Inter-alia: "...Poverty is to be studied in the context of fundamentalism prevalent in many parts of the world. The days are not very far when the number of fundamentalists will be so high that democracy will suffer in a big way....terrorism, too, should be rigorously conceptualized and better defined...."*

Dr. Shashi, who has advanced degrees in Sociology and Literature (PhD., D.Litt), has published, in Hindi and English, more than three hundred books, both fiction and non-fiction, among them the poetic "Agni Sagar" ("Sea of fire"), a socio-anthropological epic which deals with man's origin and his cultural history through time. Dr. Shashi's present project is a pioneering study of the history of Indian literature for which undertaking he is soliciting material from creative Indian authors and poets in the diaspora. (Contacts via WHC).

Dr. Shashi was born to an agricultural family sixty years ago in a village, near the famed Haridwar on the bank of India's idyllic river, ganges. Having gone through school both at home and abroad, Shashi took mainly government jobs rising to the top position of Director General of the largest publishing house with the Government of India. During his ten-year stint he was involved in the editing and publishing of some twenty magazines in as many as seven languages. Currently he is the Chair of Research Foundation International, the President of the International Academy of Children Literature, and the prestigious Editor-in-Chief of *his magnum opus-one* hundred fifty volumes of the *Encyclopedia Indica.*

In his seminal work on the dawn of history Dr. Shashi has made a singular contribution. He has informed me, for instance, that his work on debunking the euro-centric interpretation of India's early cultural history has gained greater currency in college and universities not only in the East but across the West as well. Previously, the scholars of Empire taught that the Aryan peoples, the Roma Gypsies, descended into India, some one thousand years before Christ, from their original homes in the arctic north, by way of Central Asia and Afghanistan into the Indo-Gangetic plains of India. In his books, *Roma the Gypsy World and Roma Culture and Heritage,* he has demonstrated that contemporary scholarship proves otherwise. Indeed, the reverse was the route : the Roma people emigrated from India into the plains of Central Asia and beyond all through to Europe.

The professor states: 'These ancient migrants were known as' 'Aryans' which etymologically means noble and honourable people. There is irrefutable evidence sufficient to disprove the theory of an Aryan invasion of India. It is a proven fact that the Roma gypsies are of Indian origin and they migrated from India to western countries in different periods and carried their language and civilization with them. Their foreparents lived in various parts of India...The number of Roma today is between 15 and 20 million in Europe and about 10 million in the Americas.'

On leaving NYC, Mr. Shashi will address audiences in California, North Carolina and Austin, TX, before returning to speak here at a time and place to be announced. He then continues to the United Kingdom. Interviewed by Kenneth Persaud) August 03 issue.

***Courtsy :*** *"Caribbean New Yourker", (New York), May 30,2003 (Front Page). Reports from New York, California, Austin, Taxas, Birmingham, London and other places have been published in detail in "SABHYATA SANSKRITI" (Magazine)*

### (7) Dr. Shashi's Interview in Germany

Dr. Shashi perception of cultural understanding through books and the wider environs of the publishing world is a viewpoint not given to many. More so when it comes to a regard and love for. German literature as has been the case with Dr. S.S. Shashi, who is better known as a prolific writer than in his current portfolio as a director of the publications Division, Ministry of Information and Broadcasting, Government of India. His tour of the Federal Republic of Germany has proved both interesting and educative.

Ever since he took his doctorate in social anthropology in 1968 with a thesis on "Nomads of The Himalayas," Dr. Shashi has embarked on his first love-Literature—and apart from editing the *Sainik Smachar* during a brief stint in the armed forces, went on to write a number of books on a variety of subjects including sociology, children lit., art and Indian culture. His extensive travels, which have already taken him several times to Europe, Scandinavia and the United States as well as to the Far-East, have enabled him to widen his horizons in anthropology, poetry and children's literature as well as facilitated a study of different and even primitive societies all over. Meeting authors and publishers was his special delight.

Dr. Shashi also utilised his visit to the Federal Republic of Germany to participate in the international book fair in Frankfurt which, according to him, "mirrored the cultural heritage of mankind as well as the fast changing literary scene the world over." The march of computer technology and electronics and their impact on the printing industry has impressed him favourably and he considers it necessary for Indian publishers to develop and awareness of the need to conform to sophisticated printing standards as soon as possible. The Publications Division is the largest publishing house in the public sector and serves as a distributor for twenty two government publishing houses in the country, including the Sahitya Academy, Indian Council Of Cultural Relations, National Council Of Educational Research and the National Book Trust.

His bureaucratic background has not hindered accomplishments in the literary field as the thrust of his writings has mainly been in the quest for a New Man embodying the very negation of the Selfish Man that now inhabits the world at large. His new image, strangely enough, tends to be "found more among primitive societies" than outside them as being unsullied by the filth of lucre and aggrandisement, their humanity was more lovable.

While Indological studies have come quite naturally to him, he has been very appreciative of the organised interest displayed by German universities in this direction and regards the inclination as indicative of common cultural aspirations basically. He has formed the distinct impression that German literature was very close to Sanskrit too. In this context, he has considered it most appropriate that the Frankfurt Book Fair would be focusing on India as its main theme in 1986. The event, which would be encompassing all branches to the country's literature, is being looked forward to with interest. **(Coutrsy 'German News' Embassy of the Federal Republic of Germany, 20 Dec. 1984).**

### (8) Anthropologist-Poet (By R. L. Pathak )

Dr. Shyam Shashi is a distinguished anthropologist-poet who drove about his literary journey of writings so fast, that at 40 he has already authored as many as 35 books maintaining a 2:1 ratio in Hindi and English respectively.

Though fundamentally a scholar-poet of Hindi, he has an equally felicitous pen in English.

He is a writer-poet of hope and optimism and avoids melancholiac situations which bring in some negative thoughts in their wake.

"I take life as sacred trust of God and endeavour to serve mankind through the 'spin and flight'" of my pen to cheer the desperate, sick and have-nots and enthuse them to rise and fight their adversaries," says Dr Shashi. He aspires to achieve the goal of human wellbeing by practising the eternal doctrine of "Satyam-Shivam-Sundaram."

Dr Shashi, who hails from a village near Hardwar, was promising right from childhood and maintained his high standards upto his doctorate.

Lyrical musings came natural to him. He composed his first lyric when still in High School. His first, collection of poems, titled "Lal Savera," brought him warm commendation from veteran Maithilisharan Gupta. Thereafter, Dr Shashi continued to add to his literary accomplishments both with speed and solemnity.

His collection of poems 'Lahu Ke Phool' was leading lights of the Hindi world, such as Ramdhari Singh Dinkar, Sohan Lal Dwivedi, Sumitra Nandan Pant and Bhawani Prasad Mishra. His poems in this collection were essentially poems of hope and optimism. The couplet:

> Mein rone ke nahi
> Hansne ke geet chahta hun
> Mere meeto
> Mujhe rulao nahin
>     Hansao
> Mujhe sulao nahin
>     Jagao'

demonstrates the poet's optimism.

His Hindi works include 'Ekadashi,' 'Bhoodan Dashak,' and 'Pranaya Poornima.'

His book on children 'Vanvasi Bachche Kitne Sachhe' ranks among the best literature on children, inspiring them to brave deeds and finer ways of life. He was awarded a prize by the Government of India for his pioneer work for children.

He was the Editor of 'Sainik Samachar', a pictorial weekly of the Defence Ministry published in 10 languages and lent the magazine a new dimension and vision by making it literature-oriented.

Including his martial poetry, he accomplished some terminological work also. He has evolved some 5,000-odd technical terms for use in social anthropology.

Quite a few of his works have been translated into Tamil, Telugu, Marathi, Urdu and Punjabi. ("*Evening News*", Hindustan Times, 14 Nov 1978).

### (9) Anthropologist Felicitated

New Delhi December 22, 1971, Mr. Uma Shankar Joshi eminent Gujrati litterateur and Member of the Rajya Sabha, said here today that the social life and customs of the nomadic and tribal people in India offered a highly interesting and almost virgin field for aspiring young writers to study and write about, reports PTI.

Mr. Joshi was speaking at a function held under the auspices of the Nagri Pracharini Sabha to felicitate Dr. Shyam Singh Shashi, anthropologist and writer, who has just received an award from the Union Ministry of Education for his Hindi book about children of various nomadic and tribal communities in different parts of India.

(*Times of India*, 23 Nov. 1971)

### (10) Book on Shyam Singh Shashi

New Delhi, June 30, 1988 (UNI)—Eminent poetess Amrita Pritam today released a critical work "Evaluation of Dr Shyam Singh Shashi's works" and said such books could be useful references not only for Hindi literature, but also for other languages in India and abroad.

At a simple function here, attended by prominent litterateurs, poets and critics, Mrs. Pritam said that Dr Shashi's Writings were both optimistic as well as related to society.

### (11) Dr. Shyam Singh Shashi : A Profile and List of Books
***(Complied by Dr. S.G. Hieremath)***

**Dr**. Shyam Singh Shashi, a renowned Anthropologist-Poet, Litterateur, Academician and Journalist was awarded **Padmashri** in the Republic Day Honours-1990 for his multifaceted achievements in the field of literature of two languages i.e., Hindi and English. He has written over 300 books in both the languages. Poet Shashi has to his credit 20 collections of poems and one epic "Agni Sagar," two dozen books and monologues on tribals and travelogues, dictionaries, five encyclopaedias and 25 books for children. His over 200 books in English include *'Nomads of the Himalayas, 'Tribal Women of India,' Roma- The Gypsy World,' Nehru and the Tribals,' Gaddis of Himalayas,' A Socio-History of Ex-criminal communities OBCs,' White Darkness'* (Poetry) *etc. 'His first book 'Lal Savera"* (poetry) appeared when he was still in his teens and a dozen before he joined Govt. service. He has over thirty publishers in India and abroad. He has edited 50 volumes of *Encyclopaedia of Humanities and Social Sciences*, 12 Volumes of *Encyclopaedia of Indian Tribes*, 10 Vols. of *Encyclopaedia of world women* and 150 vols of *Encyclopaedia Indica* etc.

Rating him as 'one of the few Hindi Poets who have shown human concern, the doyen of Indian literature Dr. Mulk Raj Anand says, "Your poems promise survival...... I hope you will one day face the challenges to man like Alen Ginsberg and the other poets who are aware of the dangers before humanity." His anthropological epic *Agnisagar* based on the unending journey of man-Manu of Menes interpreting *Manusmriti* in social change has been acclaimed as the best model of modern poetry in Hindi and world literature. Scholars conducted research on this monumental work and obtained Ph. D., D. Phil, M. Phil etc.

His creative literature in Hindi has been admired by Sumitranandan Pant., Ramdhari Singh Dinkar, Viyogi Hari, Sohanlal Dwivedi and various contemporary Hindi writers. Eminent poets like Umashankar Joshi, Thakazhi Sivasankara Pillai, G. Sankar Kurup, Dr. Dasarathi, Amrita Pritam and Dr. C. Narayana Reddy have spoken very high of Dr. Shashi's poetry that underlines basic issues haunting the humanity today.

First in many fields, Dr. Shashi is the first scholar to get his Doctrate in sociology on Himalayan nomads from Agra University under the able guidance of Dr. R.N. Saksena, an eminent social scientist of international repute. He is again the first scholar to be conferred upon with a D. Litt. in Anthropology for his pioneering work on Roma of Europe and America by the International University Colombo, Sri Lanka. He topped in his classes from his 8th standard to M.A. He his post-Graduation in Man Management and Man Power Planning from Manchester University U.K. He taught Mass Communication and delivered lectures on Indian culture, nomadic tribes, poetry etc. in various Universities/Insts. On the one hand, he has been the examiner for Ph. D.,D. Litt. in social sciences, Hindi literature and Journalism, on the other, various universities viz Agra Uni., Delhi, Bangalore, Meerut Garhwal, Rajasthan, Ajmer, Sagar, Madras, Kerala, Ranchi. Osmania etc. have conferred Ph. D.D. Phil etc. on his literature and his works have been included in the international Who's who of intellectuals and various "*Who's Who*" published in India and abroad. As Intellectual-Sociologist and creative writer who has equally proved to be an outstanding literary, research and academic manager in civil services as Head of the Deptt.

Dr. Shashi has been honoured by Government of Uttar Pradesh. H.P., A.P., Bihar and various leading institutions at home and abroad for his contributions to literature. In 1991 Hindi Akademi (Delhi State) honoured him with a cash award for his outstanding achievements in Hindi literature and Uttar Pradesh Hindi Sansthan (U.P. Govt) awarded him for his epic *'Agni Sagar'* On 14th Sept. 1993 after he left Govt. service, the President of India. Dr. S.D. Sharma awarded him *Mahapandit Rahul Sankrityayan, Samman* for his contribution in lit. On 2nd October 1993, he got yet another national award- *Mahakavi Jai Shankar Prasad Puruskar* for his epic *Agnisagar* besides felicitations in India and abroad. He was honoured by various organisations in USA and UK in 2003 and Hungary and Germany in 2004.

Widely travelled. Dr. Shashi's studies and researches into tribal life and culture have taken him to numerous travels within India and abroad to 55 countries in Asia, Europe including USA, UK, Canada, Russia, Ukren, Mexico, Japan, Thailand, Bangladesh etc.

A versatile genius, Dr, Shashi though a Poet-Anthropologist, is known as a dynamic Administrator, Researcher, Academician, Journalist and Social activist also. He has been a very successful Media Head and Director/DG., Field Publicity and Publications Division. I&B, Government of India, for 10 years. He had been Editor of Sainik Samachar (Armed Forces). He also controlled 20 journals in 12 Indian language viz. *Yojana, Employment News, Ajkal. Bal Bharti* etc. and published thousands of books for his Dept, in various languages. He is associated with number of literary, research academic, socio-cultural and welfare organisations viz. *ISA, IAA,*

*AGI, Translators' Association.* He fought in the interest of Indian languages and resigned from Govt. Service. Though he succeeded in his mission, he decided to leave Govt. service on voluntary retirement and to work for International Institute of Culture & Languages, Research Foundations as Chairman Media Research Centre and also as Chief of *Encylopaedia, Social Sciences in Hindi* and Indian languages. He keeps himself engaged as Visiting Fellow/ Professor/ Consultant in various Universities/ Institutions in Indian and abroad including Indira Gandhi National Open University where he is working as Professor (Coordinator-Head) and teaching social sciences; Lit. and Journalism. He is associated with a number of Govt. Departments and NGOs as an expert in the field of Mass Communication, Media, Social Sciences and Hindi Committees etc. He rendered his hony. Services as Chief Editor of *Collected Works of Dr. B.R. Ambedkar* (Min, of Welfare) in 8 Indian languages. He edited and published 13 volumes of Baba Saheb's Speeches and writings. 5 in Hindi, 2 in Tamil, 1 in Punjabi, 2 in Gujrati besides more than 50% translation in Hindi and partly in other languages. Dr. Shashi again resigned as he was not happy with the system and red-tapism. Dr. Shashi is also the President of the International Academy of Children Literature, Executive Head/Chairman International Institute of Nomadic Studies, Roma Research Centre and Indological Studies. He has been regular talker of AIR and appeared on T.V. occasionally in literary programmes. He had miraculous escape from death several times during his journeys. Once his aeroplanes was hijacked on which his articles. *A brush with death appeared in Hindustan Times* (8 may 1993) and its Hindi version *Navbharat Times* (31 Mar. 1993). Due to heavy burden of work, he fell seriously ill and had been bed-ridden for 2 yrs. (1996-97) due to his spinal cord operation.

As social activist, he has been working for *Indian Tribes*, Dalits, backwards, war hero families, weaker sections and children. Dr. Shashi is man of *Charaiveti* Philosophy. He is the founder of Research Foundation (International) having its own building as (Charitable Vaidik Mandir) in Rohini, Delhi and the emblem of 'Vasudhaiv Kutumbakam' (World is one family). His motto is: service to man is service to God.

## BOOKS BY DR. SHASHI

### Original and Edited ( मौलिक व संपादित)

1. Nomads of the Himalayas
2. Roma-The Gypsy World
3. Nehru and the Tribals
4. Shepherds of India
5. Himachal-Nature's Peaceful Paradise
6. Night life of Indian Tribes
7. Tribal Women of India
8. Defenders of India - Victory of Peace and Liberty
9. Roma Children Round the World (Child Lit).
10. Our Tribal Children (Children Lit.)
11. Uniform to Civvis
12. White Darkness (Poetry)
13. A Socio-History of Ex-Criminal Communities OBCs
14. Gaddis Today
15. A Sociological Study of Gaddi Tribe in H.P.
16. Mini Encyclopedia of Hinduism
17. The Women of Janunsar Bawar of Himalayas
18. Jawan-The Pride of the Nation
19. Ambedkar and Social Justice Vol I
20. Ambedkar & Social justice Vol II

21to 70. Encyclopaedia of Humanities and Social Sciences (50 volumes) Ed.
71 to82. Encyclopaedia of World women (10 Vols) Ed.
83 to 93. Encyclopaedia of Indian Tribes (12 Vols) Ed.
94 to 231. Encyclopaedia Indica (150 Vols) Ed.
232 Roma Culture and Heritage
233 A sayings of Deendayal Uapadhyay.
234 The World of Nomads

### हिंदी काव्य (Hindi Poetry)

235. अग्निसागर (प्रबंध काव्य)
236. शिलानगर में
237. एक दधीचि और

238. ढाई आखर
239. यायावरी (विदेशों में रचित)
240. लाल सवेरा (हाई स्कूल में प्रकाशित प्रथम लघुकृति)
241. एकादशी
242. भूदान दशक
243. प्रणय पूर्णिमा
244. प्रतिनिधि कविताएं
245. आस्था के स्वर (संपादित)
246. युद्ध के स्वर : प्रेम की लय (सं.)
247. लहू के फूल
248. व्हाइट डार्कनैस (अंग्रेजी काव्यानुवाद व मौलिक)
249. स्वर तुम्हारे अक्षर मेरे (रूसी कविताओं का अनुवाद)
250. एकलव्य और अन्य कविताएं
251. विश्व कविता की ओर
252. एक और यायावरी
253. आपके लिए (कुछ कथ्य : कुछ कविताएं)
254. चरैवेति चरैवेति
255. रोमा-विश्व के यायावर
256. हिमालय के यायावर
257. हमारा समाज
258. भारत की पशुपालक जातियां
259. इतिहास बनती यात्राएं
260. देशभक्त बिरसा (जीवनी)
261. सूर्य मंदिरों की खोज में (यात्रा वृतांत)
262. जीवन-पथ पर
263. कालशंख (साक्षात्कार)
264. भारत की आदिवासी महिलाएं
265. सफलता और सफलता
266. जवान-भारत का गौरव

267. हिमालय के खानाबदोश
268. हिन्दी हम सबकी
269. प्रेमचंद के मदनगोपाल
270–280 हमारी जनजातियां
281. दीनदयाल उपाध्याय ने कहा था

**बाल साहित्य** : 281. देश–देश में रोमा बच्चे
282. समाज के सुपुत्र (जीवनी)
283. बहादुर बंग्लादेश के
284. जंगल में मोर नाचा
285. जंगल की गुड़िया
286. आज के अस्त्र–शस्त्र
287. अच्छे बच्चे कितने सच्चे (स्वामी दयानन्द सरस्वती कृत व्यवहारभानु पर आधारित)
288–289. आदिवासी लोककथाएं
290. बालक दयानन्द (जीवनी)
291. शौर्य गाथाएं
292. अनकही कहानियां
293. स्वतन्त्रता सेनानी बिरसा मुंडा (जीवनी)
294. मेरी बाल कहानियां : किंगरी
295. ताले वाली गुफा
296. हमारे प्रधानमंत्री (जवाहरलाल नेहरू से अटल बिहारी वाजपेयी तक)
297. आओ गीत गाएं (बाल गीत)

**विविध** : 298. हमारे राजवंश तथा अहिल्याबाई होलकर
299. हमारा समाज वंशावली
300. सम्पूर्ण डा. अम्बेडकर वाङ्मय सं. (5 भाग)
301. समाज मनोविज्ञान (अनू.)
302. डा. रानी चेनम्मा (अनू.)
303. कूरियर
304. वर्ल्ड पोयट्री

**डा. शशि पर पुस्तकें** : 1. Selections from Shashi (Ed. Dr. S.G. Hiremath-Foreword by Dr. Mulk Raj Anand 2. श्याम सिंह शशि का सृजन मूल्यांकन 3. समकालीन शोध में शशिकाव्य-डा. चन्द्रिका प्रसाद शर्मा तथा डा. एम. रामनाथन, भूमिका : डा. सुरेशचन्द्र गुप्त - '92 4. अग्निसागर से गुजरते हुए - डा. हरिमोहन 5. अग्निसागर की अग्निपरीक्षा (सं. निशांत केतु) 6. अग्निसागर - चेतना और शिल्प - डा. वीरेन्द्र भारद्वाज 7. श्याम सिंह शशि का काव्य : चेतना और शिल्प - डा. मीना यादव 8. पद्मश्री साहित्यकार डा. श्याम सिंह शशि (फोल्डर) 11. A Literary Profile of Padmashri Dr. Shyam Singh Shashi 12. श्याम सिंह शशि : एक सृजनशील व्यक्तित्व 13. श्याम सिंह शशि का रचना संसार 14. S.S. Shashi-A Literary Profile (English and Hindi) 15. Anthology-Dr. Shashi's Literature 16. कामायनी तथा अग्निसागर का तुलनात्मक अध्ययन - डा. राजपाल सिरोहीवाल 17. उत्तर आधुनिकता भूमण्डलीकरण तथा शशि-काव्य-डा. सम्राट सुधा, 18. Folders on Dr. Shashi's Life and Works (10).

## डा. शशि के साहित्य पर प्रदत्त पी-एच.डी. की शोध उपाधियां

पी.एच.डी. प्राप्त शोध ग्रन्थ :- 1. A Critical Study of Shashi's Poetry by Dr. M. Ramanathan (Ph.D. awarded by Bangalore Univ.) (श्याम सिंह शशि के काव्य का आलोचनात्मक अध्ययन) 2. श्याम सिंह शशि का काव्य: चेतना और शिल्प - डा. मीना यादव, आगरा विश्व; 3. समकालीन युगबोध और शशि का काव्य - डा. कुसुमलता चमोली, गढ़वाल विश्व, 4. डा. श्याम सिंह शशि के काव्य में मूल्य अवधारणा-डा. अनिल कुमार चड्डा (मेरठ विश्व.) 5. शैली विज्ञान के निकस पर अग्निसागर की समीक्षा - डा. अजिता भदौरिया (आगरा विश्व.) 6. कामायनी और अग्नि सागर का तुलनात्मक अध्ययन - डा. राजपाल सिरोहीवाल (राजस्थान विश्व.) 8. कामायनी एवं अग्निसागर-एक तुलनात्मक विश्लेषण (अजमेर विश्व.) 9-13. अन्य विश्वविद्यालयों के शोध ग्रंथ (अप्राप्य) 14. अग्निसागर : मिथक द्वारा अभिव्यंजित युगबोध-राधा जनार्दन (उच्च शिक्षा शोध सं., मद्रास) 15. श्याम सिंह शशि कृत अग्निसागर : एक विश्लेषण-जेकब बेनोजी (उस्मानिया विश्व, हैदराबाद) 16. डा. श्याम सिंह शशि का काव्य संसार-नरेन्द्र कुमार (सागर विश्व.) 17. श्याम सिंह शशि का यायावरी साहित्य : एक अनुशीलन-कु. वत्सला ब्रह्मदत्त गिरि (नागपुर विश्व.) 18. श्याम सिंह शशि रचित 'शिलानगर में' काव्य संग्रह : एक अध्ययन-कुमारी कविता जैन (आगरा

विश्व.) 19. समकालीन हिन्दी कविता और श्याम सिंह शशि का काव्य-कु. माधुरी खंडूरी (गढ़वाल विश्व.) 20. श्याम सिंह शशि का काव्य : एक विश्लेषण-कु. ऋता भट्टाचार्य (हैदराबाद) 21-24. (रांची, मुजफ्फरपुर, मणिपुर, केरल आदि विश्वविद्यालयों में अप्राप्य) 25. श्याम सिंह शशि के काव्य में उत्तर आधुनिकता तथा भूमंडलीकरण-डा. सम्राट शर्मा, 26. अग्निसागर में यायावरी तथा आर्ष तत्व-डा. ममता सिंह (आगरा), डा. श्याम सिंह शशि का बाल साहित्य में योगदान - डा. वीर सिंह (कुरूक्षेत्र विश्व.), 27. श्याम सिंह शशि विशेषांक : 'अथाह क्रांतिमन्यु' (डा. श्याम सिंह शशि शोध संस्थान दिल्ली में उपलब्ध, 28. श्याम सिंह शशि के काव्य में उत्तर आधुनिकता तथा भूमंडलीकरण-सम्राट सुधा। 29. महापंडित राहुल सांकृत्यायन तथा पद्यमश्री डॉ. श्यास सिंह शशि के यायावर साहित्य का तुलनात्मक अध्ययन डा. माधुरी आर्या। अन्य प्रकाशित शोध ग्रंथ - 'अग्निसागर से गुजरते हुए'-डॉ. हरिमोहन, 'अग्निसागर की अग्नि-परीक्षा' - डॉ. निशांतकेतु, समकालीन शोध में शशि काव्य - डॉ. चन्द्रिका प्रसाद सिंह

**श्याम सिंह शशि विशेषांक** - 'अथाह', 'क्रान्तिमन्यु' (1997) (डा. बेकल), बाल साहित्य समीक्षा (डा. राष्ट्रबंधु) तथा अन्य शोध ग्रंथ रिसर्च फांउडेशन (डा. श्याम सिंह शशि शोध संस्थान, दिल्ली) में उपलब्ध।

**उक्त ग्रंथों के शोध-निर्देशक** :- प्रो. देवकीनन्दन शर्मा, प्रो. राजकिशोर सिंह, प्रो. योगेन्द्रनाथ शर्मा 'अरूण', प्रो. जगतपाल सिंह, डा. घनश्याम व्यास, डा. उषा यादव, डा. कुलदीप चन्द्र गुप्त, डा. उमाकान्त गोयल, डा. हरिमोहन, डा. केवलिया, डा. के. रामानायडु, प्रो. के.के. गोस्वामी, डा. जगमल सिंह, डा. रतन प्रकाश, डा. सुधा पांडे, डा. रामसनेही शर्मा 'यायावर', डा. महेश चन्द्र, डा. रमेश गुप्त, डा. तुकाराम पाटिल आदि।

**Publishers of above books :** Sterling Publications, Concept Publishing Company, Agam Prakashan, Sandeep Prakashan, Kitab Ghar, Rajpal and Sons, Atma Rama and Sons, Pustaayan, Anmol Prakashan, Praveen, Shilalekh and other publishing houses including Govt. Organisations viz., National Book Trust, NCERT, Publications Division, Lotus Printers Pub. etc. Dr. Shashi's books are available with these distributors—1. Central Book House, CSC-5, Shiksha Bhawan, Rohini Sector-9 (Opp. Akash Kunj Appt.), Delhi-110085, Ph. : 27862461, 2. Suryaprabha Prakashan, 2/9, Ansari Road, Darya Ganj, New Delhi-110002. Ph. : 23285915

## (11) DR. SHASHI IN HUNGARY

### Hungarian Writers Association Honour

### Dr. Shashi: Talk to TV & Radio

Established in 1932 under the great prose writer Zsigmond Moricz, the HWA has seen many ups and downs. It has association with PEN Clud, MAOE, Writers Union, FISZ etc. Dr. Shashi after delivering his lectures in World Congress and speaking to TV and Radilo Budapest, attended the Writer's Symposium on 4th June where he spoke about Indian literature in general and poetry in particular. He emphasised the need of translation of contemporary literature in Hungarian from Hindi and Indian languages and vice-versa.

(Media Research Centre)

### Dr. Shashi Felicitated in Germany

After a short stay in Budapest, Dr. Shashi left for Berlin via Slovakia and Czech Republic by train on 7th June and met a number of NRIs, Roma Sinti people who love India very much. The members of Bharat Majlis honoured Dr. Shashi for his outstanding work on variety of subjects. According to Mrs. Susheela Sharma, an NRI writer of Berlin, the organisation Bharat Majlis has also felicitated (Nejtaji) Subhash Chandra Bose, Jawaharlal Nehru, Indira Gandhi, Pt., Ravi Shankar, Bismillah Khan etc. in the past. Mrs. Sharma said that Dr. Shashi is currently engaged conducting research on *Gotras* and *Alhs* of various castes and tribes besides his creative work. This will help the historians in writing or rewriting history of India and also PIOs and NRIs.

### Dr. Shashi Honoured in Hungary

President of the World Hungarian Federation Mr. Patrubany Miklos honoured Dr. S.S. Shashi, as a social Anthropologist with special medal and Commendation Certificate for his outstanding contribution in the field of anthropological history of Shakas and Hoonas in India and Hungary. Mr. Patrubany paying his deep regards to Dr. Shashi, suggested him to write a book on this subject also. Dr. Shashi accepted the proposal to complete with the help of Dr. Eeva Aradi who is a learned scholar and Indologist.

(Media Research Centre)

## (12) History of Research Foundation

(Regd. by the Govt of India in 1972)

"Social developments are basic to the progress of a happy and well adjusted mankind. Those are also the forerunners of all other developments.

The man must learn to adjust and steadily integrate the political, economical, sociological, psychological and other aspects of his life for achieving progress, peace and harmony." This is an excerpt from the Foundation's Journal *"Contemporary Social Sciences,"* published in 1972. The foundation's motto is *"vasudhaiv Kutumbkam"* (the world one family) )वसुधैव कुटुम्बकम्।

### Aims & Objectives

1. To encourage, co-operate and co-ordinate research work in various branches of social sciences, literature, religion and other allied subjects. 2. To conduct research, surveys and to hold seminars for discussion on various topics among the social scientists and other scholars. 3. To publish research works and allied literature of a high standard. 4. To conduct educational, social, cultural and various activities for the welfare of the society, particularly the upliftment of weaker sections, illiterates, women, orphans, war widows, war hero families, disabled soldiers, ex-servicemen and any other class considered for welfare activities.

### Field of Study and Research

(1) Sociology, anthropology and Social Work, (2) Political Science, Public Administration and law, (3) Economics and Commerce, (4) Education, Psychology and Philosophy, (5) Literature and Linguistics, (6) Fine Arts, (7) Geography (8) Historical sciences, (9) Mathematics, Statistics, (10) Religion and Indology, (11) Tourism, Transport and Public relations, (12) National Integration, International Understanding, Defence Studies and Journalism, (13) Agriculture, Industrial, Marketing and Media Research, Value Education.

### Medium of Research

English, Hindi and Indian Languages as per the availability of resources and manpower.

*Gadulia Lohars with a foreign scholar.*

*Dhangar women and children of Maharastra.*

*Author being honoured in Kannada University by Vice-Chancellor and Dr. B K Ravi, Dr. K M Metri, Head, Nomadic Studies.*

Author with educated Banjara couple.

Swamiji Tarakanadpuri of Karnataka blessed the author with Kanaka Award.

International conference organized by Research Foundation and IICCA in Chandigarh.

Banjara conference presided over by Prof. I P Singh, Anthropologist.

The Red Indians

Calender of Mexico's Aztec culture.

Author in front of Sun Temple of Mexico.

Research Foundation's International Conference (language session) presided by Dr. Bindeshwari Pathak.

*Author being honoured with Shawl in Birmingham UK Literary Circle by Dr. Krishna Kumar (2003).*

*The author is being honoured by Vishwa Hindi Samiti America during his 2 month's stay. He addressed number of conferences in USA (2003-L to R) Dr. Dauji Gupt, Dr. V K Mehta and Mr V P Singh.*

*Honoured in Budapest by President & Secretary General Hungarian Writers Association.*

*Being felicitated by Mr. Patrubany Miklos, President of Hungarian Federation, Dr. Eva Aradi and others.*

*With Mr. Sudhanshu Pandey Counsellor Embassy of India Berlin, Mrs. Sushila Sharma and Mrs. Katarzyna Pollok.*

*Participants professors from Kazakhstan and Mangolia.*

*With Japanese scholars in Tokyo.*

*Author being honoured with SAROPA by Rakab Ganj Gurudwara Prabandhak Committee, New Delhi.*

*Author being honoured by the Secretary Gaddi VS Mr. Ratan Pahl Mr. Joginder Thakur, Gaddi officers in Govt. of India.*

*Pema Bhotia and his grand daughter of Uttranchal Pradesh.*

*The Gaddi IAS officer Mr. Suresh Kumar Director, Govt. of India being felicitated by the Minister of Himachal Pradesh Mr. G S Bali.*

*The Young Gaddi dancers at a function organized by Gaddi Vikas Samiti on 19 Oct 2004 in New Delhi.*

### Indira Gandhi National Open University Study Centre

The foundation has a recognised study centre for Indira Gandi National Open University at its Rohini Shiksha Bhawan, in which thousands of students of graduate and PG courses get counselling from the highly qualified professors, readers and Lecturers (Counsellors). There are over 100 part time/Guest/Visiting Faculty-members and Associates in various branches of the Foundation including **Media Research Centre.**

### Shiksha Bhavan

Besides IGNOU study centre, we have international institute. We have started Value Education Programmes for teachers and others. Many more courses are being launched, including children university's projects.

### Historical Background

Research Foundation was established in 1970 under the Chairmanship of eminent Sociologist of International repute Late Dr. R.N. Saksena, Ph. D., D. Litt, the then Director, Institute of Social Sciences, Agra University (Vice-Chancellor, Kashi Vidyapeeth) and Dr. S.S. Shashi, Ph. D., D. Litt., Anthropologist-Poet (Padma Shri Awardee) Former Director General Publications Division, Govt. of India, the Founder, Gen. Secy. Hony. Director who is currently the executive Chairman of the Foundation. Dr. Shashi has donated his royalty of number of books for Foundation's building and other activities. The Foundation is affiliated and associated with number of research, educational and cultural organisation in the country and abroad. It completed various research and publication projects successfully with the grant-in-aid from Indian council of Social Science Research, Ministry of Human Resource Development, Min. of Welfare, Govt. of India, etc. The Foundation conducted Social survey and social research in the field of Tribal welfare sociological Studies, Weaker Sections including women and children of backward classes.

### Achievements in Nutshell

1. The Foundation has conducted research work in various fields of national interest. 2.- The Foundation has completed a research study of tribal women in Jaunsar Bawar (Dehradoon) financed by Ministry of welfare. 3. The Foundation has published over two dozen

issues of its Quarterly Journal *"contemporary Social Sciences"* edited by Mrs. (Dr.) Deepa Malaviya. 4. Documentation of 8000 books of social sciences in Hindi. 5. Documentation of articles of social sciences published in Hindi journals during 40 years' period 6. It has undertaken a monumental work Hindi Encyclopedia of Social Sciences and published 3 vols. 7. The Foundation has successfully organised an international conference on Art, Culture, Literature and Human Rights in 1995 in cooperation with ICCR and other organisations 8. The Foundation has successfully run MEG, MHD, MSO, MARD, PG, BCA, BDP, and BPP courses of Indira Gandhi National Open University at Rohini. 9. The Welfare Wing of the Foundation had brought out a monthly bulletin/magazine ""Yudh Veer Nari", distributed among 10,000 war hero families and ex-servicemen free of cost and continued for 13 years. The inaugural issue of the magazine was released by Mrs. Abida Begam w/o Janab Fakhruddin Ali Ahmed, the Former President of India at Reshtrapati Bhawan, Vocational courses for war hero families and others were also organised from time to time. 10. Organised a number of national conferences and seminars in Delhi and elsewhere. In 2003, the Foundation organised a two-day seminar on *"Terrorism : Concept and Counter"* with the grant in aid from ICSSR, govt. of India. 11. The Foundation constructed its own building at Rohini. The Foundation stone was laid by Mr. P.K. Dave, Former Lt. Governor of Delhi And Mr. R.K. Takkar, IAS, Former Chief Secretary, Delhi,

## International Conferences

To commemorate Silver Jubilee of the Foundation, an International conference on Indian Art, culture, literature and human rights was held at Azad Bhawan on 9-10 Dec. 1995 The conference was inaugurated by justice Ranganath Misra, the former Chief Justice of India and Chairman Indian Commission for Human Rights and was presided over by the former Union Minister Mr. Vasant Sathe. The Executive Chairman Dr. S.S. Shashi, Col, Bhisham Pal, Mr. Jagdish Chaturvedi, Prof. Asis Sanyal, Mr. Dev Bhardwaj and others were the main organisers.

A large number of social scientists and Roma and other scholars, India and abroad namely Prof. Kazua Azuma, Prof. Teiji Sakata, Mr. Yoshikichi Furui, Ms. Keiko Azuma, all from Japan, Dr. Vania

De-Gila-Kochanowski (France), Ms. Agnes (Belgium), Dr. Suresh Shukla (Norway), Dr. V.P. Vatuk (USA), Professors, scholars from universities of Delhi, Pune, Bangalore Gujarat, Vidyapeeth, Patna, Meerut, Agra, Garhwal, Varanasi, Awadh, Aligarh, Kanpur, Indore, Raipur, Bhubaneshwar, Surat, Itanagar (Arunachal Pradesh) etc. attended the conference. The then Chief Minister of Delhi Mr. M.L. Khurana and Mr. Sahib Singh Verma graced the occasion. The conference was organised in cooperation with Indian Writers Association, Calcutta, India Continental Cultural Association, Chandigarh and with the financial support from Indian Council of Cultural Relation and others.

**Media Research Centre**

The Foundation conducts socio-political Gall-up-Polls on national level through hundreds of research scholars and journalists utilizing modern techniques. It has chain of Associate journals, magazines and newspapers. Prof. J.S. Yadav, former Dir, IIMC and Prof.. Devesh Kishore, IGNOU are among the Advisers.

**Encyclopaedia of social Sciences and Documentation**

The Foundations' two publications were released by Mrs. Indira Gandhi, Former Prime Minister of India. These pioneer works contain documentation of articles on social sciences appeared in Hindi Journals /Magazines during 40 years before and after independence and were published in dictionary form *"SAMJIK VIGYAN PRALEKH KOSH."*

Another monumental and pioneer work entitled *"SAMAJIK VIGYAN HINDI VISHWAKOSH"* (Hindi Encyclopaedia of Social Sciences) in 10 volumes (now 5) was undertaken by the Foundation with the grant-in-aid from Ministry of Human Resource Development, Govt, of India. Dr Shankar Dayal Sharma who has been the Chief Adviser of the project, released it's two volumes at Rashtrapati Bhawan, Eminent scholars and social scientists-Prof.. S.C. Dube, Prof Moonish Raza, Dr. Prabhakar Machwe, Akshay Kumar Jain (Padma Vibhushan), T.N. Chaturvedi (Padma Vibhushan, Governor of Karnataka), Prof. Iqbal Narain, Prof. Yogendra Singh, Dr. H.G. Hiremath, Dr. S.P. Agrawal and Padma Shri awardee Dr. Shyam Singh Shashi (Hony., Chief Editor) and others were nominated by ICSSR in a national committee for this work. Subsequently, Dr. A. Padmanabhan, Prof. I.P. Singh, Prof,

Anil Mahajan, Dr. Dharamvir Mahajan, Dr. Ratnakar Pandey, Dr. Raj Kishor Singh, Dr. Lakhan Singh, Dr, Parmanand Panchal, Dr, Puran Pal, Prof. Asis sanyal, Mr. M. Bandopadhayay, Dr. Majida Asad, etc. were associated.

Foundation's other publications are *"Reaction to frustration," "Nomads of the Himalayas, "Attitude change"* etc. Associates of the organisation have published hundreds of books through private publishers and national organisations. Dr. Shashi, edited 50 vols. of *Encyclopaedia of social Sciences* and *Encyclopedia of Indian Tribes* (12 vols). He is also the Editor-in-Chief of Encyclopaedia *INDICA* (150 vols). He has over 300 books in English and Hindi to his credit.

**Patrons, Presidium - Seminars**

The Foundation had the privilege of having blessings of various national leaders viz., Indira Gandhi, Dr. Shankar Dayal Sharma, Mr. Rajeev Gandhi etc., and association of Late Presidium members—Mr. Aziz Imam , Kr. Mohan Swroop, Mr, Chandu Lal Chandrakar, Mr. M. Basvaraju, Dr. Shankar Dayal Singh, Pt. Sohanlal Dwevedi etc. It has organised various national and International conference including the Roma-Barjara conference of the World and Literary symposium in collaboration with Wishwa Hindi Samiti, Sahitya Bharati Kavi Sabha, Ahilyabi Holkar Vidyapith etc. In addition, it has convened seminars, symposium on-addiction, Police and citizen relation, NRI literature in cooperation with NDMC, Delhi Police etc.

A conference on Roma heritage and culture in collaboration with other NGOs and Ministry of Culture was held in 2001 in which 33 Roma scholars from dozen countries participated.

**(14) PM "Baro Rani" of Roma Gypises**

Roma, the nomadic people who migrated from India to different parts of Europe some 1000 years ago, still cherish the memory of their lost land and worship Rama, Krishna, Kali and a host of other Hindu deities.

This is the observation made by noted Indian anthropologist Shyam Singh Shashi in the course of his door-to-door survey of hundreds of Roma people in Scopje, a city in Yugoslavia where more than 50,000 Roma live.

Even today, the Roma carry Indian names like Ramkali, Meenakshi, Sudhakant, Asha, Ibrahim, Devasaran, Kaity and Rahman. They call India their "Baro Than" (great land) and talk of their "Baro Rani" (great queen), meaning Prime Minister Indira Gandhi.

— Indian Express, 21 March 83

# Bibliography

Agnihotri, B.S. : Kinnar Desh.

Atkinson, Edwin T. : Kumaun Hills.

Bailey, T. Grahame : Kanauri vocabulory in two parts—in Royal Asiatic Society of Great Britain.

Bose, Nirmal Kumar : Tribal Life in India.

Bose, S.C. : Geography of the Himalaya.

Bamzai, P.N.K. : Jammu and Kashmir.

Bruce, C.G. : Kulu and Lahaul.

Cunningham, J.D. : Notes on Moorcraft's Travels in Ladakh and on Genard's Account of Kanawar including the general description of the latter distric, in-J.

Cunningham. A. : Ladak.

Das, S.R. : A note on the Kineras-in-"Man in India."

Francke : Antiquities of Indian Tibet.

Gerard, Alex : Travels in the Himalayan Country.

Gore, F. St. J. : Lights and Shades of Hill Life in the Afghan and Hindu Highlands of the Punjab.

Himachal Pradesh Directorate of Economics and Statistics : Facts and Figures of Kinnarur District, Simla.

Hugal, Baron Charles : Travels in Kashmir and Punjab.

Ibbetson, D. and Maclagan : A glossary of the Tribes and Castes of the Punjab and N.W.F.P. compiled by H.A. Rose.

Montgommery, Maj. T.G. : Routes in the Western Himalayas, Kashmir and Chilas.

Hunter, W.W. : Imperial Gazetteer of India, London, 1881.

Mishra, P.K. : Nomads in the Mysore City.

Punjab, Government : Gazetteer of the Kangra District Pts. II to IV-Kulu, Lahul and Spiti.

Shashi, S.S. : Himachal Nature's Peaceful Paradise.

The Gaddi Tribe of Himachal Pradesh. Sterling Publishers Delhi.

The Tribal Women of India. (Sandeep Publications)

Nomads of the Himalayas – Sandeep Publication, Delhi.

Shephards of India – Sandeep, Delhi.

Roma — The Gypsy World — Sandeep, Delhi.

Night life of India Tribes. Agam Delhi.

Nehru and the Tribals Concept, Delhi.

K.M. Metri : The South Indian Nomads

Saraswat, H.C. : Himachal Pradesh P.D.

Saxena, Dr. R.N. : Sufi.

Swen, Hedin : Trans. Himalayas.

Titus, J.T. : Indian Islam.

*Tribal Journal* : Tribal Institute, Udaipur.

Tarachand, Dr. : Influence of Islam on Indian Culture.

*Vanyajati Journal :* Adim Jati Sewak Sangh, Delhi.

*Hill Resorts of India :* Deptt. of Tourism.

*Gazetteers.*

Punjab Gazetteers.

Gazetteer of Kashmir and Adjacent Distts. of Dishtwar.

Rajputana Gazetteers of India, Kashmir and Jammu. Gazetteer of India, 1965.

H.A. Rose : Glossary of Punjab Castes and Tribes, Races of the North Western Provinces.

TVRAN, Budapest Ref. Dr. Eva ARADI and Dr. Shashi.

Misc. *Material from Books / Journals* Mr. Ranjit Naik, Dr. S.P. Malhotra, Dr. S.P. Ruhela, Little India (USA).